PRAISE FOR
Raising the Barre

"This delightful story of one woman's personal quest will be enjoyed by anyone who thinks age is just a number, but *Nutcracker* fans will find it especially appealing."—*LIBRARY JOURNAL*

"[Kessler] inspires readers as she realizes that 'you can't feel the thrill unless you take the risk.'"—*PUBLISHERS WEEKLY*

"With a funny and warm writing style, Kessler describes a history of doubts, from the poking comments of her early dance teachers to her powerful drive to succeed in Eugene Ballet Company's performances— by any means necessary."—*EUGENE WEEKLY*

"[An] adventurous immersion into the subculture of ballet, this is a great, inspirational story for someone who is looking for a push to take that leap and do that thing they have been putting off for a really long time. If Kessler can do it, you can do it."
　　—*OREGON ARTSWATCH*

"Lauren Kessler's new memoir *Raising the Barre* sits at the intersection of two different popular genres: self-actualization and behind-the-scenes reporting."—*SEATTLE WEEKLY*

"Lauren Kessler's resolution to dance in *The Nutcracker* late in life was more than a pet project, it was a lifestyle revolution. And her new book about the journey to Eugene Ballet Company's stage, *Raising the Barre*, is more of about kicking yourself in the ass than Balanchine."—*WILLAMETTE WEEK*

"Kessler's book is well structured, generates suspense and culminates with amusing stories of performance mishaps and the rigors of touring."—*MEDIANDER*

PRAISE FOR
Counterclockwise

"Kessler takes on the marketing, (sometimes pseudo-) science, and the psychology of the anti-aging industry in this funny personal tale . . . Her journey through the temptations of quick-fix anti-aging options treats the fountain-of-youth–seeking side of us with humor and compassion."—*PUBLISHERS WEEKLY*

"An entertaining and informative investigation into growing old."
—*KIRKUS REVIEWS*

"[Kessler's] breezy style conceals an aptitude for reasoned analysis, and she incorporates a cogent summary of clinical research on aging into her tour of the fountain grounds, a one-woman guinea pig gamely trotting down a dozen different paths in search of the bubbling waters."—*NEW YORK TIMES SCIENCE TIMES*

"A fascinating new book . . . Essential reading for every woman who wonders whether problems ranging from brain fog to wrinkles can be reversed as she ages . . . Take charge of your health and your options for feeling and looking younger with Lauren's ultimate guide to anti-aging empowerment."—*EXAMINER.COM*

"You could not hope for a smarter, savvier, more committed guide to the multibillion-dollar anti-aging industry than Kessler."
—*THE OREGONIAN*

"[Kessler is] an intrepid explorer of all things anti-aging."
—*PSYCHOLOGY TODAY*

"Kessler is fun to read as she perkily pushes herself to become biologically younger."—*HARPER'S*

"Informative and witty."—*WALL STREET JOURNAL*

PRAISE FOR
My Teenage Werewolf

"Straight from the trenches, a mom's tale of weathering her daughter's transformation from sweetheart to snark mouth."—*PEOPLE*

"A hilarious and insightful read that's sure to resonate with any mom."—*LADIES' HOME JOURNAL*

"Readers who live with Lizzies of their own will enjoy this glimpse into the adolescent brain, which is 'not yet open for the business of wise and measured living.'"—*MORE*

"If you're battered by a daughter who's 10 times smarter and 100 times cooler than you are, this book could save your sanity. It turns out that that teen monster is still your little girl—just don't let her know that you know it!"

—BARBARA EHRENREICH, BEST-SELLING AUTHOR OF *BRIGHT-SIDED*,
THIS LAND IS YOUR LAND, AND *NICKEL AND DIMED*

PRAISE FOR
Stubborn Twig

"Excels in its historical sweep and in Kessler's flair for dramatic story telling . . . an eye-opener."

—*SAN FRANCISCO CHRONICLE*

Winner of the 1994 Oregon Book Award for Literary Nonfiction

PRAISE FOR
Clever Girl

"A spellbinding tale of a woman who fell prey to her idealism."
—*LIBRARY JOURNAL*

"Compelling . . . Kessler masterfully explores and exposes the myriad, competing facets of Bentley's tumultuous life."—*BOOKLIST*

"*Clever Girl* vividly traces the dramatic life of New England blue blood Elizabeth Bentley."—*ELLE*

"Superb . . . [brings] to life the loneliness, the fear and the thrill of [Bentley's] life as spy and anti-spy."—*SEATTLE TIMES*

"An insightful biography of an extraordinary American woman [and] a thrilling character-driven drama . . . Reads like good fiction . . . fascinating."—*SAN FRANCISCO CHRONICLE*

"A well-paced and sympathetic chronicle."—*BOSTON GLOBE*

Raising the Barre

ALSO BY
LAUREN KESSLER

Counterclockwise: My Year of Hypnosis,
Hormones, Dark Chocolate, and
Other Adventures in the World of Anti-Aging

My Teenage Werewolf:
A Mother, a Daughter, a Journey through
the Thicket of Adolescence

Finding Life in the Land of Alzheimer's:
One Daughter's Hopeful Journey

Clever Girl: Elizabeth Bentley,
the Spy Who Ushered In the McCarthy Era

The Happy Bottom Riding Club:
The Life and Times of Pancho Barnes

Stubborn Twig: Three Generations in the
Life of a Japanese American Family

Raising *the* Barre

Big Dreams, False Starts, & My Midlife Quest to Dance The Nutcracker

Lauren Kessler

Da Capo Press

Da Capo Press
Hachette Book Group
1290 Avenue of the Americas, New York, NY 10104
www.dacapopress.com
@DaCapoPress

Printed in the United States of America.

Originally published in hardcover and ebook by Da Capo Press in November 2015

First Trade Paperback Edition: November 2017

Published by Da Capo Press, an imprint of Perseus Books, LLC, a subsidiary of Hachette Book Group, Inc.

The Hachette Speakers Bureau provides a wide range of authors for speaking events. To find out more, go to www.hachettespeakersbureau.com or call (866) 376-6591.

The publisher is not responsible for websites (or their content) that are not owned by the publisher.

Print book interior design by Trish Wilkinson.

Library of Congress Cataloging-in-Publication Data has been applied for.

ISBNs: 978-0-306-90327-4 (paperback); 978-0-7382-1831-1 (hardcover); 978-0-7382-1832-8 (ebook)

LSC-C

10 9 8 7 6 5 4 3 2 1

To Kim
and to AE: So there!

To dance is to be out of yourself. Larger, more beautiful, more powerful. This is power, it is glory on earth and it is yours for the taking.

—AGNES DE MILLE

I don't understand anything about the ballet; all I know is that during the intervals the ballerinas stink like horses.

—ANTON CHEKHOV

Contents

Prologue

THE TROYANOFF BALLET Academy is a single-studio dance school, a storefront wedged between a dry cleaner and a pizza joint in a Long Island strip mall. My mother drives me there twice a week, Tuesday and Thursday after school, to take classes with Professor Troyanoff and his seriously arthritic wife, Madame Troyanoff. They were Russian dancers of little renown who left the motherland between the two world wars. My mother calls them "white Russians" to distinguish them from the Reds, this being the Cold War.

The distinction is lost on me. The inelegance of the academy is lost on me. I am six, seven, eight, nine, and what matters is pulling on pale pink tights and a black three-quarter-sleeve leotard in the tiny dressing room no bigger than a closet, sitting on the bench on the side of the studio and carefully slipping my feet into soft leather slippers. What matters to me is standing at the barre: first position, demi-plié, plié, relevé, second position, third, fourth, fifth; tendu, battement, rond de jambe, arabesque; and later, in the center of the room, glissades, the thrill of the grand jeté. What matters is dancing.

The Professor is a kindly middle-aged man with a handsome fleshy face and a luxuriant head of silver hair who wears snug T-shirts, billowing trousers, and black leather ballet slippers. While he instructs, his accent so thick one or another of us has to ask him to repeat, again and again, his wife, stern and crabby, stalks the studio, leaning on a cane. When one of us gets sloppy, when our grand pliés are not grand enough or our turnouts are not turned out enough, she raps the backs of our legs with the cane. It doesn't hurt as much as the idea of it hurts. I learn much later that her ballet career in the old country crippled her before she turned forty.

The Professor loves to choreograph. He puts together bits and pieces of what my mother tells me are the classics, each little dance ending in dramatic grand tableaux with all sixteen or eighteen or twenty of us young dancers striking and holding poses. The academy presents two parent-pleasing recitals a year, held in whatever elementary school the Professor manages to persuade to host us. I love the music. I love learning the steps. I love the costumes, the lavender tutu edged in silver with matching silver-sprayed ballet slippers, the white satin *Swan Lake* costume with yards of netting, so gorgeous that, after the recital, I find reasons to wear it: several "performances" in the backyard, show-and-tell at school, Halloween. But it's not just the trappings, it's how it all makes me feel: a part of something big and important and glamorous, a (pointed) toehold in a world of romance and pageantry so very different than my small suburban life. I don't think of it as "my small suburban life" at age nine or ten, but already I feel the insularity of it, the ordinariness. Already I feel the need to look elsewhere.

Now I am almost eleven, and I am leaving the Professor. I am about to move to a more serious ballet school, one run by the legendary André Eglevsky. Eglevsky is a French-trained Russian who retired from a stellar career in the United States. He had been a leading member of the Ballet Russe de Monte Carlo, a premier dancer with the American Ballet Theatre, and, for the final years of his performing career, a principal with Balanchine's New York City Ballet. He had danced pretty much every great ballet there was to dance, partnered with the world's prima ballerinas. In his early forties, he left the stage to set up his own ballet school. Eglevsky wasn't some guy who wanted to put on shows for parents in elementary schools. He was in the business of training ballerinas. For the New York stage. This was the big time. The school he opened was in Massapequa, just minutes from my house.

My family is sitting around the dinner table. My mother is telling my father that I will start lessons at Eglevsky's school next week.

"Well," my father says to me, after my mother explains what a big deal this is, "you'll need a Russian name. All great ballerinas are Russian." He smiles, then squints to think.

"Laurissa Kesslova," he says. "That's what we'll have to call you." And we all laugh.

1

The Binge

MY HUSBAND ANNOUNCES he's going on a three-week business trip in early December, and no, he doesn't ask me along. I decide to view this as a personal enrichment opportunity rather than an invitation to begin divorce proceedings.

I write this with a flippancy I do not feel. In fact, I am stung, even knowing that I would decline the invitation. The trailing-spouse thing is not me. I make my own way with what others might, from time to time, consider annoying persistence. Or bull-headedness. But still . . . he is going to *Paris*. So when I say, "I decide to view this as a personal enrichment opportunity," I mean I really do *decide*. It's a purposeful act. I make up my mind to move from hurt to I-have-a-plan, which is pretty much my m.o. in life. The moment I do that, the moment I decide a plan is called for, one emerges.

With my husband about to be occupied sampling pain au chocolat throughout the 3rd and 4th arrondissements, no kids living in the house at the moment, my flock of chickens decimated by a family of raccoons, and a light teaching schedule, I am free to do exactly what I want to do. And I know *exactly* what that is: a solo trip, the kind of trip no one in my family would dream of accompanying me on, even if they were available and even if I paid their way. I will indulge my lifelong love of ballet (shared by neither my husband nor my children) and my near obsession with one particular production, *The Nutcracker*, by gorging myself on this ballet. I will use this non-Paris time to attend *Nutcracker* performances. Lots of them. I will, I decide in a flash, hopscotch the country attending the performances of some of the top ballet companies in the United States. It will be my Transcontinental *Nutcracker* Binge Solo Tour. Who needs Paris?

MY LOVE AFFAIR with this ballet began the year my mother took me to see a New York City Ballet performance. I was five. I may not have blinked through the entire show. Did I know what I was seeing? Did I realize it was Maria Tallchief, one of the greatest ballerinas of the twentieth century, onstage? No. Was I transfixed, transported, and transformed? Did I feel I had stepped into a dream, into Clara's dream, into a dream I wanted to make my own? You bet. (A few months of concerted begging later, I began ballet classes with the Professor.) My mother took me again when I was six, and seven, and every December thereafter until I left for college. It was an Event, a velvet-dress-and-upswept-hair event, which, even during those teenaged years when I could barely stand to breathe the same air as my mother, I looked forward to. When my own daughter, Lizzie, turned five, I started taking her to the performances of our resident ballet company. Her lukewarm interest was a disappointment, but it did not discourage me. I have strong-armed her into going to every holiday performance since. I myself have watched twenty-six performances of *The Nutcracker*. This doesn't count several dozen video viewings of the iconic

Mikhail Baryshnikov and Gelsey Kirkland performance. (I keep an ancient VCR in a closet in the house for the sole purpose of viewing this video.)

Part of me is embarrassed to admit this. Not the secret VCR thing but the lifelong love affair with *The Nutcracker* thing. I know that no true balletomane loves—or would publicly admit to loving—*The Nutcracker*. I am well aware that *Swan Lake*, *Giselle*, *La Sylphide*, *Sleeping Beauty*, and *Cinderella*—all of which I've seen—are considered greater works of art, purer forms of expression, more richly and deeply emotional. But they don't have leaping Russians or tiny adorable children who come running out from under a voluminous skirt, do they? I believe I've made my case.

When I begin to plan the tour, Googling my way through literally hundreds of *Nutcracker* references (7,630,000 results in 0.32 seconds for "Nutcracker Ballet"), I am disturbed but not all that surprised to read outright *Nutcracker* slander. In a piece in the *Washington Post*, for example, the writer despairs of the ballet's "pervading tweeness." Tweeness is not good, in case you didn't know. I didn't know. I had to look it up. It's a Britishism meaning "sweet or cute in a way that is silly or sentimental." Hard to argue with that. The ballet *is* sweet, and a big chunk of Act II is both cute and silly. This is why children—my daughter notwithstanding—love it. And "sentimental" is not necessarily a bad thing. Sentimental can be tender and nostalgic without being cloying, can't it? I say yes.

The same writer correctly pegs *The Nutcracker* as the cash cow of the ballet world. Apparently, it is not just *my* favorite ballet. It is *everyone's* favorite ballet, as in everyone in the United States, as in everyone in the world. It is the most popular ballet on the planet. I read one estimate that says *Nutcracker* performances account for 40 percent of the revenue of major companies. The executive director of the Milwaukee Ballet—I happen upon the site in the midst of a clicking frenzy—says *The Nutcracker* makes up 55 percent of his company's annual ticket sales. It seems that this single production, this one twee ballet, is indeed keeping ballet alive, and ballet companies in business, from coast to coast.

It *is* a good thing, tweeness notwithstanding. But, in terms of planning my Transcontinental Nutcracker Binge Tour, it is a confusing thing because the choices are overwhelming. Every company everywhere puts on performances during December. It's not just the megacities—New York, Chicago, LA—or the cities that are known for attention to the arts—San Francisco, Boston, Atlanta, Minneapolis. It's Memphis, Louisville, and Boise. It's Dayton, Madison, and Detroit. It's Wilmington, Lincoln, and Peoria. It's Lubbock, Texas, for goodness' sake. Everyone wants a piece of the action.

Which performances should I see? I'm determined to partake of the work of the "best" companies, but which are the best? This seems like one of those questions made for my friend Siri, but she leads me down crooked paths. Where art is concerned, subjectivity reigns. And in the ballet universe of state- and city-branded companies, regional loyalties are ferocious. That said, I find general agreement about the excellence of New York City Ballet (NYCB), American Ballet Theatre (ABT), and the Joffrey Ballet. They go to the top of my list. After that, the field opens up: Houston, Miami, Boston, San Francisco, Pacific Northwest? Pennsylvania, Atlanta, Milwaukee, Washington, Colorado? I have to make tough choices. More digging. Two conversations with twenty-something ballerinas I know, a hard look at performance schedules, logistics, and the cost of airline tickets, and I narrow the tour to six: NYCB, ABT, and Joffrey with the addition of Boston, San Francisco, and (even though it didn't make anyone's top ten) Eugene Ballet Company because it is the home team, and because it is unbreakable tradition. And I don't want to deprive Lizzie of her yearly forced march into High Culture.

―☙

MY TOUR BEGINS the second week of December. There is a reason people don't travel in December unless they have to or unless they are headed to the Cayman Islands. I make it to Chicago just in time for back-to-back snowstorms. But, dressed in my *Nutcracker* special (simple black velvet dress with, yes, a ballet neckline), bundled up in arctic outerwear borrowed from an old college friend, I am in high spirits. What a way to begin—with the Joffrey, "America's Company of Firsts," as it likes to (and correctly) bill itself. The Joffrey was the first dance company to perform at the White House (invited by Jackie Kennedy), the first to appear on television, the first and only dance company to appear on the cover of *Time* magazine. It is performing at the perfect venue, the grand and elegant Auditorium Theatre (where, a lifetime ago, I saw a not-so-grand-and-elegant Frank Zappa concert).

It is a jaw-droppingly beautiful theater with twenty-four-carat-gold-leafed ceiling arches, intricate bas-relief designs, ornate stencils, murals, and mosaics. The place glitters and shines. Frank Lloyd Wright, who was really not about glitter and shine, once called it "the greatest room for music and opera in the world—bar none." He could easily have added "ballet." Next to me, in the very decent section I paid more than $100 to sit in, just far back enough from the stage to experience the tableaux but not so far back as to require binoculars, sits a fiftyish woman and her equally stylish mother who have, together, seen *The Nutcracker* "too many times to remember." The daughter never wanted to be a ballerina, never took ballet lessons, and has never seen any other ballet. How do I know this? Because, unlike other busybodies who strike up random conversations with strangers, I have an excuse: I'm a journalist.

When the orchestra—that would be the Chicago Philharmonic—starts up, I realize how long it's been since I've heard a real orchestra. These people don't just play music; they *are* music. When the ballet begins, I realize how long it's been since I've seen a major company perform. It is a grand production, with expensive sets and lavish costumes, dancers at the top of their form and at the apex of their careers. How do they manage to make it all look so light and playful when I know how impossibly hard it is? How can dance look so effortless when it takes so much effort? It must be like writing—you work impossibly hard in order to make it look easy. But what is happening onstage seems more like magic than work to me. Did I really once dance? Not like this, of course, not at all like this, but still, in a tutu, en pointe, a long, long time ago. And it was magic. That much I remember.

After a pleasant seven hours at O'Hare awaiting the passing of a second snowstorm, I finally make it to my next stop, Boston. The performance the next night takes place at another gorgeous venue, the Boston Opera House. But unlike the elegant Auditorium Theatre in Chicago, this place seems a bit tarted up. It doesn't surprise me to find out, when I look up its history, that it was originally built for vaudeville performances. The production befits the environment, intensely theatrical with sets that move and morph, a huge stage-transiting cloud, buckets of snow, a dancing bear, and a stiff-legged gingerbread man who gets nibbled on by little mice. It is witty and fanciful, full of broad, silent-movie-style acting, grand gestures, and maybe just a tad too much mugging for the audience. Still, I watch wide-eyed and entranced, just as I did when I was five.

The children in this production don't just skip and waltz. They really dance. They dance joyously as those who have not yet experienced injury, or maybe even given it a thought, can dance. They are young, nine or ten—just the age I was when ballet was everything to me and I dreamed big dreams—but they are already highly trained and disciplined, already little perfectionists, already, it seems, committed to the life.

But, as lovely as Clara and the children are, I find myself drawn to the "older" characters. This production features characters in the first-act Party Scene who look to be as old as their roles: an aunt who fusses over the children; grandparents who dance together, at first hesitantly, presumably showing their age, but then with growing confidence and liveliness. The grandfather looks to have a legitimately gray beard.

The lady sitting next to me (she came with her daughter-in-law because her daughter is in New Mexico and can't make it this year) is a psychiatric nurse who wanted to be a Rockette but was too tall. She's seen *The Nutcracker* just about every year in one or another of the five cities she's called home. She scribbles her e-mail address on the back of her ticket stub, just in case I find myself in Albuquerque next *Nutcracker* season. At intermission, she hands me another scrap of paper with her information and asks for the ticket stub back. She almost forgot: She saves all of them.

The next day, temporarily snowbound in my hotel room and amusing myself online, I stumble upon a Boston-area show that I, unfortunately, have just missed. It's *The Slutcracker*, a naughty burlesque version of the ballet that incorporates tango dancers, drag kings, Hula-hoopers, acrobats—and, yes, ballerinas—to tell a tale of sexual awakening. Here's the plot: Instead of receiving a nutcracker as a gift, Clara (a consenting-age adult, of course) receives a vibrator. Which, you guessed it, transforms into *The Slutcracker*. Who takes Clara into the realm of sexual fantasy. Where (in Act II) the Arabians are lesbian bondage belly dancers; the Russians are a trio of black-PVC-clad dominatrixes; and the Sugar Plum Fairy performs a striptease en pointe. Not exactly mother-daughter date-night material. But, with apologies to Pyotr Ilich: It would have been a hoot.

This gets me thinking about the other entertaining (and perhaps borderline alarming) ways in which this classic ballet has been embraced and adapted by pop culture. Of course there was Disney's *Fantasia*—a classic to end all classics—with its long and enchanting series of ballet suite dances featuring fairies, fish, flowers, and mushrooms. The omega to that alpha was Mattel's straight-to-video *Barbie and the Nutcracker*, which I force myself to watch a few minutes of (remember: I am snowbound) if only to see how those little (apparently size 3 if extrapolated to a human) molded plastic feet meant for high heels manage the choreography en pointe. Let's just say it's fortunate that Barbie had more than 150 alternate career paths—from aerobics instructor to paleontologist—to keep her busy because ballet was decidedly not her thing.

Once I start looking, *The Nutcracker* appears everywhere. Duke Ellington composed jazz interpretations of the score. Ogden Nash wrote verses inspired by the ballet. Cartoon cats Tom and Jerry starred in a 2007 version of the ballet. The Simpsons, Smurfs, Care Bears, SpongeBob SquarePants, and, gulp, Beavis and Butthead all riffed on *The Nutcracker*. A $90 million British-Hungarian production, *The Nutcracker in 3D*, was the biggest box-office flop of 2010. On the other hand, a Belgian rapper had a hit single with "Nutcracka," and a Canadian electronic music producer successfully released the charmingly titled "Distorted Dance of the Sugar Plum Fairy." Happily, the snow lets up, and I'm on my way to New York before I have time to consider checking out Jerry and his little nephew Tuffy as they watch Nelly the Pony and Paulie the Christmas Ornament come alive.

───⟡───

NEW YORK IS, as any New Yorker will tell you, *It*. That's an arguable point—but perhaps not in the world of American ballet. I'm here to see performances by what just about everyone considers the two top companies in the country, and I couldn't be more excited. It's like Chicago and Boston were the warm-ups. Now I'm ready for the big time.

New York, on the other hand, doesn't seem all that excited. New York takes this ballet in stride. It's just another show on another night. Lincoln Center Theater is just Lincoln Center Theater—no floor-to-ceiling posters and showy Nutcrackery decorations in the lobby, as in Boston and Chicago, no strings of lights, no flower garlands, no giant nutcrackers providing photo ops for the mothers and their dolled-up little girls who pack the theater on this frigid night. I was once a dolled-up little girl walking through this lobby holding on to a mother's hand. I had bangs. My mother wore a black Persian lamb wool coat with a dramatic cowl collar. Arpége by Lanvin was her scent. Once, years later, when I was a preteen, my mother stood and yelled "Brava!" as the curtain fell on the first act. We had third-row seats, almost too close. My mother's "brava" was the first voice, and it rang out, loud and distinct. I was mortified until the handsome conductor turned toward her, caught her eye, and winked. And then I thought, *That's my mom*. There weren't many times during those years that I thought my mother was cool.

Tonight I've got a great seat in the first ring. It's the most I've sprung for a ticket for any of the *Nutcrackers*—$149 plus multitudinous New York taxes. I chose the seat from a diagram of the theater back at my computer at home and am now completely reassured that my decision was brilliant because the woman next to me (in scarlet five-inch-high Jimmy Choos) is a season-ticket holder, and these are the seats she loves.

I settle in. This is the real deal. This is the Balanchine company dancing the Balanchine ballet as God—and Balanchine—intended it. It doesn't get purer than this. It doesn't get more iconic. I know. I've done my homework.

The great George Balanchine choreographed this version of the ballet for the company he founded, this same New York City Ballet, with the first performance in 1954—and the company has been performing it (up to forty-seven times) every holiday season since. "I've seen only the Balanchine," the woman in the Jimmy Choos tells me just as the house lights dim. "There's no point in seeing any other, is there?"

Back in 1919, the fifteen-year-old Balanchine had danced the role of the Prince in a Russian production of the ballet. Russia was the ballet's home, with native son Tchaikovsky writing the score and the St. Petersburg Imperial Ballet's premier and assistant ballet masters choreographing the dance. That very first performance, in December of 1892 in St. Petersburg, was—I am surprised and sort of charmed to discover—somewhat of a bomb. One critic wrote that the premier ballerina was "corpulent" and "pudgy" and that one of the other dancers was "completely insipid." The libretto was "lopsided." Children should not have been part of the cast. About the choreography of the battle scene, the critic wrote, "One cannot understand anything. Disorderly pushing about from corner to corner and running backwards and forwards—quite amateurish."

The ballet has come a long, long way since then. What is on-stage now is, to my eyes, a seamless blend of technique and artistry, of precision and grace, the absolute definition of ballet. The sets are simple, the costumes understated. That said, I read later that the Mother Ginger costume is nine feet wide, weighs eighty-five pounds, and requires three people to help lower it by pulley over the dancer's head. But this production is about dance. There is a pas de deux in the second act during which I do not believe I take a breath. The ballerina, ignoring the laws of physics (and probably gravity), strikes an arabesque poised on the most perfect point with the most astonishing arch to her foot and appears to glide halfway across the stage on the arm of her partner. She maintains the pose as if she were a still photograph of herself, yet there is nothing stiff or frozen about her body. I have never seen anything like this before. I don't understand how a body can do this. Her partner is agile, athletic, graceful. But Baryshnikov has ruined all other male dancers for me.

—☙

TWO NIGHTS LATER, I am riding the B103 down Coney Island Avenue to see the American Ballet Theatre's production of *The Nutcracker* at the Brooklyn Academy of Music (BAM). (I was born in Brooklyn back when one didn't admit such things.) The BAM arts center is split between a movie theater and a performance hall, so on one side of the lobby they are selling Milk Duds and on the other Clara dolls. To my surprise, given the modest, popcorn-scented lobby, the performance hall turns out to be an elegant opera house. (Enrico Caruso opened the place in 1908, singing Faust with the Metropolitan Opera Company.) I find my seat in the mezzanine, back two rows, in the center. Perfect.

But no sooner do I settle myself in than a big guy, burly, bald, and beer-bellied, starts to squeeze by to take the seat next to me. I get up to move. "Naw," he says, dripping Brooklynese. "Don't move. I'm not as trim as I usedta be, but I'll get by." And he does. Then, after catching his breath, he engages me in conversation as if we're old friends. In the less than five minutes before curtain time, I learn the following: His name is Victor LaRossa, and, except for two years in Vietnam in the late 1960s and nine months in upstate New York when he tried to "find myself after my first marriage," he has lived all his life in Brooklyn. He's never seen *The Nutcracker* or any ballet. His wife—"Hey, Joanie, meet this nice lady," he brays to the woman on the other side of him—got the tickets from a woman whose kid the wife takes care of. "But culture, ya know. It can't hurt," he says. I love this guy. This guy is why *The Nutcracker* is the most popular ballet in America.

That said, I am not prepared for this very different *Nutcracker*. I want to like it because, after all, Baryshnikov, after dancing with Balanchine, went on to become the artistic director of this company (a fact, unlike the Mother Ginger costume stats, that I do not have to look up, by the way). But I have problems appreciating the mash-up of ballet and contemporary dance, the broader, more sweeping, less controlled movements, the four male dancers dressed as bees wearing bright yellow swim caps. They perform this antic insect dance involving something that far too closely resembles "spirit fingers."

But what really gets me is how, in the first-act Party Scene, the grandmother and grandfather totter around in a parody of old age. They dance stiffly, awkwardly, with the other guests, at the front of a kind of minuet line until the grandmother—a twenty-three-year-old, according to the program—pretends to faint from exhaustion. This depiction of old age rankles the "counterclockwise" me, the me who spent two years delving into the research of how we age and how we can maintain youthful vitality far longer than we think, the me who wrote about turning back her own biological clock. I hate this old equals feeble stereotype, onstage, in life, everywhere.

At intermission, the lady sitting behind me asks, in a southern drawl, whether I am reviewing the ballet for a newspaper. She has observed me scribbling notes during the performance. She's just in from South Carolina to take her daughter, an NYU film student, to see the performance. They've been "nutcrackering" together, as she puts it, for twenty years, including four years when the daughter was a mouse in the local production. "I worked backstage," the mother tells me. "I loved every minute of it," she says. The daughter leans in to her mother, gives her a little shoulder bump.

At curtain call, the audience stands en masse, and the applause is thunderous. People are actually stamping their feet, and—as my mother did before it was fashionable—yelling "Brava," "Bravo." Although I love this version of *The Nutcracker* the least, I love this audience the most. They are into it like it was a Dodgers game. (And by that I mean, of course, the *Brooklyn* Dodgers.)

Victor turns to me. "That was very entatainin," he says. I ask him if he'll go again next season. "Nah," he says, helping his wife on with her fake-fur coat that looks a whole lot like my fake-fur coat. "We're gonna try opera next."

THE NEXT MORNING, hoping to beat the worst of a snowstorm that seems to have followed me since Chicago, I am on the plane out of JFK headed for San Francisco. Sitting next to me is a handsome, strapping guy wearing worn, top-quality cowboy boots. It turns out he is a national rodeo clown. Who's seen *The Nutcracker*. (Of course I ask.) His mother took him to a performance by the Tulsa Ballet Company (he grew up on a ranch outside town)

when he was twelve. There's more. He took his first girlfriend on a date to the Tulsa *Nutcracker*. "I bet that impressed her," I say. "Well," he says, in that laconic way cowboys have, "it was kind of a good-bye present. I broke up with her the next week." I'm thinking, *If a rodeo clown sitting next to you on a plane has a* Nutcracker *story—actually two—does that mean everyone has a* Nutcracker *story?*

—৩

STROLLING OVER TO the War Memorial Opera House in San Francisco for my fifth *Nutcracker* in nine days, I have to give myself a good talking-to. Do I really want to see yet another production? How many snowflakes and flowers, stiff-legged jack-in-the-boxes, leaping Russians, and really cute eight-year-olds can a person handle? Can't I hum every bar of this music by now? But as I join the excited crowd and enter the elaborate lobby of this stunning Beaux Arts building, I fall under the spell. It's another throng of high-heeled mothers corralling their high-spirited little girls. They twirl and prance in their party dresses, white tulle and red velvet, their hair adorned with bows or tiaras. Some are holding nutcrackers. I watch a four-generation family— well, more like stalk them—for a while, hoping to get a picture on my iPhone. The great-grandmother looks uncannily like Maggie Smith. The great-granddaughter, maybe five, is wearing a full-on ballerina costume, more *Swan Lake* than *Nutcracker* but impressive as hell.

The lobby is done up with massive wreaths and lights with an enormous, brightly lit Christmas tree in the center. By one of the entrances to the auditorium, the dance company has set up a photo op with a dancer in Mouse King regalia and a tutued ballerina who patiently pose with kids. In the mezzanine lobby, there's another big Christmas tree laden with *Nutcracker* ornaments for sale. (I buy two.) Next to it is a fifteen-foot-long counter displaying at least a dozen different nutcrackers as well as Clara dolls, snowflake globes, *Nutcracker* T-shirts, posters, stickers, mugs, CDs, DVDs, and books. Next to that is a special walk-through "Candyland" where little girls squeal as they fill *Nutcracker* bags with caramels, licorice, and jellybeans. This is the most merched-up of the *Nutcracker*s I've seen, but all of the venues, all of the ballet companies, have taken advantage of the big holiday crowds, the loyal *Nutcracker* fan base, and the special, needs-to-be-commemorated-by-object nature of this event.

The uniqueness of this *Nutcracker* is that it is set in early-twentieth-century San Francisco, with the scenery a depiction of modest Victorian row houses and the costumes less opulent and fanciful than I've seen so far. But this is San Francisco, so the production veers into Alice-in-Wonderland psychedelic territory, with stage-obscuring billows of dry ice, Christmas presents the size of garden sheds that slide in from the wings, an eight-foot-long mousetrap, a big red dragon, Russians who burst out of over-sized ornaments, and a trapdoor. There is also elegance here, like the Balanchine, but it is coupled with the youth and energy and nerviness I associate with West Coast culture.

—⟶

TWO DAYS AFTER returning home, I once again don my trusty velvet dress, pick up my daughter at her boyfriend's house, and head to *Nutcracker* number six, my local production. Lizzie would rather be in the dank basement of her boyfriend's house playing *SkyRim* and *Grand Theft Auto 4*. She would rather be sitting on the ratty couch *watching* her boyfriend play these video games. To put it another way: She would rather be doing almost anything than dressing up and accompanying me to a ballet performance. But she knows how much it means to me. And then there is the more powerful motivator: She knows I will guilt-trip her for weeks if she refuses.

The Eugene Ballet Company (EBC) has been on the road with *The Nutcracker* since Thanksgiving: twelve cities, four states, twenty-four performances. Now it has five hometown performances at the city's arts venue, a classy theater that is home to an opera company, a symphony, this ballet company, and the International Bach Festival. If you didn't know you were in a barely 150,000-population town tucked into an agricultural valley in western Oregon, you wouldn't know you were in a barely 150,000-population town tucked into an agricultural valley in western Oregon. I've seen this local production before—fourteen times, in fact—but I've never viewed it after seeing five world-class performances. I'm setting the bar low for this evening.

I am surprised. Delightfully surprised. The music is a bit thin, but the sets are lovely and the costumes as sumptuous as I've seen elsewhere. This is a small company, I realize, when I see that they are mounting the big scenes with fours—four soldiers, four mice—rather than six or eight or even ten with the large companies. But this stage is smaller, and the choreography is rich and substantial, so you don't miss the bodies. The dancers have confidence. There is zest to their dancing and that same combination of supreme effort and effortlessness that I've seen around the country. I learn later that they are mounting these productions with a cast and a half rather than two casts because of so many injuries on the road.

If anything, my cross-country tour leaves me more in awe of the abilities of these hometown dancers. It occurs to me that this professional world of ballet is like the world of sports—not just for the obvious reasons that both involve extraordinary physical abilities and years of training and special, genetically blessed bodies and the constant threat of injury and the short career span (as if those were not enough) but because there are all these excited young "players" who love to participate, who love the thing for itself—as I did when I was a child. And then there are those who dream bigger and work harder. And of those, a tiny percentage are able to make this activity into something more. And of those, an even tinier percentage transcend the rest: They are the Olympians. Joffrey and NYCB dancers are the gold medalists, yes. But these EBC dancers are good enough to make the team.

I drive home from the theater, dropping off my daughter—who, despite herself, enjoyed the performance—at a party along the way. I can't wait to get home. I can't wait to dig out the VCR from the hall closet and pop in the tape. You know which one: Gelsey and Misha, 1977. Pure magic.

My husband, newly returned from the City of Lights and disturbingly unrepentant, hears the Tchaikovsky from the next room. "I can't believe you haven't had enough," he yells over the music.

Enough? I am drunk on dance. I am bewitched. I am on fire.

I watch Misha leap as if gravity were a law he decided not to obey, and I cannot believe the thought that jumps into my head, the voice that whispers in my ear: *Dance* The Nutcracker, it says. *You—midlife woman, you who have not been in a ballet studio since you were twelve: Shake it up. Attempt the impossible. Take a chance.*

2

The Cure

THERE ARE REALLY two questions here: Is this dream of dancing *The Nutcracker* remotely possible? And *why am I dreaming it in the first place?* I think I need to explore the second question before I can broach the first. I need to puzzle through and make some sense of my motivation before I figure out how—or whether—to take action.

Part of me thinks the dream is just a passing fancy, a temporarily intoxicated, tour-inspired lark of an idea, something to entertain my female friends with over skinny lattes. I sit with that thought for a while, mull it over. But just the fact that I'm sitting with it, mulling it over, tells me something else is going on here. This sudden desire to dance *The Nutcracker* can't be mere personal divertissement. The impulse, in fact, feels much bigger than that, much deeper. Scary deep, the more I think about it. It may be that this ballet dream is freighted with, absolutely *saturated* and *dripping* with, the stuff of life. And by "stuff of life" I mean fear, angst, pride, self-doubt, arrogance, fragility, optimism, pessimism, discontent, happiness, restlessness.

I have to start somewhere, so I start to unpack the restlessness thing. It's true. I am suddenly, powerfully, *itchingly* restless. As I crisscrossed the country on my tour, husbandless, childless, a me I barely recognized but liked a lot, I had this realization: The last twenty years of my life—which I thought of as, well, my *life*—were, in fact, just a phase. And that phase is over. No. I'm not talking Empty Nest Syndrome. That's not it. I love my three children, really I do, but they were never my raison d'être. I didn't dream of motherhood when I was a kid. I didn't love being pregnant. Nor did I "glow." (I did, however, acquire varicose veins.) "Mother" is a part of my identity, but it has never been all of it, or even most of it. I'm betting a lot of professional women who are also mothers feel this way. For me, home is now and always has been more than a nest for growing children. So the exit of two out of three has not robbed me of identity. Nor has it made me lonely.

And this midlife dis-ease doesn't feel like that other cliché, Midlife Crisis. Apparently, women are now allowed to have these. The *Huffington Post* has an entire section titled "Mid Life Crisis Women" that directs readers to articles written by freaked-out women who can't sleep or who are having affairs. There's advice from Dr. Mona, "who knows the signs of a woman's mid-life crisis," and a quiet little piece about the possibility of spiritual wisdom at midlife. A *Psychology Today* article I read talks about the midlife career woman's crisis as a "quest for identity." A medical advice site worries that midlife crises can turn into depression. A divorce-support site worries about the breakup of marriages as a by-product of midlife crises. None of this speaks to me. My "crisis" is not about realizing my own mortality (been there, done that), doubting my achievements to date (actually, I'm proud), wanting to dump my husband (Paris notwithstanding), or that slap-upside-the-head *Wow, I've probably got only* x *number of years left* moment. I had a boyfriend in college who was, at age twenty, mourning that a quarter of his life was gone. This cured me early and permanently of such metrics.

But clearly, something *is* happening. This restlessness is coming from somewhere. It feels like an alarm clock is going off, telling me to wake up, get up, and get moving because it is now time to begin the next part of my life. Which is . . . what? I'm confused. But wait a minute: Don't I *know* what this next phase is? Isn't this "midlife"—or, less kindly, "middle age"—a time to settle into the safe and comfortable place I have labored so hard to create, to stop all that striving and start reaping some of the benefits of two or three decades of . . . all that striving? To inhabit the lovely landscape I have designed and carefully, arduously tended? To, um, await the grandchildren?

But that's not me. I am, for what it's worth, a quadruple Aries. I know, I know, you're rolling your eyes. *Don't tell me she believes in astrology?* But really, whether it's the position of the planets at my birth (sun, Mercury, Venus, and Mars in Aries, in case you were wondering) or the "prove yourself every moment" parenting style of my father or the fact that I grew up wanting to be the globe-trotting, experience-hungry Brenda Starr, Reporter, the hard truth is that I am not built to settle in and slow down. I am not at all tempted to go on autopilot. I am a woman of enthusiasms and new beginnings. This, right now, this *No one needs me to do the laundry and help them study for tests and drive them everywhere* moment, this "middle age," is a time to grab hold of, to go boldly. This is the nature of the restlessness I feel.

But I'm not some back-page feature in a women's magazine waiting to be written: the middle-aged woman who becomes a firefighter after her kids leave home. The middle-aged woman who starts a global corporation at her kitchen table. My restlessness is not about career. It is not about throwing over one life for another.

It is more about, I think, committing to staying actively (even bravely) engaged in the life I have.

This push I'm feeling comes from inside, not from the press of circumstance—and, believe me, I know how lucky I am to be in this place. I know, we all know, about the calamities that can shake us to the core at midlife. I call them the Four Ds: Divorce, Downsizing, Death, Diagnosis. We know—maybe because it happened to us, maybe because it happened to a friend—the way life sometimes wallops you, slaps you silly, and you have to recover, regroup, restart. The partner you thought you knew but learn the hard way you didn't. The good, secure job that suddenly isn't. The aging parent you know has to die sometime, and then does, and it's still a surprise, and your world shifts. The worrisome mammogram. People can and do change in big and important ways when big and important things *force* them to change. Or rather, to be Pollyannaish about it, when circumstances present them with the (uninvited) *opportunity* to change.

But what about those of us *not* pushed by external forces? Don't get me wrong. I'm not saying I am someone who has sailed through life untouched by any of the Four Ds. (In fact, I'm personally acquainted with two of them.) I'm saying this restlessness, this compulsion to *do* something, to shake it up, comes not because I *have* to but because I *want* to, not out of desperation but imagination. Isn't it possible to want something different or more not because you are unhappy or dissatisfied or laid low by the vicissitudes of life, not because a door closes behind you, but because you suddenly see so many doors ahead of you? Doesn't midlife seem to be the perfect time to start opening some of them, to start taking a few steps down those roads not taken? Say yes.

⟋⟍

THIS SOUNDS ALL upbeat and rosy, all I'm-forging-ahead-fueled-by-optimism-and-good-vibes. It *is* that, I think, but there is something else, something darker, more challenging, going on. There is also fear, angst, and self-doubt—a tidy little emotional package that, at least for me, arrived (unbidden) to help celebrate the midlife journey. Here it is, or at least what I think is a big part of it: I fear getting old, and I think this midlife restlessness may be a symptom of or closely related to that fear.

Yes, I know, "they" say getting old is better than the alternative. But the kind of old I fear getting is, in fact, *not* better than the alternative. Oddly, I don't fear getting fragile or sick. No, I fear getting repetitive, stodgy, inflexible, unimaginative, *uninteresting*. That's right: I fear becoming a boring old person. (And yes, I know Georgia O'Keefe did amazing work into her midnineties, and that Arthur C. Clarke was writing when he died at ninety, and that my own grandma was a pistol to the very end, at ninety-four.) Nevertheless, I fear becoming a stick-in-the-mud, hesitant about—or resistant to—change. Timid and overly cautious, like a little-old-lady driver. What I fear most about aging is that my world will get smaller because my ability (or desire) to seek challenges or make changes—or cope creatively and positively with changes—will diminish. I will lose the resilience of youth. And by "youth" I don't mean a bikini body or the ability to party all night (neither of which I had in my youth). I mean a vibrant, adventurous, *resilient* state of mind.

Resilience. It is fear of losing resilience that may, in part, underlie this *Nutcracker* dream. When I was delving into the science of aging for my last book, the quality of resilience came up again and again. That ability to bend—emotionally, psychologically—to remain supple and flexible, to thrive regardless of what life dishes out . . . it seemed from what I was reading that this might be the key to well-being, the cornerstone to a productive and happy life, an effective turn-back-the-clock—or at least slow-its-relentless-progression—strategy. Resilience, I learned, meant the ability to avoid seeing crises as insurmountable problems. It meant the ability to see oneself as a subject, not an object, an actor who makes things happen, not a victim to whom things happen. Resilience meant actively looking for opportunities for self-growth, developing goals instead of focusing on barriers, taking decisive action. I was delighted to read the results of an MIT AgeLab study that found resilient midlifers to be happier, less stressed, and more involved in activities and relationships than their less-resilient counterparts.

Back when I was doing that research on aging and resilience, I came across the work of Deborah Khoshaba, a California clinical psychologist who codirects something called the Hardiness Institute. (Is that not a great name—and concept?) To her, resilience is a combination of optimism and endurance. Optimism is not a looking-at-the-world-through-rose-colored-glasses thing, which is good because I don't own a pair. It's more a belief in your own efficacy, which I do have. And endurance, she says, is not some nose-to-the-grindstone slog through change and challenge, which is to say through life. Endurance is what naturally occurs when you have—and decide to pursue—a goal that is rich in self-expression. Like, for example, dancing *The Nutcracker*. The more I think about all this, the better and more empowered I feel. This rush of positive thinking almost quells my boring-old-woman fear.

But as one fear recedes, another jumps in to take its place. It's like I have this special reserved-for-fears-and-concerns zone in my psyche, and it refuses to remain uninhabited. (Tell me I'm not the only one built this way.) The other fear leaping into the breach is one that has actually been nibbling at me for the better part of a decade. But now, given a clear field, it acquires power, and I see that it too may underlie my current state of being. It's a fear that appears to attend most women at midlife: the fear of becoming invisible. You know, the dark and depressing feeling that you are no longer vital or important or noticeable to others. The feeling of being relegated to the sidelines. Out of the game. A piece in the *Atlantic* nailed it: "the narcissistic injury of middle age." Ouch. I am very much aware that this "injury," along with my fears about aging and this restlessness eating at me, are what Louis C.K. would undoubtedly include in his category of "White People Problems." (That's when, he says, "your life is so amazing that you just make shit up to be upset about.") But Louis, *it's real*, all this midlife shit. It feels important to me. And I know I am not the only midlife woman facing these fears—although, okay, I may be the only one contemplating dancing *The Nutcracker* as a way to conquer them.

The engine that is powering this midlife quest is, I am coming to realize, fueled by a combination of hope and fear: Hope that I can, by taking on such a challenge, nourish and preserve what is youthful and vital in my midlife self. Fear that if I don't force change on myself, then this next phase in my life will be one of stagnation and decline, of increasing spectatorship, of growing inflexibility to the challenges that one day I will not have the luxury of choosing.

The Nutcracker is my cure for middle-aged doldrums.

This is how I will *not* settle into midlife.

3

Cracking the Nut

ONCE UPON A time there is this prepubescent waif of a girl, Marie, who, one Christmas Eve, unwraps a special gift from her inventive tinkerer of a godfather. It is an intricate clockwork castle. She plays with it for a while, but the little mechanical people inside do the same thing over and over again (much like her own stodgy parents and their friends is the implication), so she tires of it. This little girl (note: The author of this tale has a real-life romantic obsession with . . . a little girl) then notices another gift, a nutcracker. For reasons unexplained, she takes to it in a big way. Marie, along with her brother and sister, amuse themselves cracking nuts with it until brother Fritz uses it to crack too big a nut, breaking its jaws.

Is this sounding a little familiar? Wait—the plot thickens.

When it is time for bed, the children put their Christmas gifts away in the "special cabinet" where they keep their toys—and yes, "special cabinet" should be read with incipient goose bumps. Her brother and sister are hurried off to bed, but Marie begs to be allowed to stay with the nutcracker a while longer. As she fusses over it, making promises to the nutcracker that her godfather will repair its jaw, the nutcracker's face seems to come alive. This terrifies little Marie, but she decides it's only her imagination. Then maybe she falls asleep, maybe not. What happens next is either a delirious nightmare or a portal into an alternative (and sinister) reality.

Mice begin to come out from beneath the floorboards of the family's living room, including a grotesque seven-headed Mouse King. The dolls in the "special cabinet" suddenly come alive, with the nutcracker taking command and leading them into pitched battle against the mice. At first the dolls prevail, but they are eventually overwhelmed by the mice. When Marie sees that her beloved nutcracker is about to be taken prisoner, she takes off her shoe, throws it at the seven-headed Mouse King, and promptly faints, crashing into the glass door of the "special cabinet" and badly gashing her arm.

Beginning to sound a little bit less familiar? Just wait.

Marie wakes up in her bed the next morning with her arm bandaged (So it *wasn't* a dream?) and tries to tell her parents about the epic battle between dolls-that-came-to-life and bellicose rodents. They—of course—don't believe her. They insist that she must have had a "fever dream" caused by the wound she sustained from the broken glass. Meanwhile, moving the plot right along, the godfather shows up with the repaired nutcracker (So it *was* a dream?) and entertains her with the following byzantine tale of Princess Pirlipat and Madam Mouserinks, aka the Queen of the Mice, which is meant to explain how nutcrackers came to be and why they look the way they do.

Follow closely because this story within a story gets complicated fast.

Here goes: The Mouse Queen tricks Pirlipat's mother (a human queen) into allowing her (the Mouse Queen) and her children to gobble up the lard that was supposed to go into the sausage that the King was to eat at dinner that evening. The King, enraged at the Mouse Queen for spoiling his supper, has his court inventor create traps for the Mouse Queen and her children. The little mice scamper into the traps, and they all die. The end.

—⌒⌒

NO, NOT REALLY.

Yes, the little mice all die, but then the Mouse Queen swears revenge on Princess Pirlipat. But Pirlipat's mother, the (human) Queen, is no dummy. She surrounds the Mouse Queen with cats that will thwart her plans. But the cats need to be stroked constantly to be kept awake. Alas, the royal nurses in charge of the incessant stroking fall asleep, and the Mouse Queen is free to do her dirty work. She casts a spell on the princess, turning her into a grotesque figure with a huge head, a wide, grinning mouth, and a little goatee. Got it? She now looks like a nutcracker.

The King blames his court inventor for the ugly turn of events and gives him four weeks to reverse the spell. Which he does. And they all live happily ever after. Nope. No such luck. The inventor can't figure out what to do, so he consults an astrologer who tells him that the only way to reverse the spell is to have the big-headed, large-jawed, nutcrackerlike Princess Pirlipat eat a special nut, which—wait for it—must be cracked and handed to her by a man who has never shaved nor worn boots since birth and who must, without opening his eyes, hand her the kernel and take seven steps backward without stumbling.

Yes, really.

So. The inventor and the astrologer look (Do I need to add unsuccessfully?) for the mythical nut and the baby-faced, barefooted guy for two years. Returning home in defeat, they (miraculously) find both the aforementioned guy and the magic nut in a small shop right in the neighborhood. And the baby-faced, bare-footed guy turns out to be the inventor's own nephew! He (of course) cracks the nut easily and hands it to the Princess, who swallows it and immediately becomes beautiful again. And they all live happily ever after. Um, no. Not quite yet.

On his seventh step backward, the nephew stumbles over the Queen of Mice, and now the curse falls on him. *He* becomes the big-headed, wide-jawed, bearded nutcracker. The Princess, I am sorry to say, is repulsed by his ugliness, refuses to marry him, and banishes him from the castle. Are you still with me?

Meanwhile. Yes, there is another meanwhile. Marie—remember her?—while recuperating from her slashed arm, hears the Mouse King whisper to her in the middle of the night. He threatens to bite the nutcracker to pieces. That's the Christmas-toy-that-came-alive nutcracker, not the Princess-and-then-nephew-that-turned-into-a-nutcracker nutcracker. The Mouse King demands all of Marie's sweets and dolls. She gives them up, but the royal rodent wants more and more. Enter the (animated toy) nutcracker, who instructs Marie to get him a sword so he can slay the evil and greedy mouse. He does, returning the next night to take Marie away with him to the (never before mentioned) doll kingdom, where she sees many wondrous things. She falls asleep and is somehow returned to her home, where she tells her mother of her adventures. Again, she is not believed. (And really, can you blame the mother?) Furthermore, she is forbidden to speak of her "dreams" again.

Hold on. We are really coming to the end here, I promise. Then, one day, as Marie sits in front of the "special cabinet" obsessing over the nutcracker, she swears to it that if it ever comes alive, she would not behave as the Princess did and would love it regardless of its grotesque head, huge jaw, etc. Boom. Literally, big bang. Marie falls off her chair. The inventor's nephew (Remember him from the story within the story?) enters and tells Marie that by swearing her love to the toy nutcracker, she has broken the curse on him and made him human. He asks her to marry him. (Small problem noted by the careful reader: Marie is either seven or, if the two years in the story within a story count, nine.) She accepts. A year and a day later, he comes for her and takes her away to the doll kingdom, where she is crowned queen and eventually (presumably when she is of age) marries him. The end.

Yes, actually the end.

—☙

THIS IS "THE Nutcracker and the Mouse King," a novella written in 1816 by a German author, composer, painter, and government bureaucrat named E. T. A. Hoffmann. A wildly productive but seemingly unhappy man whose intense romantic feelings were reserved for a decade-older married woman and an adolescent girl, he died of paralysis brought on by syphilis and alcohol abuse. His stories, considered the first flowering of the horror-fantasy genre that Edgar Allan Poe and later H. P. Lovecraft would make famous, focused on supernatural and sinister characters who moved in and out of people's lives, revealing hidden secrets and the more disturbing sides of human nature. His work was grimmer than the Grimms, darker than Poe, weirder than Lovecraft, and hardly the basis for a sweet, romantic kid-pleaser of a ballet.

So how did this transcendently creepy, disturbingly psychological, overly complicated, twisted tale of bloody battles, giant rodents, whispered threats, greed, death, betrayal, and lard-eating become the sugary, plummy ballet we know and love? Enter Alexander Dumas, père.

Dumas was a lavish-living, overfed Frenchman with forty mistresses (Dumas fils was one of his illegitimate children) whom a literary contemporary called "the most delightfully amusing and egotistical creature on the face of the earth." He was also one of the most prolific and popular French writers of the nineteenth century, best known for the historical novels *The Three Musketeers* and *The Count of Monte Cristo*. Twenty years after Hoffmann's death. Dumas adapted "The Nutcracker and the Mouse King" novella, titling it *Histoire d'un casse-noisette*. "Adapted," though, is not really the right word. Sanitized. Romanticized. Disneyfied. Those words better describe what the happy-go-lucky Dumas did to the psychologically complex, morally disturbing work of Hoffmann.

The plot was simplified and streamlined, with the entire Princess Pirlipat story within a story omitted. But what really changed the essence of the story was the transformation of what remained of the plot from dark and scary to fluffy and saccharine. It's as if someone made a beach read out of *The Shining*. Although the nutcracker–Mouse King battle remains, it is cast not as a delirious nightmare but rather as a childish dream. And the alternative world that the girl visits later in the story is sweet and diverting, more fairy-inhabited amusement park than thinly veiled journey into the psyche. And consider these truly interesting, although seemingly minor, changes noted by Jack Zipes, a Columbia-educated professor of German who has written and published widely on the subject of fairy tales. He notes that Marie in Hoffmann is renamed Clara in Dumas. So what? Here's what: "Marie" is from the Hebrew meaning "sea of bitterness," "sea of sorrow," or, alternately, "rebellion." "Clara," from the Latin, means "bright and clear." The family's name in Hoffmann translates as "steel tree," harsh, rigid, an off-putting combination of the industrial and the natural. In Dumas, the family's name changes to "silver tree," which brings to mind a decorated, tinseled Tannenbaum. Sometimes I just love lit crit, don't you?

Dumas's version, unlike many of his adventure tales, was not wildly popular in its day. In fact, it languished until, seventy years later, Marius Petipa, a Frenchman considered the father of classical Russian ballet and one of ballet's most influential choreographers, got hold of it. As the premier maître de ballet of the St. Petersburg Imperial Theatres, he decided to have the Dumas story made into a ballet and commissioned Pyotr Ilich Tchaikovsky to compose the music. According to ballet legend, the pairing was not a happy one, as the two had differing opinions on how to approach the work. It probably didn't help that Tchaikovsky suffered bouts of depression. (Some scholars believe that his sudden death from cholera at age fifty-three was—get this—*self-inflicted*.) It is also said that the infrequency of the composer's early successes had made him particularly sensitive to criticism. As it turned out, Tchaikovsky and Petipa probably did not do much collaboration. The ballet master was then in ill health, and it fell to his assistant, second ballet master Lev Ivanov, to create most of the choreography (under Petipa's watchful eye, historians assume).

The ballet, now titled simply *The Nutcracker*, premiered the week before Christmas in 1892 at St. Petersburg's Mariinsky Theatre. As I discovered when I first began digging into the history of the production during my Transcontinental Nutcracker Binge Tour, it was not an immediate success. Despite the czar's enthusiasm—he was in attendance at the premiere—the ballet received what might kindly be referred to as "mixed reviews." It became just another part of the ongoing Russian repertoire and was not thought of as a seasonal or holiday production. That was the state of this now iconic ballet when, in 1919, an extraordinarily talented fifteen-year-old Russian dancer by the name of Giorgi Balanchivadze danced the role of the prince. Twenty-four years later, Giorgi (George) Balanchivadze (Balanchine) came to the United States, where he became the father of American ballet and the choreographer of his own version of *The Nutcracker*. Although the San Francisco Ballet was the first to present the full-length

Nutcracker to American audiences in 1944, it was Balanchine's complex, theatrical version, performed by his New York City Ballet company in 1954, that catapulted the ballet to its current-day status. (It didn't hurt that the production was televised as a holiday special.) Balanchine played the part of Drosselmeyer.

Maria Tallchief was the original Sugar Plum Fairy. Her costume arrived just hours before the performance was to start. Her partner, her Cavalier, sprained his ankle the day before and had to bow out. His name was André Eglevsky. Yes, that André Eglevsky.

— ⌒ —

THAT'S A LONG—138 years, to be exact—and winding road from creepy phantasmagoric pre-Jungian/pre-Freudian tale to a stage full of tutus, toe shoes, snow flurries, and impossibly cute five-year-olds prancing around as harmless little mice. It is also an extraordinary, perhaps quintessentially American journey from marginal production to not just the single most popular ballet in the world but also the most heavily, consistently—I might say mercilessly—commercialized and merchandised single production on earth.

When I attended *Nutcracker* productions in Chicago, Boston, New York, San Francisco, and Eugene, I found myself awash—well, more like drowning—in Nutcrackerabilia. The lobbies of nearly all the venues were converted to sprawling retail outlets selling what I thought was "everything" that could possibly be sold related to the ballet. How wrong I was. The merchandising of this ballet is far more extensive and expansive than the scores of dolls and ornaments and trinkets found in theater lobbies during December productions. Huge online companies market Nut merch year-round. They also run wholesale operations that supply the various ballet companies with whatever gewgaws and tchotchkes sell the best.

To get a sense of the commercial terrain that exists outside the lobbies, I spend some quality time at nutcrackerballetgifts.com, "your one stop Nutcracker and ballet gift source." There I find nutcrackers ranging in size from ten to forty-two inches. That's a three-and-a-half-foot-tall nutcracker. These nutcrackers come in an astonishing variety of styles that don't merely mirror the ballet's characters (Mouse King nutcracker, Drosselmeyer nutcracker) but include an Uncle Sam–ish "sequin patriotic nutcracker" and an all-pink breast-cancer-support nutcracker. There is also a blond Clara and an "ethnic" Clara (café au lait skin). There are *Nutcracker* socks, bibs, onesies, iron-on patches, shopping bags, and forty-eight different ceramic mugs.

But really, it's not, as promised, one-stop shopping because I also discover 1,460 different *Nutcracker*-related products for sale at another site, cafepress.com. I won't bother mentioning the usual merch. But I will bother mentioning thermos bottles, flip-flops, pet-food bowls, wall clocks, coin purses, men's wallets (?), pot holders, duvet covers, iPad cases, and, my personal favorite because it just *screams Nutcracker* to me, whiskey flasks. In terms of actual nutcrackers, I find this odd subset: nutcrackers that are fashioned as football players wearing the uniforms of various college teams. Or sometimes, as with the uniquely off-putting Florida Gator Nutcracker, in the guise of the team's mascot (a sickly green alligator with bared teeth). I know that little girls hound their mothers for Clara dolls and Mouse King puppets. I know that mothers and grandmothers memorialize their *Nutcracker* attendance by springing for ornaments and snow globes. But tell me, who buys football-team nutcrackers? And are they the same consumers who purchase ballet-themed whiskey flasks?

ODDLY, DIGGING INTO the dark and sinister origins of *The Nut-cracker* story makes me love it more, not less. So does learning about the flaws and foibles (not to mention full-on neuroses) of the cast of German, French, and Russian characters involved in bringing the ballet to life. Even plunging into the vast *Nutcracker* marketplace with its profusion of occasionally laughable items does little to diminish my appreciation for the production I've seen every December since I was five. All of this just serves to human-ize the ballet for me, makes it somehow more within my reach. I mean *intellectually*, not artistically. In my head, the ballet no longer seems pristine and untouchable, a flawless, unattainable gem of a thing, the object of wonder and astonishment. Now that I see it as a more-than-century-long collaboration across three cultures, the hard work of men with, in today's parlance, "issues," I am less in-timidated. And more curious about the art form in general. If *The Nutcracker* has such an odd history, what about ballet itself?

—❧—

IS IT FRENCH? All the movements and steps—arabesque, brisé, chassé, entrechat, glissade—are expressed as French words. The word "ballet" itself is French (by way of Italian and Latin). But the form seems to have forever been dominated by the Russians: the Bolshoi Ballet, the Kirov, the Mariinsky; Nijinsky, Nureyev, Baryshnikov, Balanchine. Balanchine, the Russian who French-ified his name. So where does ballet come from?

Here's a surprise: neither France nor Russia.

It turns out that Italy is the birthplace of ballet, which does make sense given that little nudge to the arts called the Renais-sance. Apparently, the lavish events created for fifteenth-century Italian nobility, elaborate spectacles with music, dance, and costume, were the precursors to today's ballet. Dancing masters

taught steps to the nobility, and the court participated in the performances. But it took the greatest patron of the arts in the history of the arts—Catherine de Medici—to move this dance out
of the court and into the world of performance art.

A member of the richest nonroyal family in Europe, Catherine
was the granddaughter of Lorenzo the Magnificent and related
to two popes. This genealogy has nothing to do with ballet, but I
had to include it so I could mention Lorenzo the Magnificent
because, well, how could I not? Who among us would not want to
have a grandpa named so-and-so the Magnificent? Catherine
loved dance (as well as many other arts) and began to fund it.
Now, here's where the French come in. Catherine was married to
King Henry II of France (not one of the better husbands), and
the fetes and festivals she sponsored became a popular part of the
French royal court. The Italian connection remained, though, as
Catherine imported an Italian violinist to help orchestrate these
occasions. His *Ballet Comique de la Reine*, in 1581, is considered
the first "ballet de cour." That was the name for performances that
included dance, sets, costumes, song, music, and poetry.

A century later, King Louis XIV helped to popularize and
standardize the art form. Louis was a ballet enthusiast from a
young age, and by "enthusiast," I don't mean a keen and passionate
observer. I mean a dancer. Encouraged by an Italian-born (yes,
Italy again) cardinal in his court, Louis made his dancing debut
at thirteen. Two years later, resplendent in a golden costume,
he danced the lead part of Apollo in *Le Ballet de la Nuit*. (The
spectacle lasted twelve hours.) The careful reader will note that
Apollo is the sun god. The historically knowledgeable reader will
remember that Louis was known as the Sun King. It was that
fancy glittering costume, that *ballet* costume, that earned him the
nickname we know him by. (And if that's not one of the great
pieces of trivia, I don't know what is.) In 1661 Louis established

the world's first ballet school, the Académie Royale de Danse, in a room of the Louvre. Nine years later, at age thirty-two, he retired from dance, giving him ample time to lead the French invasion of the Spanish Netherlands, fight the Dutch, and embroil France in the Nine Years' War.

Meanwhile, ballet survived the king's retirement (and his wars), flourishing in the royal court, in the dance academy, and onstage. Did I mention that at this time ballet was performed almost exclusively by men? That's right. Men in tights. Then, in 1681 a ballet master imported from—guess where—Italy staged *Le Triomphe de l'Amour*, featuring, for the first time, ballerinas. One of them, Mademoiselle de Lafontaine, is known as the "Queen of Dance." By now, ballet had permanently moved from court to stage. One trained to be a ballet dancer. It was a profession. In France.

So where were those vaunted Russians? Not yet in the picture. Isolated and under strict czarist control that allowed for little influence from the West. It wasn't until the rise of Peter the Great that Russia opened itself up to the art and culture of France and Italy and the rest of Europe. The first Russian school of dance— two rooms in the old Winter Palace—was established in 1738 by a Frenchman. That school later became the St. Petersburg Imperial Ballet School, the very birthplace of—that's right!—*The Nutcracker*. What a tidy little narrative package that was. That's the end of this series of grand jetés through the early history of ballet. Except for this last bit because the Italians just don't get their due when it comes to ballet.

The first ballerina to dance en pointe was probably the Italian Marie Taglioni. The technique was a result of a desire for female dancers to elongate their line, to appear even more lithe, willowy, and weightless. Taglioni and her contemporaries stuffed the toes of their soft shoes with starch and other materials, but soon Italian cobblers were employed to make boxy, stiff-toed shoes from leather, paper, burlap, and satin. And, fyi, the classical tutu, much shorter and stiffer than the diaphanous, calf-length romantic tutu, was introduced around this time to better reveal and focus attention on the ballerina's legs and the intricacies of the en pointe movements.

—◌—

WHILE I EDUCATE and entertain myself (and I hope you) with anecdotes about the saga of *The Nutcracker* and the history of ballet, I am also immersed in novels about ballet. Why? Well, research, of course. But there's also this: I am good at reading and thinking about what I'm reading and taking notes on what I'm reading. I know how to do this. In fact, I'm kind of a natural. And the longer I do this thing I am good at, the longer I don't have to face my trepidation about launching myself into the thing that I am not good at. You know: ballet.

And so I find myself entranced by *Ballet Shoes*, a charming children's book written in the 1930s and given to me by a friend sympathetic to my new cause. In it, three spunky British orphans make their way (or at least the most talented of the three do) in the world of ballet. I read and weep over *Painted Girls*, a vivid imagining of belle epoque Paris, which is not so belle for a poor, underfed little Paris Opéra dancer who becomes the model for Degas's famous *Little Dancer Aged Fourteen* (and the consort of an older male ballet patron). And I read and marvel at the virtuosity of Maggie Shipstead's *Astonish Me*, a steely-eyed (but lyrically written) glimpse into the world of professional ballet.

The central character is Joan, a dancer whose childhood, writes the author, "was dominated by discipline, fear, repetition—her small self in an endless, tearful hurry to get better." Joan is talented—but not talented enough. She makes it into the corps of a top New York company, but, knowing she will never be a prima ballerina, realizing she does not have the exquisite genius that would allow her to partner with the man she loves (a narcissistic Russian, but of course), she makes a different life for herself. Does she yearn for the world she leaves behind? That's not just a question the book asks but also one I ask myself. Do I yearn, today, so many decades later, for the life in dance I never had, never could have had? When I sit in the audience in these ornate theaters and watch *The Nutcracker*, awestruck every damn time at the grace, the precision, the extraordinary effort made effortless, part of me imagines that it could have been me up there. Part of me wishes it had been. But then I read what Maggie Shipstead writes about Joan's friend, who did make her career in ballet. She had "the minimalist body of the survivor." She had "reduced herself to the most essential pistons and gears," her body "offered up" and "spoken for." At one point in the book, the friend describes a career in ballet as "best case scenario . . . a lifetime of feeling inadequate."

The more I learn about the nitty-gritty of this path that was closed off to me, the smaller my sense of regret. I finish *Astonish Me* and exhale a breath I didn't know I was holding. Coming to ballet in midlife, as a rank amateur, on a quest not to be Laurissa Kesslova but to be a slightly braver, energized, and empowered me feels right. Feels just right.

4

Reality Bites

YES, *IT FEELS just right.*

In theory.

But how to convert theory to practice, how to stop thinking and reading and dreaming and start doing? Oh, I know: *Be bold. Take risks. Go for it.* I am familiar with the pep talks. I've given them to myself over the years. I've given them to my children (except the "risks" part. They don't need to hear that one from me). I've read them in women's magazines and self-help books. And yet, now all I can think about are the many and varied and *completely logical* reasons I cannot possibly realize this midlife *Nutcracker* dream:

Allow me to enumerate:

I haven't been in a ballet studio since I was twelve and a half.

Although I am flexible for a midlife woman, in the world of ballet I would be considered just this side of rigor mortis.

Although I am HWP, as they say on the dating sites, I am a hippo in the ballet world.

Although I am "in shape" for a midlife woman, I am a basket case for a dancer.

Although, thanks to my "counterclockwise" lifestyle, I am biologically much younger than my years, I am probably two and a half times older than almost all of the dancers I saw perform.

This is a challenge that exhausts and injures genetically blessed twenty-year-olds. Which I am not.

It might actually be that you can't teach an old dog new tricks.

Or: It very well might be that you can't find a trainer willing to *try* to teach an old dog new tricks.

And: What dog show is going to allow entrance to some elderly mutt?

In other words, who would *allow* me to dance in *The Nutcracker* even if I could?

Why is it so much easier to play the *I can't* tape? Why is self-doubt the go-to place? I think the Indigo Girls had it right: "Darkness has a hunger that's insatiable / And lightness has a call that's hard to hear." Somehow negative self-talk sounds like the truth, and attempts at positive self-talk sound like New Age blather. You know: *affirmations*. Delivered daily to your smart phone. Spare me. Still, I need to pull myself out of this negativity. It feels like it has a life of its own, a fierce headwind, a deep gravitational pull.

I know this terrain. I've been here before. Like when I had all but convinced myself that career and motherhood were incompatible because *I can't* do both. Like when I played the *I can't* tape for far too many years and didn't get on an airplane because of one (admittedly) harrowing experience. Like the years I spent smoking cigarettes because I told myself *I can't* write without smoking.

I need to get to the other side of this newest *I can't* iteration. It's not so much about my ability, or lack thereof, to dance. It is about change and how hard and how scary that is.

Rather than attempting to silence the oh-no-you-can't internal monologue, rather than be angry at myself (more negative self-talk!) about the insistence of the voice, I decide to listen carefully. But with detachment, as if I were listening to someone else.

When it's not personal, I can really hear what I'm telling myself. And what I hear are excuses. Reasons this person (that would be me) is fabricating to put obstacles in her path because she (that's me) doesn't want to, is afraid to, venture out of her comfort zone. What's so great about residing in a comfort zone anyway? Well, it's safe—"anxiety-neutral" is how it's been described—and safe is good. Safe is restful. But, as my father used to say (this was his idea of motivation), "You can rest when you're dead."

Thanks, Dad.

But he's kind of right. There's plenty of time for inertia when you don't have a choice. I *do* have a choice. I have an adventure in the offing, an adventure that requires bidding adieu to the C-zone. Best now to focus on the many and varied benefits of discomfort, of self-induced anxiety. Here's what I find.

I'll have an easier time dealing with new and unexpected (read: unwelcome) changes in the future if I take controlled risks now and challenge myself to do what I don't normally do. The idea is that if you learn to live outside your comfort zone when you choose to do so, the experience can prepare you for the times when you don't get to choose. Kind of like disaster preparedness. Also, I will presumably find it easier to brainstorm and harness my creativity for future endeavors, the thought being that when you open the door to new experiences and new skills, the door stays open. Venturing outside the comfort zone forces you to seek new information, which can help break open the stultifying, limiting way most of us deal with the world around us. It's called "confirmation bias"—the tendency to seek information we already agree with. In the absence of that bias, with the door open, we are free to be our most creative selves. Or so they say.

And here's something particularly interesting for a restless midlifer: Apparently, the more you step out of your comfort zone, the easier it gets. You feel increasingly confident. You venture out more often and go further. This makes sense, and I like it. I like it because this *Nutcracker* dream better not be all I am capable of dreaming. If I can push open this door, who knows what other doors will beckon?

But I wonder just how wedded I am to my personal C-zone. Like a fish that doesn't realize it's swimming in a special environment called "water," I may not even know the landscape and the boundaries of this zone I so happily (and unconsciously) inhabit. How can I go about figuring this out? It turns out that miraculously—oh, okay, not so miraculously—there is an online test for this at www.whatismycomfortzone.com. Of course, I take it. I am actually a sucker for self-tests: emotional-intelligence tests, parenting-style tests, what-famous-dead-person-would-you-be tests. I once took a "scientifically validated" test to determine if I could "take negative feedback like a pro." (I really didn't need to take that one.) And, one day a few years ago, I devoted a full eight hours to taking every "How old are you really?" test I could find on the Web. (In case you're wondering, I might be as young as twenty-seven or as old as fifty-six. I have the eyes of a twenty-five-year-old. I have the bone density of that twenty-five-year-old's mother.)

The comfort-zone test is divided into three questionnaires: the adrenaline survey, the professional survey, and the lifestyle survey. The adrenaline survey asks if I've ever skydived, bungee jumped, or hang glided (no, no, and no) and if I'd like to (uh, no, no, no). I do get points for scuba diving and once having climbed a mountain, but this does not save me from a poor score of 43.1 out of 100. I love the ".1." It's so *scientific*.

The professional survey is interesting because most of the outside-the-zone activities being asked about are actually well within my zone. The creators of the test deem earning an advanced degree, writing a book, speaking in front of a large crowd, and networking at an event as C-zone busters. Not for me. I rack up some points here, scoring a respectable 87.7 out of 100. Note that ".7." But, had the survey asked such questions as *Have you tried (as an adult) to play a musical instrument? Have you participated in a major collaborative project? Have you written outside your genre?*, my score would have plummeted. It just so happens that I have learned to be comfortable in areas where others are not. I think that means I inhabit a different, but not necessarily a more spacious, zone than others.

I do give myself a pat on the back for the lifestyle section. Here I score a 94.3 by virtue of, among other achievements, starting a family (way, way outside the C-zone for me at the time), traveling alone, and overcoming an irrational fear (flying). After answering all the questions, I arrive at a final screen that tells me my comfort-zone average is 75 and offers this bit of good news (I guess): "If your overall comfort zone score is above 66%, congratulations— you're above the statistical average!" I love being above average! Even if I have no idea what that means.

I have to say that, meaningless as I am betting the survey is, it is both boosting my confidence and making me angry. The confidence comes from realizing that I have already done many of what at least the creator of the survey thinks are C-zone-busting activities. That puts the *Nutcracker* dream in some perspective, makes it feel a little less intimidating. After all, I am brave enough to be a mother. Times three. I stand up in front of people and talk. Yay, me. The anger? The average scores listed, divided by gender, are also segmented by age, and the oldest category maxes out at fifty. Fifty? What's the message there? That those fifty and up are not C-zone pushers? Not interested? Not worthy of inclusion? Just plain *invisible*? If challenging yourself and experiencing new things are keys to staying youthful in mind and spirit (and maybe body), wouldn't fifty-somethings be particularly interested in venturing outside the zone?

I call a therapist friend of mine to tell her about the comfort-zone website and my "above average" score. She is, herself, a midlife woman who changed course out of choice, not necessity. She laughs. When I ask for her personal definition of "comfort zone," she pauses to think for a moment. "It's where you are when you don't have to tell yourself to breathe deep," she says, adding quickly, "Of course, sometimes it's a *very* good idea to be conscious of your own breathing."

I THINK I'VE learned what I need to know about the comfort zone. What remains is the trivial matter of busting out of it. Or at least taking that first step. As I continue to contemplate this—because, well, contemplation is much more *comfortable* than action—I'm struck by what seems like paralyzing contradictions: A comfort zone is a *good* place in that it is stress-neutral. We have far too much stress in our lives. Stress makes us sick. But it's a *bad* place because, being stress-neutral, it can lull us into living our lives on cruise control. Also: Midlife is a time to look at and take pride in personal and professional accomplishments, to enjoy an earned sense of satisfaction. But it is also a restless time with (at least for some of us) an insistent urge to shake it up. It's confusing.

I'm puzzled, also, by the popular assertion—a cliché, really—
that the older you get, the braver you become, that the older you
are, the less you care about what others think of you. It's that
"older women just go for it" message promulgated, heralded, and
celebrated for the past decade and a half by the Red Hat Society,
a vast global organization with (I looked it up) 40,000 chapters in
the United States and thirty other countries. That's *a lot* of women.
I ran into a gaggle of them at the Salt Lake City airport not too
long ago. They were a boisterous lot. And they were, indeed, all
wearing red hats, too many of which were so egregiously ugly that
the only conclusion to draw is that, true to the motto of the society, the women really didn't care what others thought.

To be bold. To not care how that boldness looks to others.
That's powerful stuff. But here's the equally powerful message I've
been listening to as I contemplate my dance dreams: *Watch out!
You have so much to risk! You have more to lose now than ever before!*
(Yes, the message comes with exclamation points. Also in italics.)
*You do things you are good at, and people admire you for that. What
will happen when you try to do something you are not good at? Are you
actually willing to be a beginner again? Are you seriously willing to
look foolish? You are queen of your comfort zone. Do you really want to
abdicate the throne?* I'm finding it difficult to argue against these
cautions.

So, let me get this straight: I'm supposed to be enjoying my
hard-earned midlife successes, but I'm not. I'm supposed to be
more self-accepting, but, if anything, I have become harder on myself with age. I expect more. I place the bar higher. I am supposed
to jolt myself into experiencing anxiety, but this sounds like a very
bad idea. I'm supposed to be braver and less concerned with the
opinions of others, but I'm not. I want to dance onstage in the
most beloved ballet on the planet, but I haven't had a pair of pink
slippers on my feet since Spot was a pup. Or since people used the

expression "since Spot was a pup." My head is about to explode. I don't think an exploded head will be good for my dance career.

It occurs to me that *I could fail at this*.

It also occurs to me that not trying would be the bigger failure.

5

A Good Talking-To

IT WAS A little more than a year into my training with erstwhile principal dancer André Eglevsky—he of Balanchine's American Ballet Theatre and, incidentally, the man who conducted private lessons in Manhattan for Caroline Kennedy and her friends. I was, I thought, just about to start taking three or four classes a week, like the more serious students did. I didn't know then—and neither did my mother (or she just didn't let on) that this was a much bigger deal than merely signing on to take additional classes. This was a sea change. I had been what I now understand was a "community student," one of a group of suburban tweens whose mothers enrolled them in ballet lessons so the girls could learn to be graceful and have good posture and dabble in High Culture (not much in evidence otherwise in Massapequa).

But Eglevsky was also busy developing his own little corps de ballet, promising youngsters whom he could place as apprentices or aspirants with Balanchine or in some other major company. Those were the girls who took three and four and five classes a week. Those were the girls whose mothers drove them an hour each way to get to Eglevsky's academy. In moving from one or

49

two classes a week to three or four, I was looking to cross this divide I didn't even know existed. When my mother came to pick me up after class that day, the day she thought she would be arranging for my additional classes, Eglevsky called her into his little office. I was outside in the hallway, sitting on the floor, unwrapping the pink grosgrain ribbon from around my ankles and calves, carefully removing my boxy, painful, completely wonderful toe shoes. Just three months before, Eglevsky had allowed me to go en pointe.

I was a few feet from the door. Of course I eavesdropped. *Her shape is wrong*, I heard Eglevsky telling my mother. *She will never be a dancer with that shape. She has the wrong body.* I heard the words "bottom heavy" and "thighs." And my throat closed. I walked, quickly but with all the grace I could muster, to the bathroom, where I shut myself in a stall and cried.

I never told my mother what I had heard, and she never told me what Eglevsky had said. That's the way our family worked. Or didn't.

A few days later, feigning disinterest, I told my mother I wanted to drop ballet altogether. She tried—halfheartedly as I now see it—to convince me to continue with my weekly class. But I was unpersuadable. Now that I knew how Eglevsky saw me, I saw myself that way too. And so this moment was not just the end of my ballet lessons and the end of my girlhood fantasy of becoming a ballerina. (In truth, I was both anatomically and temperamentally ill suited. I can say this now. I did not know it then.) This moment, this eavesdropped moment, was the end of my girlish lack of self-consciousness about my body, the end of that carefree period during which I didn't give a thought to my physical self. My legs, my arms—they got me where I wanted to go and allowed me to do what I wanted to do. What I looked like, what others thought of my body? This wasn't on my radar. I wore whatever clothes were in the drawer (or on my floor). I passed by mirrors without a glance. I threw my body around with abandon. Many of us enjoy this joyful body oblivion as children. It may be that boys enjoy it longer. Or forever. Most girls do not.

Most girls awaken to body self-consciousness around the age of my own rude awakening: twelve. We lose that innocence. It's often about "developing," about breasts and blood. Or sometimes about others noticing. The gaze. The way a boy (or girl) looks at us that instantly shifts the paradigm. Or it's about the comment. After Eglevsky, I went from oblivious to self-conscious—and from self-conscious to self-critical—in a leap so quick I didn't know it happened. All I knew was that suddenly I was looking in mirrors and not liking what I saw. There was now this voice inside my head that listed faults. The faults my ballet teacher saw. The faults he pointed out to my mother. The faults I heard him point out to my mother.

—◌⁓—

ALL RIGHT: NOW you know. You know how freighted this ballet dream really is, how many layers I need to work through, why my hesitation is so great. You know why it is so challenging for me to silence the "Are you kidding me, you (bottom-heavy) fool?" internal monologue and replace it with something a bit more, shall we say, inspirational.

In search of such inspiration, I mine the Internet for the better part of the next two days, journeying from the National Health Service site to Oprah to a gaggle of angsty teenaged bloggers, an activity that temporarily relieves me of the responsibility of thinking original thoughts. Instead, I am the recipient of a steady stream of predictably underwhelming Web wisdom and clichéd encouragement. However, by some irreproducibly circuitous route, I come across a guest post at a site for "personal growth for passionate living" that does spur a thought or two. It's a column about being fearless written by a counselor who works with university students. She writes about something I knew but had forgotten I knew: the joy and openness of the beginner's mind. In fact, she quotes a book I have on my bookshelf and have read at least three times, Suzuki's *Zen Mind, Beginner's Mind*, which opens with this wonderful statement: "In the beginner's mind there are many possibilities, but in the expert's mind there are few."

This is so much more interesting and enlightening to ponder than the circumference of my thighs. How could I have forgotten this? It is not only okay to be a beginner—as I will be, once again, in ballet—but beginner status can actually confer enormous benefits. A beginner's mind is open, curious, enthusiastic, eager, and creative. Anything is possible. Everything is possible. I have been stuck thinking that being a beginner is all about being clueless and awkward. Being a beginner is a source of embarrassment and potential humiliation. Being a beginner is about fear of failure. But maybe—here's an idea!—being a beginner can be about discovery and the possibility of success.

I hold that thought as I scour the world of self-help books via Amazon.

The key words "mastering fears" net me 566 possibilities. Omitting those works that appear to focus on (alphabetically) conflict, difficult mothers, emotional commitment, flying, insects, loneliness, nightmares, panic attacks (bookmarked for later), public speaking, sex, stage fright, and stuttering and discounting those written to embolden people for the purpose of their own financial enrichment, I narrow the list to a handful. I am tempted by the upbeat imperative of *Be Fearless!* and momentarily enticed by the wildly optimistic *Change Your Life in Thirty Days.* But *Life Unlocked* has a ring to it I cannot ignore, and the subtitle, *7 Revolutionary Lessons to Overcome Fear*, implies great ideas. Plus, it's written by a Harvard psychotherapist! A quick download later, and I am reading about the science of fear and how our brains work, about the split-second timing of the amygdala (our lizard brain), about fear circuits and traumas, brain imaging and Buddhism. Of the seven lessons (which are, I'm disappointed to learn, somewhat less than "revolutionary"), number 3 speaks loudest to me. *If it's hard to change, it is not unchangeable* borders on bumperstickerese, but that's hardly damning. I've read some mighty profound bumperstickers. However, the most powerful lesson I derive from the book is this: You can challenge fear by turning up the volume on positive emotional states. Like hope, for example. If fear focuses on the obstacles and terrors that stand in the way, then hope zeroes in on the possibility of achievement and success. By amping up hope, you shout down fear. Or something like that. It's a good concept, not just for this mildly insane—but of my own choosing—*Nutcracker* challenge but for anything any of us might face, especially the tough, unpleasant challenges that present themselves, unbidden.

I'm on a roll now. I think I'll delve into one more book on the short list, *Master Your Fears: How to Triumph over Your Worries and Get on with Your Life*, by a Long Island psychologist named Linda Sapadin. I like the tough-love implication at the end of that subtitle: *Get on with Your Life.* No whining. No years of therapy. Just get on with it. This attitude is one of the only things—maybe *the* only thing—I miss about New York. I download the book and meanwhile investigate its author, who, it turns out, has an information-rich website.

At the website, I take a fourteen-question personality test—of course I do—and discover that I qualify as a dual personality, "perfectionist worrier." This makes perfect sense, and, although it seems like a heavy cross to bear, there is something quite comforting in conforming to type. Even if it's two types that work together to more than occasionally make life difficult, if not for me, then for those around me. As a veteran of many such tests, I am impressed by the thoughtfulness of the questions. Most online surveys lack nuance. This one is pretty smart. I speed-read Dr. Sapadin's book, then e-mail her and ask if we can talk. She is also the author of several books on procrastination, thus, unsurprisingly, she answers my e-mail in less than an hour and agrees to a phone conversation.

After we exchange the usual pleasantries, I manage to convince her that I am a writer working on a story, not a patient looking for free therapy. Which is almost true. We talk about a concept I particularly like in her book: her reframing and reclaiming of the idea of "difficulty." *Difficult* doesn't have to be synonymous with burdensome, demanding, even impossible, she writes. "Difficulty isn't just something to tolerate, endure, and suffer through; it can also be a source of pride, delight, or self-fulfillment."

Right.

Suffering: No. Self-fulfillment: You bet. I tell her about my dream to dance *The Nutcracker*, and then, without thinking, launch into the many and varied obstacles that stand between me and that performance. I catch myself before I veer into blather and rant, but just barely. It's time to switch back to journalistic mode. It's time to pose a big and important question.

"Where does courage come from?" I ask Dr. Sapadin. "I don't mean skydiving or going to war," I add, probably unnecessarily. "I mean the courage to change, to try new things, to shake things up, to risk failure." I emphasize that last one: *to risk failure*.

"Well," she tells me in that warm but authoritative voice we love to hear from therapists, "courage is not the absence of fear." That's good news. I can't imagine obliterating this fear. Drowning it out with a tidal wave of hope, maybe. I'm still pondering that one. But fear can be both persistent and powerful. I know that from experience. "You don't defeat fear," she says, as if reading my mind. "You don't cure fear. You learn from it. And then you tell yourself, *I'm fearful, and I'll do it anyway.*"

We are both silent for a long but not awkward moment. Or maybe it just seems long because we're on the phone, and I can't read her face. At any rate, it's not awkward. I assume we're silent for the same reason: to let the words sink in. As they sink in, part of me thinks, *Oh, jeez, an affirmation.* But then another part of me thinks, *Yes, this is what you have to say to yourself. This rings true.*

"'I'm fearful, and I'll do it anyway,'" I say, repeating her line, breaking the silence.

"You got it," she says. Warm. But professional. "We push through because we have to leave the harbor and go out into the deep water to see what's out there."

YES, I GET it. *Embrace the beginner's mind. Turn up the volume on hope. Delight in difficulty. Acknowledge fear and do it anyway.* Now I have to work it. I will need to heed all of this advice, and more, because the uphill climb to *The Nutcracker* is steep and rocky. Clearly, the journey is not, at its core, about getting myself in shape and relearning to dance and finding a ballet company willing to take me in and, gulp, performing. It is not merely about the mildly terrifying, potentially humiliating act itself. It is the whole midlife-shake-up thing. The whole fear-of-aging thing.

The whole body-image thing. On this climb, I will be attempting to silence an old tape as I engage with a demon that's been haunting me since I was twelve, since that overheard moment from outside Eglevsky's office.

—☙

THE FAMOUS STUNKARD scales, a series of silhouette figures of female body types ranging from an anorexic 1 to a morbidly obese 9, had not yet been created when I was a young about-to-be non-dancer. First published in 1983, the scales are frequently used in research that measures body-image perception. Subjects are asked to choose a body silhouette that they believe most closely resembles how they look. Before eavesdropping on the conversation in Eglevsky's office, I would have said I looked most like silhouette 3, not skinny, not slender, but not padded either, just a serviceable, healthy-looking body. It would have taken me a moment to make the choice, though, as I didn't relate to my body as something "other" that could be viewed this way, by me or anyone else. Post-Eglevsky, I would have seen that very same body as a 6. A 6 is thick-waisted and chunky-thighed. A 6 still has a definable shape, but just barely. There is too much of everything on a 6. A 6 has a BMI of maybe 29 or 30, the body-mass calculation that marks the entrance into the Kingdom of the Overweight. Was I a number 6 when I was twelve? I thought so. Photographs of that time tell a different story, but the only image I believed was the one inside my head. (Do not worry! This is not about to turn into a teenaged binge-and-purge tale. I didn't do any of that. I just quietly disliked and consistently criticized my body.)

Did I say "dislik*ed*" and "criticiz*ed*"? As in past tense? I wish. Number 6, it turns out, is a damn tough self-image to lose, objective reality (and decades of maturity) aside. I know. Just this morning, I took a quick peek at the Stunkard scales, and I thought, *Yep. That's me. Number 6.* Really? Still? What's going on here? Do I really have such an out-of-whack self-image? Maybe I *am* a 6.

I consult the experts. Well, I consult what passes for "the experts" in our culture. Which is to say, in rapid succession I zip through a series of online self-tests that promise to tell me just how skewed my body self-image really is. I wish these tools, superficial as they turn out to be, had been available back when my self-image changed from 3 to 6. At least I would have known there was such a thing as self-image and that it might not be particularly trustworthy.

On the "How good is your body image?" test I score a 45 (top score is 50). Yay! Oh, not so fast. Apparently, the higher the score, the worse your body image. In fact, along with the results of the test comes this dire diagnosis: I suffer from BDD—body dysmorphic disorder—and am instructed to see a therapist. Thank you, Dr. Internet. BDD, I discover, is a serious mental illness characterized by a person obsessing about her body, or some part of it, for hours on end. The obsession leads to high anxiety, depression, and problems functioning day to day. Someone with this disorder may be so focused on a physical flaw (generally one that appears insignificant or even invisible to other people) that she cannot go out of the house because she does not want anyone else to see it. I don't think I qualify, although there were dark moments in high school when I might have come close. I believe I can safely ignore this diagnosis. Results from the next test reveal that "You are not overjoyed with your physical appearance—to put it mildly." That is correct. To put it mildly. I am most satisfied with my score on the third test. (My m.o., by the way, is to keep taking these online tests until I get a result I like.) The generalized but still insightful summary reads, "You are a product of much of society: self-conscious and somewhat self-judging. You feel uncomfortable with your body some of the time, while other times you feel pretty good." That sounds about right.

This number 6 on the Stunkard scale, the silhouette that's been haunting me since I hung up my toe shoes, is that of a weighty woman. But the image has a weight of its own that has nothing to do with poundage. Sallie Tisdale, in a much-anthologized essay published two decades ago in *Harper's*, wrote about "a weight that women carry." She wasn't talking beefy Stunkard silhouettes. She wasn't referring to what the bathroom scale said. She was talking about the weight of thinking and obsessing and making oneself miserable over what the bathroom scale said. She was talking about the weight of the self-criticism, the heavy burden of measuring your worth by the size of your jeans. The weight of body shame. That's the weight we carry. I carry. I have carried this weight since I was twelve.

So here's my semicrackpot notion: Given that my loss-of-body-innocence moment was a ballet moment, given that leaving Eglevsky's school led me to shoulder "the weight that women carry," could going back to ballet reverse the process? In other words: What André Eglevsky took away, could *The Nutcracker* restore? Doesn't this sound at least a little bit logical? It does to me. I see this midlife foray into ballet as an opportunity to unburden myself of "the weight" and, in the act of dancing, perhaps recapture, if only for a moment, that uncomplicated joy I once felt inhabiting this body. And how wonderful would it be to delete those Stunkard silhouettes from my brain?

Now to the "semicrackpot" part: As anyone who knows anything about ballet knows, dancers have a complicated, uneasy— and often unhealthy—relationship with their bodies. So the notion that I could nurture a *better* relationship with my own body by immersing myself in a world inhabited by the body-obsessed is, well, as deeply flawed as many dancers think their bodies are. And how deeply flawed is that? I'm a little reluctant to find out. But forewarned is forearmed.

———&

YEARS AND YEARS ago, I read Gelsey Kirkland's memoir, *Dancing on My Grave*, about her anorexia, bulimia, and cocaine addiction. (Also about what a jerk Baryshnikov was. I hated that part.) This was jaw-dropping stuff back in the mid-'80s, when the book was first published. Kirkland was one of the most acclaimed ballerinas of her generation, a Balanchine phenom, a prima ballerina who danced the lead in just about every important ballet there was, including, of course, *The Nutcracker*. She partnered with Baryshnikov in the 1977 American Ballet Theatre *Nutcracker* video I rewatch every season.

But all that was more than a generation ago. Surely things aren't as bad now, are they?

Oh, yes, they are, according to a study I find that focuses on the current generation of young dancers. Based on interviews and questionnaires with five hundred of them, the authors conclude that dancers exhibit more pathological attitudes toward weight and eating, have higher rates of eating disorders, and have higher levels of body dissatisfaction. This puts my decades of thigh-dissing, mirror-scowling behavior to shame.

Next I come across an apparently infamous 2010 *New York Times* review of that year's Balanchine *Nutcracker* production. Prepare to gasp. In it, *Times* dance critic Alastair Macaulay slammed New York City Ballet principal dancer Jenifer Ringer, who danced the Sugar Plum Fairy on opening night, for . . . her *weight*. She "looked as if she'd eaten one sugar plum too many," he wrote. Oh, what a clever fellow. Ringer, then a forty-year-old pro who had been dancing with the elite company since she was sixteen, had been anorexic, bulimic, and suicidal earlier in her career. She'd come back to dance after curing herself of anxiety-fueled binge eating and giving birth to two children. In an interview she did with an *Elle* magazine writer, she talked about how her stomach dropped when she read the review. She told the reviewer that she considered it a "huge personal triumph" that she was able to move beyond the words—and the sting—of that sentence.

Misty Copeland, another Balanchine ballerina—she was born exactly thirty years after Gelsey Kirkland—writes about eating a dozen Krispy Kreme donuts after performances. At 108 pounds, she was told she needed to "lengthen," which is ballet code for *lose weight*. "I had always been proud of my body," she writes in *Self* magazine. "Now it had become the enemy." I read about a National Ballet Company of Canada dancer, a bulimic since puberty, who was told she needed to be thinner. She was five foot six inches and weighed 105 pounds.

Finally, I read what is supposed to be an inspiring story in *Dance* magazine about dancers making peace with their bodies. But it could easily be read as a cautionary tale. One dancer who experimented with bulimia criticizes her large breasts. Another admits she continues to struggle with insecurities about her body so severe that at times she can't stand to look at herself in the mirror. A third admits she knows what it's like to be in a "dark place" about weight, then goes on to tell a story about eating entire baguettes at one sitting. And these are the *inspirational* stories.

Regardless of—or maybe *because of*—what I am learning about ballet's obsession with the body and the serious struggles ballerinas have with body image, I am still thinking my own *Nutcracker* journey may offer a way for me to move beyond Stunkard 6. I'd like to find a path that could lead to appreciating, maybe even celebrating, what my body can do rather than dwelling in the land of Not the Right Body. Why should what some long-dead guy told my mother half a lifetime ago continue to affect me? Why, indeed.

Could *The Nutcracker* be my cure? Could giving myself over to the world of ballet, a world ruled by the very demons I want to exorcise, act like a vaccine? Or maybe that "hair of the dog" cure for a hangover? I don't know. But there's a chance.

This is scary, but do it anyway.

This is hope outshouting fear.

This is me pep-talking myself into action.

6

The Door Opens

TONI PIMBLE LOOKS like Joan, the main character in *Astonish Me*. Or she looks like what I imagine Joan would look like if she stepped, with simple elegance, practiced self-possession, and a kind of steely fragility, from the pages of the book I've just finished reading. As I watch Toni enter the coffee shop we've settled on for our rendezvous, as I study her scanning the tables in search of me, I note her small, perfect oval of a face, her lifted chin, her slender neck, but mostly I notice how she carries herself. I have sat in theaters for scores of performances and watched perhaps hundreds of dancers do their thing, but I'm not sure I've ever seen one out walking in the world, and certainly not one dressed in trim slacks and a little red leather jacket making her way toward me. It's not just that she moves with grace. It's that she moves with a studied poise that seems unstudied, each step a purposeful, precise, yet effortless movement of hip, leg, and foot. Her posture is extraordinary: perfectly balanced, erect without being rigid, tightly controlled but seemingly relaxed. How is that possible? And how is it possible for such a small woman to look downright willowy?

I cold-called Toni last week. Actually I cold-e-mailed her, but that's not an expression. At any rate, although I was well acquainted with her name, I'd never met her. And I wanted to. Badly. She was the key to my dancing *The Nutcracker*. I needed to sell her on this project and, most especially, on me. I needed her to see me as the hardworking, determined Little Engine That Could that I am. I needed her to *believe* in me. Toni is a nationally known, National Endowment for the Arts award–winning choreographer who has created more than sixty original works, some of which have been performed by the New York City Ballet, Atlanta Ballet, Washington Ballet, and others. She's been written up in *Dance* magazine, the bible of the trade. She is also the artistic director and cofounder of the company I want to dance with.

She hasn't been a dancer for more than thirty years, but you'd never mistake her for having been anything else. When she holds out her hand for me to shake, she extends a long, slender arm as if executing a port de bras. Her hand is delicate and light, but her grip is strong. She lowers herself into a straight-backed wooden chair in one smooth movement that appears to be some sort of a plié managed with knees together. You might think I'm belaboring a point here, but I'm not. I could go on about how she sips tea, reaches into her bag for her cell phone, jots a note—and sneezes—like an exotic creature, like no one you've ever sat across from at a local coffee hangout unless you keep company with ex-ballerinas who studied with a teacher who danced with Pavlova. Yes, *that* Pavlova. The principal artist of the Imperial Russian Ballet. The first ballerina to tour the world. The one who, when told a lifesaving operation would end her dancing career, replied, "If I can't dance, then I'd rather be dead." She didn't have the operation. She died. She was forty-nine.

Toni is sixty, with—I probably don't need to add given my previous descriptions—the body, muscle tone, and fluidity of movement that any twenty-five-year-old would be proud to call her own. She started dancing at age seven. This is the first story I ask her to tell me. I want to know her background. I want her to see how interested I am in who she is and what she does. And I want her to relax before I pitch her.

Toni tells that she grew up in a small village in sleepy, rural southern England. Her mother wanted her to take music lessons, but instead of sitting at the piano bench practicing—"I just couldn't manage to sit still," she says—she flitted around the living room, twirling, leaping, and dancing. (She illustrates with a sweep of her arms.) Her mother enrolled her in dance classes twice a week and soon on Saturday also—"so she could get rid of me, I think," Toni says with a laugh. Her laugh is soft, faint, gone almost before you can hear it. Toni's teacher at this little local dance school happened to be a former dancer who had performed with the great Pavlova. It may have been one of those career trajectories that was meant to be. It also so happened that Camberley, her small village, was home to one of the United Kingdom's oldest and most prestigious schools of classical ballet, Elmhurst. One day, in the bath, as she remembers it, eleven-year-old Toni announced to her mother, "I am going to Elmhurst." It took her father, who had escaped the life of a coal miner, a while to get used to the idea.

Toni auditioned, got in with a scholarship, and for the next five years advanced through the grueling Royal Academy of Ballet syllabus, from elementary to intermediate to advanced, while attending equally rigorous academic classes. At sixteen, full of hope, she auditioned for the Royal Ballet. And was not accepted. She remembers the day, more than forty years ago, with a kind of clinical precision. The audition was in a particularly grim part of London. It was pouring rain. After the audition—"I was crushed, absolutely crushed," she says—she spent a month moping around the house in the doldrums. "If you love to dance," her father the ex–coal miner told her, "you'll find a way to dance."

She auditioned for Tony Taylor, a British-born dancer who had made a significant career in Germany, and won a place with his ballet in Kiel. There she happily danced for four years and met a man—a fellow company dancer from, of all places, Eugene, Oregon—who would become her husband. They moved to a company in Bonn and later Mannheim when opportunities to work with directors and choreographers presented themselves. But Mannheim was a disappointment. The city was dirty, she says, and the artistic director whom she went there to work with was barely there. When she and her husband heard about a ballet school for sale in Eugene—the very academy her husband, Riley, had attended as a boy when he first fell in love with dance—they shifted their lives, their careers, and their home and took a chance.

At first, Toni thought she would dance and choreograph for the company as well. By then she was thirty-two, juggling the *me me me* of the dancer with the *everyone else* of the director/choreographer. She was running rehearsals and didn't have enough time to warm up properly. She was starting to hurt in ways she should not have been be hurting. She remembers dancing *The Firebird* one night with the company and knowing, just knowing, *I'm done. I cannot do both.* And so she closed the door, abruptly, on her dancing career. She says she had intense dreams for the next seven or eight months, dreams in which she pirouetted across an endless stage.

We talk a lot about what it takes to be a dancer, the alchemy of artistry and athleticism, of passion and discipline. And the body. The body. I tell her the Eglevsky anecdote. I know she will know the name—I see one thin eyebrow arch upward when I mention it—and I know (shamelessly) that my now ancient association with him will boost my cred. In the world of ballet, in the world of the arts, it's all about whom you studied with. Or whom the person you studied with studied with. She listens carefully to my kicked-out-of-ballet tale and then surprises me with her reaction.

"He was being kind," she says. She maintains that it was better to tell me then when I was young than to encourage me and set me up for disappointment later. Good point. She also thinks it was "ethical" of him to, essentially, kick me out. He could have charged my mother for a thrice-weekly class for years knowing I wasn't going to make it—but he didn't. Also a good point. But you know how sensible, solid information, new and even insightful information, doesn't make a dent in a long-held belief? I still curse the guy.

I ask her to tell me about the company she cofounded thirty-six years ago. Of course, I have already done deep research. I know Eugene Ballet is a successful professional company with a long history. Since she and Riley founded it in 1978, it has grown from a community-based dance group to one of the West's busiest (and most versatile) companies. The resident company in a stunning performance hall that really has no business being in a minor-league town like Eugene, Oregon, it has performed in more than a hundred cities in thirty-three states as well as internationally in Canada, India, Sri Lanka, Bangladesh, Syria, Jordan, Tunisia, and Taiwan. The company performs full-length classical ballets (*Swan Lake, Cinderella, Sleeping Beauty*) as well as contemporary works by some of the country's top choreographers. But more to the point—my point, that is—in November and December of every year, EBC mounts a full-on production of *The Nutcracker*, taking it on the road to five western states. The tour spans six weeks, includes twenty-five performances, and ends with a three-day (generally sold-out) run in Eugene, my town.

And I want a piece of that.

No, it's not the Joffrey. No, it's not the Mariinsky. But these EBC folks are true professionals. The bar (barre) they set, that Toni sets, is high. And the company is right here, in my (delightfully undervalued) hometown. And I am right now sitting across from the company's artistic director, the one person who can make my dream come true. Will she allow me to immerse myself in the life of her ballet company, take classes with the dancers? Could I earn a spot in *The Nutcracker*? Join the troupe for the 2014 holiday production of the ballet?

I'm thinking all this as I listen to Toni talk about her company. She speaks in a cultured but understated British accent that has been softened and flattened by almost four decades of living in the former colonies. She talks about the lean years, the very lean years. In the '80s, facing shrinking dollars for the arts and unsustainable budget deficits, the company paired with the neighboring Ballet Idaho to become Western Ballet Theatre, a rich but crazy-making collaboration that lasted almost fifteen years. Toni is matter-of-fact about the struggles. And equally matter-of-fact, although obviously proud, of the successes. Today, she tells me, 60 percent of the company's $1.8 million budget is "earned income," which makes the company less dependent on fund-raising than many arts organizations. "How much of that earned income comes from *The Nutcracker*?" I ask her, ever so gracefully (I think) moving the conversation in the direction it needs to go. She has to double check with her production manager, she says, but "a lot." (A few days later he gets back to me with the exact figure: 44 percent of the company's entire earned income.)

We talk about *The Nutcracker*. I tell her that my mother took me to see Maria Tallchief dance the Sugar Plum Fairy. (She is impressed.) I tell her that I've taken my own daughter to see the EBC production for the past fourteen years. (She's pleased.) I tell her a bit about my Transcontinental Binge Tour. (She laughs, then quizzes me about each production.) Then I get her to talk about her production, her interpretations in choreography, the number of dancers onstage, the costumes and sets, the use of children— different children in each of the cities on tour—and what it means to mount such an ambitious endeavor. I'm thinking that I can somehow seamlessly segue into my pitch, but I can't. I just take a breath and plunge in. Do I sound ridiculous? I try not to listen to myself.

Toni sits, quiet and composed. She takes a sip of her tea. I finish the pitch, stopping myself from excessive babbling, stopping myself from pointing out my (obvious) flaws and defects: wrong body, way too old, ancient, ancient training. She doesn't laugh or, oddly, even act surprised. But she pauses for a long moment. I see her holding herself back from giving me the once-over. I know what she'll see. But I also know what she heard. And I'm a pretty good talker. Still, I am ready for her to tell me, undoubtedly with more kindness and tact than Eglevsky did, that this ballet dream, this fantasy of dancing in *The Nutcracker*, is and should remain just that: a fantasy.

But she doesn't.

"Interesting," she says. Now she does, in fact, give me the once-over. Happily, I am sitting with my best parts (large eyes, long dark hair, decent shoulders) showing and my decidedly unballetic butt hidden from view. Should I say more? What more could I say? I'm busy constructing new arguments in my head. In fact, my internal *Trust me trust me trust me I would never embarrass you, the company—or myself* monologue is so loud that I almost don't hear her when she finally breaks silence.

"Yes," she says.

Whaaaat?

"With conditions," she quickly adds. I must be in shape. I must relearn the vocabulary of dance. I must awaken my long dormant muscle memory and begin to walk and move and gesture like a ballerina. I must take lessons and classes, lots of lessons and classes. I must prove myself worthy.

"And," she adds, unnecessarily, "we're not talking Sugar Plum Fairy here."

I am so stunned by her immediate and positive response that I don't ask her why she's taking this chance on me. Only months later, when I'm braver, when I am more sure of my place, do I ask.

7

The Ballerinas

A WEEK LATER I find myself sitting on the floor of one of the exercise studios in my gym. Across from me is Tori, a six-year veteran dancer of Eugene Ballet Company whom I've contacted on Toni's suggestion. I wanted to talk to a couple of dancers to discover how they got to where they are. I am intensely curious about the nature of a life in ballet, a life I tried to imagine for myself when I was twelve, and about how young professional dancers do what they do. Do they have a life outside ballet? Are they happy? Do they like themselves? After reading so much about the horror show that is ballet and body image, I wonder how these objectively extraordinary physical specimens feel, subjectively, about their instrument, their body. On a more practical level, I need to quiz them about how they stay in shape, what they do to promote strength, flexibility, and stamina. I need advice. Badly. It's not that I am a couch potato—far from it—but I'm sure that what I do to stay in shape has almost nothing to do with what a ballerina must do.

Also, truthfully, I need to make personal connections within the dance troupe. I can't, a few months from now, march into the

71

first company class of the season as a stranger. A stranger who is twenty-five years older than everyone else. With flappy midlife arms and a peasant butt and a back leg that, in arabesque, is raised barely two feet off the floor. I need friends! I need a couple of dancers who know me, who are—because I am asking for their advice and counsel—invested in how I do.

Tori, whose e-mail moniker is "yellowtutu" and whose full name is the very ballet-friendly Victoria Harvey, is sitting across from me in a position that defies my understanding of human anatomy. Her legs (long, slender, subtly muscled) reach out from her hip sockets at almost 180-degree angles, as if she is doing a split but facing me. Her back is straight, her shoulders down—not hunched like the rest of us mortals—her arms (long, slender, subtly muscled) resting lightly on the tops of her thighs. Her neck is long; her chin is lifted, and she is smiling. She is smiling, not grimacing like a normally constructed human being would be if that normally constructed human being could ever manage to force her body into this impossible position.

Tori is twenty-five and, just in case it isn't clear already, looks every inch the ballerina. I want to start our conversation by asking her about her background, but we immediately begin talking body. It's my fault. I just can't get over the extraordinary flex in her hip flexors, the long, tapered muscles of her legs, her single-digit-body-fat torso. I ask her to evaluate her body because if ever there was a body about which a dancer should have a good body image, hers is it.

But no. She makes no mention of the "good parts" that are so obvious to me, but instead directs her focus—and my attention—to her "bad feet." Apparently, they do not exhibit the demi-circle curve of great ballerina feet. "Cashew feet" is the expression I've read that refers to this magic top-of-the-foot arch. She takes off

her ballet slippers to show me and points her toes. I see a beautiful arch with the tips of her toes in almost perfect alignment with
her heel. "Almost" being the operative word, I guess. As if these
terrible feet were not bad enough, Tori, at a willowy five foot
seven, is two inches taller than what has been decreed the tallest
optimal height for a ballerina. Between five foot and five five is
the range because, as Toni explained to me last week, toe shoes
add five inches in height—and it doesn't look right if the ballerina
is taller than her male partner. ("But what about Maria Tallchief?"
I immediately countered. "She was five nine." "Ah," Toni replied,
"that was a different time. And the exception that proves the rule."
She asked if I knew how tall Mikhail Baryshnikov is. I did not.
He is five foot six.)

I wonder aloud how Tori can be so critical of such a tuned and
toned body. She points and flexes her feet as she answers. "You
look at yourself, you *stare* at yourself, in the mirror every day," she
says, "and, really, that's not a healthy thing." She bends over at the
waist, stretching her arms in front of her, laying her stomach almost flat on the studio floor. Ten years ago, when I used to practice yoga with some regularity, I worked on just this position.
After two years, with a borderline unbearable tension down the
backs of my legs, I could get my elbows to touch the floor. "Some
days," Tori is saying as she lifts her upper body to vertical, "some
days I say, 'I'm having a fat day,' but really I know that you can't
be 'fat' all of a sudden one day and then not the next. But in
tights and a leotard, you can see everything, And I mean *everything*. And you look at the dancers around you, and of course you
compare."

But mostly, she says, she likes herself. The hardest time she had
with her body image was when puberty hit. (Join the club.) As a
budding ballerina, she did not want to be a budding woman. She

did not want the hips. She did not want the breasts. She wanted to keep her twelve-year-old body.

The "budding ballerina" comment gets her talking about what brought her to ballet. She was not, as I had imagined, one of those precious three-year-olds who fell hard for ballet when her mother took her to see *The Nutcracker*. Her first love was actually figure skating. She took ballet to help with her technique on ice. But an injury that kept her from skating and a summer ballet intensive changed her direction, and her life. At thirteen, she was completely committed, balancing school and daily ballet classes until she auditioned for the prestigious Royal Winnipeg Ballet, got in, and moved to Canada. Then at nineteen she landed an apprenticeship at Eugene Ballet Company and has been here ever since. She tells the story matter-of-factly. Her voice is soft, and everything about her is light and airy. But this delicacy masks what has to be an iron will and a ferocious work ethic.

Her life, I learn, is rigidly scheduled and narrowly focused. And exhausting. I listen as she details her in-season daily agenda: Up at 6:00 in time to wash her face, eat a bowl of oatmeal, and throw back a cup of coffee. Oh, and make up her face, especially mascara. (Large, dark eyes are part of the ballerina's look, apparently offstage as well as on.) She preps everything the night before: ballet clothing, shoes, towel, water. She arrives at the studio a half-hour early to warm up. She warms up her feet a lot, those less-than-perfect feet she worries about. Class runs from 8:00 to 9:30 with one fifteen-minute break. And then there's rehearsal all or most of the day until 4:00. (How much she rehearses depends on the role she has in that ballet.) From 4:30 to 7:00 she works at the Dancers' Closet, a small retail outlet selling clothing and shoes for dancers. Then it's dinner and early to bed. Her social life is with the other dancers during rehearsal and, wedged in between the end of her workday and bedtime, with her boyfriend. I work hard. I am disciplined and focused, but this is something else, this passion, this drive that trumps . . . well, everything.

We're still on the floor of the studio, she spread-eagled, I cross-legged. I tell her I thought I wanted to be a dancer too, but hearing about her life, how challenging it is, how much energy (body, mind, spirit) is takes to do what she does, I know my love for ballet would not have been equal to the task. I tell her about wanting to rename myself Laurissa Kesslova. She laughs knowingly. "I wanted to change my name to Viktoria with a 'k' because it looked Russian." Okay! A bit of bonding across a generation and a yawning talent gap. Good!

I quiz her on what she does to stay in shape, looking for pointers. I need pointers. I run, which I know tends to shorten the hamstrings, the opposite of what you want in ballet. And I weight train, which creates bulky muscles. I don't mean weight-lifter bulky or "show me your guns" bulky. It's almost impossible for women to visibly bulk up. But there's a difference between the shortened, thick muscles one cultivates doing squats and bench presses and the long, loose muscles one wants for ballet.

"Pilates?" she says, more a question than an answer. "I heard that was good." But she doesn't take classes. How could she? She is in the ballet studio six or seven hours a day. *That's* how she stays in shape. Me . . . I need to *get* in shape. I'm not going to get the advice I'm looking for from Tori. So I switch gears and ask her to take me through her warm-up. My warm-up, on the rare occasions I actually do warm up, consists of jumping jacks and a few runners' lunges. Tori's warm-up lasts forever and involves a tennis ball, two different foam rollers, a painful white one and an even more painful black one, and far too much attention to something I never knew I had and now wish I had never discovered: my iliotibial band.

I MEET SUZI, another EBC dancer whom Toni suggested, a few days later at the ballet company's home, a modest, clean-lined glass-and-brick building that looks vaguely Scandinavian. Or maybe that's because I remember it used to house a Danish modern furniture store before EBC and two other arts groups raised enough money to buy the place. We meet in one of the smaller practice studios. Suzi is already there when I arrive, and here's the maybe-not-as-odd-as-I-think-it-is thing: She is sitting on the floor, her legs opened almost 180 degrees, just like Tori was, in that forward-facing split. And, just like Tori, she is pointing and flexing, pointing and flexing her feet. Suzanne Haag is, at thirty-three, the oldest dancer in the company, which may be why Toni suggested I talk with her. Or she may have pointed me in Suzi's direction because—as I discover during the first few minutes of our conversation—Suzi is smart, self-reflective, direct, articulate, and generally an interviewer's dream. Not that I am *interviewing*. I'm trying really hard not to interview. Just talk. Just learn about her life and get her interested in my quest. Just make some friendly overtures.

Suzi is henna-haired and blue-eyed, small and lithe, trim and ever-so-slightly muscular. Which makes her look not at all like a classic ballet dancer. But I've seen her onstage—in fact, in *The Nutcracker* dancing the Arabian—and she is fluid, sinewy, and supple, simultaneously precise and passionate. She dances with the assurance and self-possession of a veteran performer. (She's been with EBC for a decade.) I don't tell her any of this because it would sound like sucking up. But I think it as I watch her point and flex and as I listen to her tell me that she's been dancing since she was two. And yes, it was a *Nutcracker* moment! She saw the ballet with her mother and said, "I want to do that," or "Me do dat, Mommy," or whatever a two-year-old would say. She doesn't remember. The story comes from her mother. What she knows is that she cannot remember a time without dance.

Her first lessons were at Miss Nancy's School of Dance. "The name tells you everything you need to know," Suzi says, deadpan. At six she saw Suzanne Farrell on *Sesame Street* showing "big bend, little bend" (plié, demi-plié) to the Sesame Street characters, and she thought, *Her name is Suzanne, and my name is Suzanne, so I can be a real ballerina too.* Take that, you critics of TV-watching and children. When Suzi was eight, Miss Nancy told her mother the happy news that her talented and enthusiastic daughter had outgrown the teacher's eponymous studio. "Take her to Hartford," Miss Nancy said. That would be the School of the Hartford Ballet, a rigorous preprofessional program that aimed, like Eglevsky's academy on Long Island, to train dancers, not to give kids an after-school enrichment activity. She started classes there in the third grade. A year or two later, when the teachers did a detailed analysis of her body (finding various faults and imperfections), she remembers thinking, *Well, I guess I'm not going to be a dancer. . . .* But she had what I didn't have, and I don't just mean talent. I mean passion and drive. She would not be discouraged. By her early teens, she was taking ballet classes six times a week. Which possibly explains the vertebra stress fracture she suffered at fourteen.

Maybe she shouldn't pin all her future hopes on ballet, she thought during the nine long months of rehab. Maybe her injury wouldn't get better. Or she'd suffer another one. With her parents' encouragement, she decided to go to college, which is not a route, or at least not the fast track, to a career as a dancer. She majored in arts administration with a dance concentration, deciding along the way that yes, her body *could* take it, and yes, she *did* want to dance. After graduation she sent out scores of videos and auditioned for maybe forty companies, landing a job with the Lexington Ballet Company in Kentucky just a month before it folded. So she went out on the audition circuit again and got a handful of offers for unpaid apprenticeships, the position that seventeen-year-olds take when they first join a company. Finally she got what she wryly describes as a "nominally compensated" position with Nevada Ballet. And then, in the summer of 2003, Toni Pimble called. And Suzi has been a member of the EBC corps ever since.

I wonder if that means she has made peace with this highly trained, well-used body she was told long ago was not a dancer's body. In a word: no. When I ask her for a head-to-foot evaluation, she jumps in with no hesitation, describing her "flaws" with clinical objectivity—not the kind of deprecating self-talk the rest of us (okay, I) engage in.

"My head is, well, okay," she says, cupping the sides of her jaw with her hands. A dancer's head is supposed to be smallish, I learn, with, of course, the perfect oval face. "My neck is too short," she says, "and my shoulders are too broad." She squares her shoulders, which look lovely and sculpted to me. "I have linebacker shoulders," she says. "My torso is . . ." She hesitates, looking for the word, placing her hands on either side of her waist. "Toni says it's square, too square, not tapered enough." She extends her arms, slender, slightly long for her body (a good thing), and very pale, red-head pale. "My arms are too muscular. I bulk up very easily." I can't see the bulk, and there's no apparent muscle definition, but ballet standards are . . . what's the word? Extreme? I steal a look at my own arms, where the muscles I've been working on so assiduously are fighting it out with the underarm flab that (literally) flaps in the wind. (Okay, it has to be a pretty strong wind. But still.) "My chest isn't flat enough," she says, which is a sentence one does not often hear from a woman. "But my legs are long for my body," she says, extending one beautifully shaped gam with a curving calf, slender ankle, and arched foot. This is a good thing. Also, she likes her feet. Or, at least, she proclaims them "okay," which, in this context, appears to be high praise.

At five foot three she wishes she was either shorter so she could partner with short guys or taller so she had a nicer line. Oh, and she thinks she could be ten pounds thinner. (She weighs herself every morning. I was going to modify "weighs" with "obsessively," but I think I don't need to, right?) To my eye, if Suzi were ten pounds lighter, she would float away. Like Tori, she talks about the mirror, the wall of mirrors in the studio. "I am always looking at myself. I am looking at the other dancers too and comparing myself."

Her typical day is, not surprisingly, a lot like Tori's, from the 6:00 a.m. wake-up to the long warm-up at the studio, from the tough morning class to the day-long rehearsal schedule, which she calls "brutal." I ask what she does in the little spare time she has. "I know this sounds weird," she says, "but I like to go dancing." To make this life of dance work—she and the EBC dancers are paid only during their twenty-six-week season—she travels elsewhere to teach dance and lives close to the bone, in a one-bedroom apartment, with her cat. That sounds a little pitiful when I write it, but Suzi is doing what she wants and loves to do and says she can't imagine stopping. Her namesake, Ms. Farrell, danced until she was forty-four.

The advantage, to me, of Suzi's age and her long tenure and her various injuries along the way is that she has thought hard about— and spent years practicing—ballet-centric workouts. When I ask her what she does, what I should be doing to get myself in ballet shape, she has lots of ideas. Maybe a few too many.

First there's yoga, she says, for opening the chest and hips, for centering and balancing, and for lengthening, especially the hamstrings. She is also a fan of Pilates. I tried it a few times, but it didn't make me sweat, so it didn't feel like a workout. "Ah," she says, "it is *quite* a workout. You'll see." She mentions something called Gyrotonics, which I've never heard of. It's some sort of guided, machine-based, stretchy, dancery, semicultish thing. She hasn't done it herself—it's too expensive—but she's heard great things from dancers who have. I'll have to check it out. So far, nothing she's endorsing is anything I'm doing, which is not good news. "What about cardio?" I ask. Cardio is probably two-thirds of what I do, most of it running. Her answer is yes on the cardio (great for stamina) but a big no on the running. "Keep stress off the joints!" she says, more command than statement. She jogs in the water. I can't imagine anything more boring, but I see her point. As for weight training (the other third of what I do), she cautions "very light weight . . . arms and chest only . . . no legs." I have to say that I won't be sad to give up the squats and lunges. And oh gosh: no more burpees? C'est dommage. Finally, as if the rest were not enough, she likes ab work. She suggests crunches on a stability ball and planks, lots of planks. I'm glad I asked. I guess.

I am daunted by the physical challenge of getting myself to a place where, when the season begins in September and company classes start up every morning, I can participate without hurting myself and/or incurring the shocked looks of my classmates (I was going to write "fellow dancers," but that strains credulity at this point). I *should* be daunted. It is daunting. I will have to—in who knows what order, probably all at the same time—lose ten pounds, develop an entirely new fitness routine, make myself more flexible than I have been since I lay on my back and did Happy Baby in my crib, create strength and articulation in my decidedly uncashewlike feet, figure out what to do about my flappy midlife underarms, and relearn ballet from the ground up.

And, oh, yeah, reorganize my life to make all this possible.

It's not like I have nothing to do and ballet will fill a void. In fact, my current life is virtually voidless. I've got a family that includes a teenaged girl who may not think she needs me, but oh, yes, she does, and two sons who have grown into people I love spending time with. I have a husband who probably occasionally wants to see me and a good friend, Kim, whom I more than occasionally want (and need) to see. I have a full-time job teaching writing at a university. I have pets and a huge garden and a several-afternoons-a-week hanging-out-at-espresso-joints habit that I enjoy. I have a time-consuming Facebook obsession, and I blog every Wednesday. Also, I love to cook.

On the plus side—if the above could be considered minus— I have been blessed with prodigious energy, the nose-to-the-grindstone work ethic of a newly arrived immigrant, a lifelong devotion to/bordering on obsession with list-making that keeps me superorganized—and an enormous desire to do this. To make this happen. To succeed.

Yes, this will take sacrifice. I'll have to rejigger my days, reorder my priorities, forget about the garden, do takeout from Tasty Thai. Maybe even—dare I say it—cut back on Facebook time. Oh, there will be sacrifices. But a dancer's life is all about sacrifice, isn't it?

8

Prep for the Prep

IT IS NOW the beginning of March. Six—count them, *six*—months until the new season begins for EBC. But even more importantly, and ever more urgently, it is *N minus nine*, as in a scant nine months between this moment and the moment I hope to be onstage dancing in *The Nutcracker*. Miracles have happened in nine months. An entire house can be built in nine months. Astronauts can travel to Mars in nine months. A fully formed human baby can be gestated in nine months. Surely I can be stage-ready in nine months. She says with bravado.

Let's see: I've delved into the murky depths of why I want to do this. I've ferreted out the fears and anxieties and bolstered myself with the collected wisdom of others. I've got my you-can-do-it affirmations and mantras all lined up. I know more about the origins and permutations of *The Nutcracker* than any person not completing a doctoral dissertation on the subject. The artistic director of a vibrant professional ballet company is giving me the go-ahead. Two talented ballerinas have my back. What's left? Oh, yeah. Relearning ballet. Or, first things first: getting in shape to relearn ballet.

I'm not starting from zero here. (Or so I think.) I have been
working out, concertedly, for more than two decades. For my last
book, I spent an intense, very sweaty (and slightly crazed) year
exploring every form of exercise that promised high-level fitness.
I've taken aerobics classes and aqua-aerobics classes, step classes,
step-sculpt classes, spinning, circuit training, cardio-drumming,
Zumba, NIA, CrossFit, TRX, and Tabata. I've worked with bar-
bells, kettle bells, resistance bands, medicine balls, stability balls,
BOSU balls, sandbags, and sledgehammers. I've hired personal
trainers, grunted through the entire P90X regimen, and run two
half-marathons. But, as I've learned from my two ballerina experts, pretty much nothing I do or have done for the past twenty
years has any relation to getting in shape to dance. In fact, I have
been suddenly confronted with the unhappy truth that my various physical exertions have actually done things to my body—
added square, muscular shoulders and chunky quads, tightened
and shortened my hamstrings—that are the opposite of what a
dancer wants.

SO I HAVE a new list now: active stretching and lots of it, yoga,
Pilates, water jogging, and this machine-assisted workout called
Gyrotonics. Toni, Tori, and Suzi all mentioned it, and when I quiz
another dancer I know about it, she mentions that in fact she's
studying to become a Gyrotonics instructor. It's one of those
things that you've never heard of until you start attending to it,
and then it seems to be everywhere, and everyone has heard of it.
An old friend from college e-mails me that a studio just opened
in Evanston, and she's signed up for weekly sessions. A day later I
see an informational brochure tacked up on the bulletin board of
one of my coffee hangouts. All roads apparently lead to Gyro. I

think I'll take the hint and start with whatever this method or regimen is, if only because I know nothing about it, and curiosity energizes me. Especially now, at the beginning of this long haul, I need something new and different.

I'm happy to discover that a movement studio in town run by a woman I know in passing—a no-nonsense, midlife ex-dancer—offers personal Gyrotonics sessions. Because I have never heard of Gyro before, it comes as a surprise when Marilyn, the studio owner, tells me her schedule is full. She has no room for another client. But, she says, taking a long minute to check her date book, she will have space in about two months. I'm in *Nutcracker* count-down mode. Two months is unacceptable. I tell Marilyn I need this Gyro thing, and I need it now! She suggests another instructor who, luckily, does have space in her schedule.

Three days later, I present myself to Jean Nelson for a quick tour of the movement studio and a brief orientation to what she calls "the work." I don't like that she calls it "the work," which sounds cultish to me, but I do like Jean, who doesn't have to tell me that she's a dancer. I recognize that telltale extended-neck, lifted-chin, relaxed-shoulder posture. And the small, slender, toned but not noticeably muscled build. I fear that writers have equally recognizable physiques: hunched shoulders, rounded backs, wide butts. Or, wait a second: Is that just me? If you saw Jean from a distance, you'd think she was in her twenties. Yes, *that* good. She has a son who's about to graduate from college.

In the first room we walk through, a middle-aged man and a sixty-something woman are moving and stretching on two ceiling-high structures with straps and pulleys and bars that look like a cross between a adult jungle gym and a medieval torture apparatus. I'm delighted to discover that this is not Gyrotonics equipment. The towering structures, along with two additional pieces of equally intimating equipment on the floor, are for the practice of Pilates. The machines have names like the Universal Reformer and the Spine Corrector and the Tower and make you want to go lie down on a soft bed in the fetal position. I am well aware—and not overly thrilled—that Pilates is in my future.

The next room, the inner sanctum, is Gyro-land. The bare walls are painted in warm earth tones. The only objects are three imposing machines that have so much going on—wheels and weights and pulleys and pegs, leather and steel and blond wood—that it's hard to imagine exactly what one does with them. Unlike the sharp rectangularity of the Pilates equipment, the Gyro machines are all curves and swirls. If machines can be feminine, then that's what these are. Jean had told me on the phone when I was setting up this appointment that one "danced" with the machine. Although I have not a clue how that might happen, the soft contours give a hint that it might be possible.

Jean raises one of her lovely dancer's legs and lifts it, gracefully and effortlessly, over the leather-padded bench of one of the machines. She sits, with that self-contained, pulled-together body language that I've noticed is common to the dancers I've met, and tells me she's been a Gyrotonics trainer for more than eight years. She is also a yoga teacher at several studios in town and teaches a class called Yoga for Dancers (note to self). She talks about "the work" with reverence, with a sense that this is something grander, more one-with-the-universe-y, than just exercise. She speaks about "Jului," the Hungarian-Romanian ex-dancer who invented Gyrotonics, the way one would talk about a guru. Later, at home, I do some quick research on Jului Horvath, and boy, is he ever guru material. In a video I watch, he walks the grounds of a Edenic retreat in flowing trousers, his gray hair pulled back in a ponytail, several lithe young women trailing behind. Jului's biography reads like a legend-in-the-making (his making, I assume): A principal dancer for the Romanian National Ballet Company, he defected while on tour in Italy in 1970, received political asylum in the United States, and "did whatever he needed to do to survive" in New York—including painting houses and "dancing on cars in Central Park." He went on to dance with the New York City Opera and several special tour companies before securing a position as a principal with the Houston Ballet. And here the Defector Success Story takes a twist, as did, apparently, Jului's ankle. He ruptured his Achilles, ending his career as a dancer but opening the door to what would be his life's work—and "the work." Back in New York, he began a yoga practice to heal himself and started having "profound energetic experiences," according to his bio. To delve more deeply into those experiences, he moved to St. Thomas in the Virgin Islands, built a one-room hut in the mountains, and spent the next six years studying yoga and meditation. To which I say, no disrespect intended: Nice work if you can get it. During this solitary and contemplative time, he gained new insights into movement and healing and began to create his own exercise method. Thus spake Gyrotonics.

With roots in yoga, Tai Chi, and dance, the Gyrotonics exercise sequences are performed on the specialized patented equipment upon which the lissome Jean is perched. As I pepper her with questions about "the work" and "the apparatus," she engages with the machine, swoops her arms in circles, rotates her shapely dancer's shoulders, snakes her spine, moves backward, forward, sideward, up, down in one long, fluid motion. She is sitting, but she is, indeed, dancing. Jean says it is all about expanding and lengthening the spine, creating space between vertebrae, space within the joints. It's about the natural spirals of the body, about mobility and flexibility, fluidity and motion. She says that it's a little like yoga, but the machine offers resistance. And it's a little bit like Pilates, but the movements take place in all planes, not just the linear. Because of the pulley system and weights, Jean says that you almost feel like you're in traction. In a good way. The body gets pulled into positions you couldn't get into all by yourself.

Now she lies down on the bench and puts her small, high-arched dancer's feet into the fabric stirrups hanging from the back pulleys. She moves her legs in huge circles, opening them up to near split position, then rotating them around, up, and back to form a perfect L with her torso just for a second before she begins a more complex spiraling choreography. The machine is like your partner, she says, your dance partner. And so it seems. It's impossible for me not to sip a little of this Kool-Aid. I sign up with Jean for an introductory Gyrotonics session next week.

MEANWHILE, WITH ATTENTION to the ticking clock—and because I really don't know how to do anything halfway—I show up for both the Pilates and yoga classes at my gym. I download three different morning yoga routines and vow to "create a practice," as they say. Then, walking downtown one morning to investigate a newly opened coffee shop, I come across a fitness studio called Barre3, "where yoga and Pilates meet ballet." Bingo. Maybe my life just got easier.

Overcome with excitement—okay, maybe that's an exaggeration—I walk in, find out from a lithe and lovely woman, who I hope owes her body to Barre3, that I can get a great deal on three introductory sessions, and immediately pay up and register for my first class tomorrow at 7:30 a.m. Then I rush home to research the method, which, of course, I should have done before I plunked down the money. But I am happy to discover that Barre3 "evolves the dancer's workout by combining the grace of the ballet barre with the wisdom of yoga and the strength of Pilates." It is a combination of isometric holds, low-impact dynamic movements, and recovery stretches that promises to "create the strength of an athlete with the long, lean, graceful lines of a dancer." The only long line that in any way relates to me is the long line of sturdily constructed peasants I have evolved from, so achieving the "long, lean lines" of a dancer may stand outside my genetic capabilities. But toning muscles I haven't paid attention to (foot, ankle, hamstring), creating a truly solid core, and stretching and lengthening—these are things I can (and must) do.

I arrive at the small, classy studio fifteen minutes early, dressed in my raggedy, well-used, gym-rat-style workout togs—a shapeless tank and even more shapeless cut-offs that were once sweatpants—to find a bevy of 10-percent-body-fat twenty-somethings in fashion dancewear, several of whom are wearing those incredibly cute, flirty workout skirts over colorfully printed spandex capris. I attempt not to feel completely intimidated by saying to myself, *Oh, yeah, well I bet none of them have written seven books, have they?* And that sort of works. A little like imagining your audience naked, I guess. I need to get used to this uncomfortable out-of-my-depth feeling, this stranger-in-a-strange-land sensation that threatens to overcome me. The World of the Lithe and Lissome will be my world for the next eight months. I'd better start dealing with it now.

The instructor, Summer Spinner—a name that pretty much destined her for this kind of work—is the lithe-ist and lissome-ist of all. Also one of those instructors who actually knows and understands the human body, knows how and when to cue, is funny. And is one tough cookie. The class, nonstop routines for sixty minutes, is surprisingly difficult with interminable mini-pliés that burn followed by fifteen-count holds that leave me shaking all over. "Let's see those shakes and quakes," Summer says. This is apparently a good thing. We do triceps squeezes using two-pound weights—two pounds! I regularly work out with twenty-pounders—that make me want to scream. We do a thigh-squeeze, side-plank routine that could easily replace waterboarding as effective torture. The sweat is pouring off me, running down my legs and puddling on my yoga mat. If I only had a pair of those cool grippy socks like everyone else, I wouldn't be slipping between moves. Or at least a French pedicure like the girl next to me. The routines, at the barre, in the center of the studio, on the mats, are equally grueling. Summer is constantly reminding us of form, cuing us to which muscle groups we should be working, egging us on to go deeper, extend more fully, find engagement, "dial it in," find the "ease in the effort."

That last one will take a while. It's all effort and no ease for me this morning. This class is like nothing I've ever done before, one of those it-sucks-but-you-can-brag-about-it-later experiences that exercise hounds like me thrive on. I figure that the core work and the excruciating little movements done on demi-toe and the use of light weights are all ballet-friendly. When the class is over, I hose myself down in the locker-room shower, put on a clean pair of sweatpants, and go to the front desk to sign up for a package of ten classes. I am going to swap out my daily morning run for Barre3.

The next day I show up at an afternoon Pilates class, the kind performed on a mat, not the version that uses the jungle-gym/torture machines I saw in the movement studio. I know Pilates has been around for a long time and enjoys significant popularity. Ten years ago, a story in the *New York Times* estimated that there were 14,000 instructors in the United States and eleven million regular practitioners. I've just never been one of them. I haven't been much interested in the stretch-and-flexibility world of exercise until now. Sweat-and-grunt is more my style. But Joseph Pilates, the sickly son of a gymnast and a naturopath who invented the method back in the mid-1920s, was apparently on to something. The Pilates workout is touted to build core strength, emphasize alignment, increase flexibility, develop control and endurance, and improve coordination and balance. Which sounds to me like this protoballerina's wish list. George Balanchine and Martha Graham thought so too. They became Pilates devotees (Mr. P. operated a gym on Eighth Avenue beginning sometime in the 1930s) and sent their dancers there for training and rehabilitation. I figure that if it's good enough for Balanchine and Graham, it's good enough for me. So I try hard to like this mat work. But it's slow-moving and kind of boring, and there's no music! What are those eleven million people seeing that I'm not? This is one of those regimens I'll do because it's good for me, not because I enjoy it.

WHAT I END up enjoying—which comes as a huge surprise to me—is boxing. Yes, that's right: I start taking boxing lessons. But don't be too quick to judge me. I sign up for half-hour weekly sessions with a badass mixed martial arts fighter (who is, truth being stranger than fiction, also a student in a master's program in conflict resolution) because I read that Twyla Tharp, the famous dancer and choreographer, took boxing lessons. I can see why after my very first session with Roma Pawelek, the aforementioned badass. It's all about stamina and footwork. It's about moving with intensity coupled with a new-to-me kind of looseness in the body that is neither sloppy nor uncontrolled. I love the challenge of that, to throw a jab, a hook, an uppercut with power—but to keep my shoulders relaxed. To bob and weave, slip and duck, stay on the balls of my feet—but also keep my core engaged. And keep breathing. I don't hit anything but the mitts Roma holds for me. I am not at all interested in connecting a punch with some-one's jaw or solar plexus. But I am interested in this activity that feels strangely like . . . yes, dancing.

And then there is Gyro. I am back in the movement studio early the next week (after another arduous Barre3 class) for my first session with Jean. Jean is a hands-on instructor, literally, using her palms to press down my hunched shoulders, placing her hands flat against my spine to help me find the right curve. With far more patience than I would have for someone like me who has trouble distinguishing right from left, Jean guides me through the basic moves on the machine. The movements are deceptively simple: leaning forward and stretching my arms, rotating my arms using the wheels at the front of the machine, undulating my spine, scissoring my legs. But Jean cues me with such specificity, using the slightly weird, semiunderstandable language of yoga that in-volves "closing and opening the ribs" and "bringing the sit bones in toward the pelvis" and "opening the heart," that the moves are not simple at all. She places her small, strong hands lightly where they will do the most good, to rotate elbows in, squeeze together the scapula, rotate legs, point toes, flex toes, lengthen through the midthigh. And then there are the breathing cues: either the quick inhalations and explosive exhalations called "engine breath" or the whooshing in-and-out called "wave breath." And meanwhile, my body moves from position to position, curving and arching, sway-ing and swooshing.

On the one hand, everything is mindful and purposeful, and I am thinking hard about every muscle, every joint, about rotation and position, about lengthening without straining. On the other hand, the physicality of the moves and the synced breathing allow me to, every once in a while, just move. This precarious balance between extreme focus and graceful surrender is, I have to say, surprisingly exhilarating. The moves are slow, but time passes quickly. At the end of the hour I feel more in and of my body than I have in years. My limbs feel longer. My posture feels naturally erect, like I'm taller but not like I'm *trying* to be taller. As I zip down the flight of stairs from the studio to the street, my feet seem to bounce on the treads. I will be back.

—☙—

I WILL BE back to Gyrotonics and boxing and Barre3. And Pilates. And a yoga class I just discovered that Jean, the Gyro instructor, teaches on Thursday nights. And my own yoga practice that I'm supposed to be restarting. And—I almost forgot—water jogging. And. And. And. This new intensity of purpose is invigorating. And exhausting. It puts into perspective my previous busy but going-on-autopilot life. It challenges me to figure out how to restructure my days to make room for all this. It's not like I can stop being a mother, a wife, a woman with a day job, someone who has a life. This is not a *Stop Everything I Am Going on a Journey* adventure. Shaking it up in midlife doesn't work that way. By this time, one is fully embedded in one's life. One has responsibilities and commitments. But presumably, one is by now adept at prioritizing and organizing and scheduling and juggling and balancing.

And so this is what I do, with my lists and lists of lists. But organizing and scheduling are not enough. I need more time. I add two hours to most days by disappearing into my home office after dinner, which means no more binge-watching *Justified* or *Mad Men* or *Orange Is the New Black* with my husband. He's not happy, but he'll live. I start waking up predawn to make it to the earliest possible Barre3 class, which is tough but doable. I work most weekends, time I steal away from the garden I'm not putting in and the yard work I'm not doing. I Skype with my friend Kim instead of meeting her for our regular coffee dates because it saves me thirty minutes. I quit boxing lessons—which I love—because there is just so much time I can devote to physical activity. I make it work.

What is actually more overwhelming to me at the moment is not all this reconfiguring of my days but rather the realization that this is just *prep* for the real work. Or rather *prep* for the *prep* for the real work. All these classes and sessions and practices, these new activities and instructors and new ways of moving and relating to my body, are meant to prepare me to enroll in EBC's community Adult Ballet class next month. And that class is meant to prepare me to take the daily *company* classes once the season begins in September.

E. L. Doctorow's famous line runs through my head: "Writing a novel is like driving at night in the fog. You can only see as far as your headlights, but you can make the whole trip that way." For "writing a novel," I substitute "dancing *The Nutcracker*." I need to focus on what the headlights illuminate and try not to imagine the long, dark (foggy) road ahead.

9

Let the Wild Rumpus Begin

DESPITE A LONG, sweaty month of best efforts to whip myself into shape, I have to admit that, as March turns the corner into April, I am not yet ballet-ready. I am not even ballet-*class*-ready. I need to take radical action. I need to do something big to *really* shake it up. I'm managing, most of the time, to fit in all the get-into-decent-shape challenges I've committed to: Pilates, Barre3, Gyro, water jogging, even a bit of yoga. And I am immersing myself—admittedly from a safe distance—in the world of ballet by reading *Apollo's Angels*, Jennifer Homans's 627-page history of ballet. But I feel I need to make some comfort-zone-busting, decisive, and emphatic move to catapult myself into this next phase. I need to do something, pre–ballet class, to quickly boost physical stamina and, more important, to practice the kind of extreme focus and dedication I will soon need to draw, and depend, on.

And so, after pulling-out-all-the-stops negotiations with my family and filling the refrigerator with food and finding guest lecturers for the class I'm teaching, I commit to a week at a fitness boot camp. At Fitness Ridge in southern Utah, land of cerulean skies, red-rock canyons, and pink-cheeked Mormons, I wake at 6:00 a.m.; gear up for a rigorous two-hour hike; return to a lean, green, and caffeine-free breakfast; sweat through a high-intensity intervals class; change into my swimsuit for killer water aerobics; eat a lean, green lunch; attend lectures on "Cleaning Your Belief Window" (mine is quite smudged with *I'm too old I'm too fat It's too late for me* beliefs); plow through three more intense exercises classes (kickboxing, cardio circuit, core blast) in the afternoon; eat another pared-down meal of playing-card-deck-sized lean protein and bushels of vegetables; slather myself with arnica gel; down two capsules of what everyone at the Ridge calls "vitamin I" (ibuprofen), and fall into dreamless sleep at barely 8:00 p.m. And get up the next day and do it all over again. The bone-dry air, the intense physicality, the lack of culture and conversation about anything other than the experience itself scours my head of all thought. Which is what I want. I am my body. I am focus, fortitude, and grit. I don't doubt; I do.

I return seven days later minus two toenails and 2.1 percent body fat. I sport a suntan—unheard-of in Oregon in the spring—six blisters, and what I hope to be an infusion of confidence. I am now ready, I tell myself, to move forward. Eugene Ballet Company offers a Thursday-night adult class. That's the one for me. I go online and almost sign up for it. Three days later, I am once again a click away from enrolling. It's now a week since I came back from boot camp, and I still haven't gotten myself to register for it. What happened to that infusion of confidence?

It occurs to me that what I need to move forward is a wingwoman.

I need a sidekick, a ballet buddy, someone who will help me stay the course, someone with whom I can snark and carp, a midlifer like me, preferably not a sinewy swan, who is timid enough to understand my reticence and bold enough to accompany me on the next part of this journey. Who might that be? I do have a contingent of workout compadres from my erstwhile sweat-and-grunt days—in fact, we call ourselves the Sweat Chicas—but they are marathon monkeys with zero interest in ballet. I won't be able to strong-arm any of them. I have sedentary writer friends who will just laugh at me. I have casual coffee buddies who will just laugh at me. Really, there is no other choice. It has to be Kim.

My friend Kim is a tall, brainy, smart-mouthed, borderline gawky redhead with even less dance experience than I have. During the past few years we've bonded over the craziness of others we work with in the academic world. (We, of course, are the *sane* ones.) She is quirky, funny, adventuresome, and, I think, persuadable. Since my laser focus on this Nut Quest, the time we've spent together has been mostly on Skype—although we live maybe five miles from each other and work in the same building on campus. I mount a campaign to get her to be my sidekick, tactics of which include exchanging multiple daily e-mails and texts (the wittier the better), reinstituting our coffee get-togethers and insisting on paying for her lattes, indiscriminately "liking" her Facebook posts, and gushing about the intelligence of her dogs and the adorableness of their antics. I even allow her to refer to me as "Aunt Lauren" when she holds up Pilot or Comet to the camera during our continued almost daily Skype-fests. For all or none of these reasons, but mostly because she is a good friend, she agrees. I tell her about the evening class, Adult Ballet, that I've not quite gotten myself to register for and get her firm commitment to join me. She says yes—with more enthusiasm than I could have hoped for—but she also peppers me with good questions about the level of the class, who the other "adults" might be, and what we can expect. Actually, I don't really know. I just intended to show up. Now I see that it might be a good idea to first observe the class to get a sense of what we're in for.

—⟶

AND NOW FOR a seemingly random but actually spot-on aside:

A few years ago, thinking I might go back to school to study nutrition science, I took a battery of placement tests, including a harrowing series of increasingly challenging mini-exams in math. The goal was to achieve a score high enough to allow me entrance into the one (rather rudimentary) math class required for the major. Although I sailed through the first set of questions, proving I had an unshakable understanding of addition, subtraction, multiplication, and division, and almost aced the fifth grade–level fractions and ratio section, when it came to (ninth grade) algebra I was in a cold sweat, and geometry pretty much did me in. Although, in my defense, I did remember the difference between radius and diameter (but, alas, not how to calculate either of them). At the end of this are-we-having-fun-yet experience, I was handed a computer-generated evaluation of my math prowess, or rather lack thereof. It turned out that I was required to take Math 095, which did not carry college credit, to prepare me to take the Math 110–111 sequence, both of which I would have to pass in order to qualify to take the *actual* class necessary for the major. In other words, the severity of my math deficiencies would mean I would spend more than a year to get into the intellectual shape needed to be allowed entry into the one (freshman-level) math class I needed to take as part of the program.

I tell this story not merely to present myself as a pleasantly flawed character you can relate to but because this prep-for-prep-for-the-real-thing math experience was, I am discovering, an eerie foreshadowing of what's now happening with the "required class" necessary for my new "major," the Adult Ballet class I've persuaded Kim to take with me. When I go to observe that class, I have second—and third—thoughts. Standing outside the studio peering in through the long, high window, I watch as the dozen or so adults (all of whom look to be, perhaps, on the *cusp* of adulthood) arabesque prettily at the bar and execute disciplined pirouettes across the floor. The class is advertised as "all-comers," with no prerequisites. I have been thinking of it as the prerequisite to the daily company classes I will be attending when the season begins. The company classes, run by Toni or her ballet mistress (a former principal with EBC), are the super-rigorous, two-and-a-half-hour sessions designed just for the performing dancers. But, watching this adult class, it's clear to me that the "all" in all-comers does not include the likes of me (or Kim). We will need to find a more basic class, a prerequisite for this prerequisite.

Okay, then. I go back online and find a class called *Beginning Adult Ballet*. That is a bit of a comedown for me. After all, I did take eight years of classes. I have studied with a famous danseur. But, oh, yeah, right: *a lifetime ago*. A few nights later I stop by the beginning class to see just how easy it is so I can report back to Kim and we can get started. But these beginners have lovely turnouts and graceful ports de bras. Their tendus are precise and controlled, their relevés high and strong. These are *beginners*? And again, the definition of "adult" seems to be just barely out of one's teens. Apparently, I need to find a prep class for this prep class so I will be qualified to take the prep class I planned to take to prep me for the real company classes.

Which brings me (and Kim) to Introduction to Ballet, the Math 095 of the dance world.

WELL, IT DOESN'T *quite* bring us to class. First we must gear up.

Kim and I make a date to buy ballet footwear, which I know enough to call "slippers." Ballet slippers are soft-soled and fit the foot like a glove. Ballet "shoes" are toe shoes, blunt and boxy, painful to wear even after you swathe your toes in lambs' wool. I want those agonizing, foot-crippling toe shoes! I want badly to go en pointe as I did during that last year before Eglevsky kicked me out of his school. I remember the thrill of it all with a clarity that surprises me: that first time, holding on to the barre, that I raised myself up on the hard, square ends of my beautiful, unblemished pink shoes. The knife of pain from toe to ankle to calf. The way the pain didn't matter. The euphoria of height, the magic way you could twirl. The way the shoes transformed me from an ordinary fifth grader to a ballerina. But I cannot even contemplate toe shoes right now. Or, probably, ever. It would take years to get my feet strong enough. It's slippers for me.

"So, this is it," I say, when Kim and I meet up for preshopping lattes. "After we buy these shoes . . . um, slippers . . . there's no turning back." I'm joking, but I'm not joking.

"Yep," says Kim, extending her leg and pointing her toe as much as she can in her slightly dorky size 9 Keen slip-ons, "I know."

We walk across the street to the Dancers' Closet, the only ballet specialty store in town. Tori, the EBC ballerina who guided me through her exercise routine a few weeks ago, and LeeAnn, a pint-sized dynamo of a ballerina who teaches classes at the other ballet company in town, Ballet Fantastique, both work there. It's how they stay solvent on- and off-season. Today LeeAnn, whom I've seen onstage a few times, is one of the two sales clerks in the small, merchandise-packed store.

The moment Kim and I step into the Dancers' Closet, I feel as if I'm in a nine-year-old girl's fantasy—*my* fantasy when I was that age: pink tutus hanging on the wall, glitter-embellished toe shoes displayed like pieces of art, a gorgeous Black Swan costume hugging a torso-only mannequin, circular racks of brightly colored leotards, some sequined, others feathered. A little girl and her mother are shopping. The girl is prancing around in a sapphire-blue leotard with the price tag hanging off one delicate shoulder. Her mother is smiling and nodding, her arms full of other choices, all jewel-toned.

Kim and I sit down in the shoe section in between the leotard racks and the two dressing rooms. LeeAnn comes right over. She doesn't seem surprised to see women our age (without children), which I take to be a good sign. We tell her we are in the market for ballet slippers. "We're going to take a ballet class," I say, as if there could be some other explanation for buying ballet slippers. I immediately feel ridiculous for saying this, and—I can't believe I'm admitting it—I giggle. It must have something to do with being in a nine-year-old's tutu-fantasy world. Kim either mercifully does not hear this or, even more mercifully, chooses to ignore it. She is having a discussion with LeeAnn about canvas versus leather slippers. Canvas is cheaper, LeeAnn says, pulling down a 9 for Kim and an 8½ for me.

But the canvas doesn't hug tight. It doesn't feel like I remember ballet slippers feeling. Kim concurs. We ask for the leather ones. In for a penny, in for a pound. My ballet slippers, through all the years I took lessons, were black. These are a very soft blush pink, the pink of clouds just before dusk. They are lovely and supple. They fit beautifully. I will have to hand-sew the crisscrossed elastic that secures the slipper across my ankle. I remember my mother doing that, with the tiny, even stitches she had learned in a costume-design class at Pratt Institute a decade before I was born. I put on the other shoe and walk in a slow circle around the shoe area, lifting each leg hip-high with a pointed toe, holding my arms out in what I remember to be ballet position. I do this as in a trance, not thinking that I may be making a spectacle of myself, not thinking at all. I'm grinning by the time I make it back to where Kim is sitting admiring the slippers on her feet. We nod to each other.

"Sold," Kim says to LeeAnn.

"On to leotards," I say to Kim, walking over to the circular racks at the front of the store, the ones that had caught my eye the moment I walked in the door. I'm a medium, I figure, so I find that section. I am not shopping for glitz here. I just want a plain— please God a little flattering—black leotard. When I took classes, all the girls wore three-quarter-sleeved, scoop-necked leotards, but apparently that is not the fashion anymore. Everything is spaghetti strap. That's too bad. I was hoping for some upper-arm coverage. I find a row of black size Ms, grab the first one from the rack, and hold it up. I gasp. Audibly. Kim hurries over from a nearby rack. I hold up the leotard for her to see.

"Jezzus," she says under her breath.

"You got that right," I say. The leotard looks like it would fit an underfed prepubescent girl. I go over to the L section. These LARGE leotards look sized for a hipless, wasp-waisted, ninety-pound child-woman. I walk around the rack and the one next to it.

There is no XL.

I can't believe I'm tearing up. I'm standing in front of the leotard rack about to cry. I can hear that conversation that ended my ballet dreams, the one I overheard between my mother and André Eglevsky, as if it's happening right now, right next to me. I turn away so that Kim can't see my face.

Apparently, LeeAnn has been observing my efforts. She walks over with an armful of black leotards from a rack I hadn't noticed.

"These are what we have for, um, women," she says kindly, handing over the merchandise. "The adults who take classes buy these," she adds softly. I wonder if she has noticed my bloodshot eyes.

"Thanks," I say.

She's given me four leotards in different styles. I take them with me to the dressing room, a small, curtained cubicle decorated with dance posters (leaping, long-limbed beauties in stunning tutus). There's a tall, framed, freestanding mirror wedged in the corner. This is like trying on bathing suits—possibly my least favorite activity in the world (yes, including oral surgery)—but worse. When you try on a suit and steel yourself to take a look in the mirror, you know that a lot of the time you'll be wearing the suit you'll be in the water anyway, and no one will see what you look like. Or maybe you'll be on a chaise longue with a towel artfully draped over your worst parts. But a leotard is for dancing, for dancing in front of a wall of mirrors.

INTERESTINGLY, I DISCOVER that actual ballet dancers with young, lithe ballet physiques are not too pleased by seeing their leotard-clad bodies in the studio mirror either. In a sobering (and oddly reassuring) research article I find on ballet attire and body image, several dozen ballet dancers complete surveys about self-perceived body image after two different ballet classes. In the first class, they wear traditional garb—black leotards and pink tights. In the second, they wear what dancers call "junk"—loose-fitting workout clothes. The survey results? The dancers reported significantly lower self- and body-perception ratings when dressed in leotards with tights compared with wearing the loose-fitting clothing. They felt more positive about their bodies when they wore "junk" clothes, expressed more enjoyment when looking in the mirror in the studio, and—here's something weird—rated themselves as better dancers.

I balance this with another study I read about how clothing can influence us mentally as well as physically. It's a phenomenon the Northwestern researchers who studied it call (I think charmingly) "enclothed cognition." It appears that when we put on certain clothes, we may more readily take on the role associated with those clothes, and this may actually affect our abilities. Dressing in clothes designed for the task focuses your attention on the task and might, opine the researchers, offer subconscious motivation that can boost performance. I need all the performance-boosting I can buy off the rack.

AT ANY RATE, dance attire is required in a dance class. And dance attire I will wear. If I can find something that fits. The "for women" leotards that LeeAnn hands me are, *praise be*, sized for actual humans who walk the earth and eat meals. I take a deep breath and try on the one with spaghetti straps, a slight V to the front scoop neck, and a low back. I move around in the little dressing room, attempting ports de bras and piqués while studiously avoiding my image in the mirror. This is hard, as the space is about the size of a phone booth. The leotard moves with me. It *feels* okay. I glance quickly in the mirror. A ballerina does not look back at me.

"Are you out there, Kim?"

"Yep, right here. Do you need me?"

"Uh, yeah . . . I'm coming out. I need you to take a look." I take a deep breath, both to quell anxiety and to suck in my stomach, move the curtain to one side, and step with what I hope is grace out into the store. I am wearing my Nike workout capris under the leotard. It's a look.

Kim glances up from her phone. I hope she's not texting someone about this. "Turn around," she says. I do a slow 360. I'm facing her again. I keep my shoulders back. I turn out my feet to first position. My feet look big and silly in my Chaco sandals. "So?" I say, wanting but not wanting her honest opinion. She smiles.

"You have a beautiful back," she says.

This is what friends are for.

~~~

FINALLY, HERE WE are. Wednesday night. Intro to Ballet. There are four of us in the small upstairs studio, a wraithlike fifty-something woman who, by way of introduction, tells me she has osteoporosis and won't be doing any jumping (*Jumping?* This never occurred to me); a bespectacled somewhat younger woman who is wearing geeky-girl gym shorts over her tights; Kim; and me. We're both decked out in our never-before-worn leotards, Capezio footless tights, and pristine pink leather slippers. Kim is wearing this cute rib-skimming black sweater with just-above-the-elbow-length sleeves, which looks stylish without looking show-offy and has the advantage of hiding her upper arms. Not that her upper arms need hiding. It's mine that do. I can see that, with extraordinary clarity, as I look at my image in the forty-plus linear feet of mirrors that line three walls of the studio. I vow, next time and anytime I am in a mirrored studio, to not wear my contacts. My world is a kinder, gentler place with blurry edges.

Our teacher is Antonio Anacan, a wiry, darkly handsome EBC company dancer. I saw him dance Prince Aladdin in the Arabian sequence in last season's *Nutcracker*, and he was, well, gorgeous.

Sinuous, sexy, exotic—everything the part called for and more. According to his EBC bio (which, of course, I look up right after class), he joined the company three seasons ago after training with Pacific Youth Ballet, the San Francisco Ballet School, and the Central Pennsylvania Youth Ballet. The San Francisco Ballet School is major cred. He was a scholarship student there, which is even more impressive.

We four adult learners huddle at the barre, exchanging nervous glances. Antonio stands near the center of the room dressed halfway between ballet garb and "junk," looking both relaxed and poised the way only dancers can, striking a pose without even knowing he's striking a pose. His hair is obsidian black. His face is smooth and copper-skinned. He manages to look both delicate and masculine. And now I'm going to stop, lest you think I have already developed a crush. Which of course I haven't.

I wonder what he's thinking as he looks at us . . . *The Bad News Bears of ballet*? It quickly occurs to me that he is way too young to even get the reference. He starts the music, Debussy, I think, and leads us, slowly and carefully, through close to an hour of stretching, first on the floor, then at the barre. I am thrilled to *not* be dancing. Stretching I can do. Sort of. The Pilates, Barre3, yoga, and Gyro have limbered me up, at least a little. But for every move that comes with some ease, there is another where I feel the clench of a muscle (damn hamstrings) or encounter a leaden lack of flexibility (the tops of my feet). For every one thing I can do, there are a dozen I can't. Will this always be how it is?

Now, finally, we are lined up at the barre going through basic positions: first, second, fourth, fifth. Apparently, during my many dance-free decades, third position has gone out of style. Good. I always hated third position, that wimpy almost-fifth that had no reason to exist. We are pliéing as we move from position to position. I notice my death grip on the barre just a split second before

Antonio does. He nods, almost imperceptibly. I smile and ease the clenching claw that my hand has turned into. Antonio studies our pliés, then turns off the music and stands, silent, for a moment.

"So, the plié," he says, and then is silent again. He appears to be hunting for just the right words. "Imagine a string attached to the top of your head," he says, pulling at this imaginary cord at the top of his own head. His voice is soft, and there's a hint of singsong to it. "You are being pulled upward even as you plié down. It's hard to describe," he says, silent again for just a tick longer than you would expect from a teacher giving instructions. "It's this thing about gravity," he says, smiling to himself and swaying a bit. "You need to learn to feel it differently."

Next we practice tendus, extending a leg with pointed toe until only the tip of the toe remains on the floor ("tendu à terre," says Antonio), then bringing it back to position—in front, to the side, derrière—in first and second and fifth. He watches us, again turns off the music, again stands, silent. He closes his eyes and executes a few tendus. Then nods to himself. "You slide the foot, heel first," he says. "Only at the very last moment does the toe arrive." I attempt this. It's a purposeful, outward rotation—not at all what I was doing. I look over at Kim, who is also puzzling her way through the move. "And when the foot returns," Antonio is saying, "you lengthen upward, you extend inside your standing leg so you are making room for the returning leg." My face—probably all four of our faces—must betray confusion because Antonio laughs. "It's more of a feeling than an action," he says. "I don't know how to describe it."

But he does know. He takes his time with explanations. He thinks everything through. As I struggle with the movement and watch him struggling for the right words, it occurs to me what's happening. Antonio's first language is not English. It's not because he was born elsewhere (he is from Hawaii, which, last I heard, was part of the United States) and English is *literally* his second language. It's because he's a dancer, and *dance* is his first language. His body speaks it fluently. It takes extra effort to translate the language of the body into words. The effort, the silence, is him feeling his wordless first language and then searching for words to express what his body knows. This makes him a very interesting—and unusual—teacher. Not one who delivers instructions or barks corrections but one who seems to talk from a trance, who suggests what we might imagine, the visceral sense we might cultivate, not precise steps we mark. It's both frustrating and illuminating, like Gyro Jean's yoga-inspired patter to "open the lungs into the back body." Antonio's ballet lessons turn out to be as much about how a dancer thinks as they are about how we should move. Months later, reading about Vera Volkova, the famous Bolshoi ballerina who became a teacher, I see that Antonio is in good company. "Leg does not know is going to arabesque," Volkova once (mystifyingly) instructed Margot Fonteyn. "Arms are holding delicate flowers you must not crush." The language of teaching is opaque, poetic, as open to interpretation as dance itself.

The last ten minutes of class are devoted to teaching us how to walk across the studio floor. Yes, walk. No jetés or pirouettes. No arm movements. No flourishes. Just walk. And it is *hard*. We are imagining the string pulling us from the tops of our heads. We are denying the downward pull of gravity. We are pushing out with each foot, sliding the toe, transferring weight ever so lightly from standing leg to extended leg. We are lengthening, or thinking about lengthening, the now-standing leg to make room for the returning leg. If, when we were toddlers, walking had been deconstructed for us this way, we'd all still be crawling. I make my way slowly, awkwardly, across the room. It is taking forever. A rivulet of sweat is snaking down my spine, dampening the back of my new leotard.

"The floor is pushing you up," Antonio says as he watches us stumble, our eyes on the floor, laboring over every step. "The floor is *pushing* you up," he repeats, not with the exasperation I would probably feel at this moment but more as a mantra for us to repeat silently as we make our way to the other side of the studio. Kim and I exchange a quick smile. I am trying to feel the floor pushing me up. I am trying to feel the pull from the top of my head. All I feel is 140 pounds of gravitational pull keeping me rooted to the earth.

The language of dance is mute in my body. I want so badly to hear it.

10

Bull's-Eye

APRIL 12. After several bouts of travel that take me away from my ballet, fitness, and flexibility routines, I am back at the Barre3 studio working out at 6:15 a.m. with the usual roomful of tall, slender twenty-two-year-olds decked out in overdesigned Lululemons. (There goes my endorsement deal.) Horse pose. Carousel. Warrior III. Starfish. Narrow-arm push-pulls. Tabletop. Boat pose. Did this workout suddenly get harder? Could I possibly have lost 50 percent of my core strength in two weeks? Am I the only person raining down sweat on her mat as we hold planks for as long as it takes to hard-boil an egg? "Find the ease in the effort," Summer says halfway through class, as she always does. A great motto for life. I'm looking, Summer, I'm looking.

APRIL 25. Trying to wedge everything I need to do into my "real" life continues to be a major challenge. Happily (or sadly), my teenaged daughter is thrilled that I am paying a little less attention to her—although not as little as she would like, I'm sure. Happily (or sadly), my husband is doing quite a bit of traveling.

But I constantly need to hold myself back from other demands. I can't let myself be pulled in other directions. Now is not the time to repopulate my raccoon-decimated chicken coop. Now is not the time to refinish the dining room table. Or take on these three wannabe writers who need help developing their manuscripts. I'm already stretched thin (although not *physiologically* . . .) with a writing seminar I'm teaching in Portland and volunteer work that grounds me in life's realities. But: *No more skipping ballet classes*, I tell myself sternly. So what if they come at the end of a long day? So what if it means I don't cook dinner that night? So what if I have to see my bat wings in the mirror? This is it. In less than seven months, I have to transform myself into a stage-ready dancer.

APRIL 29. I have coffee with Toni. It's been a while. Too long. I courted her assiduously a few months ago after I returned from the Transcontinental Nutcracker Binge Tour. I shared my notes on the performances with her. I showed her pictures. I tried not to mention my claim to fame (and dishonor), André Eglevsky, too often. Just, you know, often *enough*. We met several times in the coffee shop across from EBC's studio to talk ballet and the business of the arts. Then came February and March, and I disappeared. From her view, that is. I was reaching out to Tori and Suzi. I was busy adding a few too many new ballet-friendly fitness routines. I was watching barre workouts on Vimeo. I left town for that boot-camp week. I traveled twice to give workshops.

You'll note in this litany of activity that I have not mentioned the weekly prep to prep to prep ballet class with the dashing and tongue-tied Antonio. So I need to 'fess up here. And by "'fess up," I mean blame my sidekick, Kim. How dare she come down with a shoulder injury? How dare her physical therapist order her to stop doing just exactly the movements we do in the ballet class? I'm not saying that an entire month went by without my going to the studio on Wednesday night. I did make it. Once. And it was a great class. Antonio was dancing in one of the EBC productions, so Miranda took his place. Miranda is not a performer. She is not a member of the company. But she was, I thought, a truly talented teacher, as verbal as Antonio was visceral. Her instructions and corrections had a precision to them that I loved. Although it had been wonderful to contemplate the floor pushing me up or my arms floating in gravity-free space—the mental images Antonio gave us—I appreciated Miranda's meticulous eye, how she saw too much of a curve to my middle finger, too much elevation in the pinkie, and how the look of my hand improved considerably when I followed her dictates. I appreciated her attention to my feet, her suggestion that I start working out with a wide stretch band to build strength and articulation. My posture changed, I actually felt it change, when she ever-so-lightly placed the palm of her hand between my shoulder blades. I left that class with new ideas, different ways to talk to my body. So really, there was no reason not to come back the next week. But I didn't. Nor the week after that.

The excuse I told myself, the next week, was that Kim wouldn't be there. The Wednesday after that, it was that I was weary after a long day of writing. But really, I knew what the problem was. I *know* what the problem *is*. It's all about the bull's-eye. Let me explain.

For years, whenever I've taught a writing workshop, I've begun by asking everyone to draw a simple concentric-circle target on a clean sheet of paper. I then tell them to scribble down a list of activities that take up their waking hours, from putting in eight hours at work to shopping for groceries, from exercising to checking in on social media. Chauffeuring kids. Reading. Cooking. Hobbies. The final task is to place each activity somewhere along the concentric rings of the target. The closer the activity is to the center, to the bull's-eye, the more time and energy the person spends doing it. What's consistently fascinating about this exercise is that, given that I'm in a room full of writers or people who say they want with all their hearts and souls to be writers, no one ever puts "writing" in the bull's-eye. Not one person. Ever. That includes the people who don't have eight or nine hours out of every day taken up with whatever they do to make a living.

And so, in my wisdom about everyone else's life other than my own, I deliver my well-practiced homily about how one cannot possibly get good at something if one does not do it, or does it erratically or sporadically; if one does not work—overtime—to bring it to the center of one's life. And so, I tell them, you don't do everything you think you need to do (not to mention the things you do *not* need to do, like spending an hour on Facebook, posting Instagram photos, and checking boot sales at Zappos) so that you can "find the time" to do that one thing you just said you wanted to do with all your heart and soul. You don't squeeze it in around the edges of your life. Not if you want to do it well. Not if you want to learn and improve. Not if you want to master it. No, I tell them, you find ways to push that activity you care most about as close to the bull's-eye as you can. And that process starts in your head, with the recognition of its centrality to your life—and your understanding that excellence (or even competence) takes time.

That's my problem. Ballet class, the current centerpiece of this whole operation, is not in my bull's-eye. If it were, I would (at least) have been planning every Wednesday around it. But that's not what I've been doing. I've just been waiting to see if it works out to go to class. Okay, time to "own" my errant behavior rather than foist the blame onto my generally cooperative and staunchly supportive sidekick/wingwoman/friend. Plus, I just texted her that she was to blame, and she responded with a deadpan but sarcastic "yay, me."

I still do have time, though. That's what I'm telling myself. And my hooky-playing has so far been confined to the prep class—not the *real* company classes I will be attending come fall. Even so, this is a lesson worth considering right now, the lesson being: *Practice what you preach. Apply what you've learned from a part of your life you've spent decades developing to a part of your life you are now trying to develop.*

But it's a larger lesson than that, really. It's not just about me and how I should apply my experience as a writer to my efforts as a dancer. It's a midlife lesson for all of us venturing bravely (but with some trepidation) into new territory. When we've never done what we now want to do (that's *why* we want to do it), it's easy to be intimidated by the novelty, by the steep learning curve, by the extreme discomfort of being at the bottom of that curve. But there are *some* benefits of having lived this long, right? And one of them is that we're rich in banked experience. Not experience in this new thing but in many *other* things. We've laid a foundation we can build on. We already know more than we think we know. For me, it's tapping into the discipline and focus I've spent years working to develop in my nonballet life.

I'm ruminating about this as Toni and I sit over our drinks, feeling powerful as I redraw the target in my head, as I zero in on the bull's-eye that must be ballet. We talk again about *The Nutcracker*, about my place in the company this fall and in the ballet during the long holiday season. It is understood that this is all contingent on my full participation in company class, on Toni seeing with her own eyes that I can do whatever it is she decides to allow me to do. That said, I am still surprised she's giving me this chance. I was afraid to ask why when she agreed to it at that first meeting. I didn't want her to think too hard, to question herself, to change her mind, But now we know each other better, and I am a little more secure. So I ask her.

"Well," she says, sipping iced tea, "if you had asked to dance in *Swan Lake*, that would have been a different story." We both laugh, imagining the impossibility of that. "But *The Nutcracker* . . . " She gestures delicately with her arm, "*The Nutcracker* is more inclusive. We perform with children. We tour. We think of it as more of a community event." I make a weak joke about me probably not messing up onstage any worse than one of the six-year-olds who prance around as baby mice. A concerned look briefly passes over her face. Apparently, I've just given her something to worry about. She takes another sip, recovers her calm.

"You'll be fine," she says. "When you've had ballet as a child, the dance is forever in you."

APRIL 30. Toni e-mails me the next season's schedule. Company classes begin September 8 at 8:00 a.m. sharp. The schedule is detailed and precise, with costume fittings and rehearsals and performances and travel time—and even a "dancer day off" every once in a while. I note that rehearsals begin two short days after the commencement of company class. But these aren't for *The Nutcracker*. They are for EBC's first fall production, *Cinderella*. We won't be rehearsing *The Nutcracker* until the very beginning of November. Can this schedule be correct? Only ten days of rehearsal? I call Toni, attempting to not let her hear the panic in my voice. She tells me—and I'm sure she means this reassuringly, but it has the opposite effect on me—that "so many of the dancers have danced this ballet that they know it by heart." I have *seen* this ballet almost thirty times and danced it not once. I decide not to remind her of this.

After the abbreviated rehearsal time, we take the show on the road, starting in mid-November with six Oregon dates, then up to Anchorage, Alaska, followed immediately by fourteen performances in cities throughout Washington, Wyoming, and Idaho before heading back for two shows in Salem and then our final four hometown performances just before Christmas. Note that I am using "we" and "our" when referring to the ballet company. It's an act of chutzpah. But a necessary one. The schedule makes everything very, very real.

MAY 6. I run into my friend Perrie at a local coffee hangout. With Kim still nursing a semidislocated shoulder, I ask Perrie to join me for tomorrow night's Beginning Adult Ballet class. She looks at me as if I've proposed interstellar travel. And laughs. I mount a spirited argument in my most engaging and persuasive manner. Her eyes glaze over.

That afternoon I go to a class billed as "Barre Fit" at my gym. It's taught by Marilyn, the former-dancer Gyro instructor whose schedule was too full to take me on. It turns out that the class is far more ballet-oriented than Barre3, with classic ballet positions and moves. It's hard in the same way the Beginning Adult Ballet class is hard. The class is too big for individual instruction or correction. But there is plenty of *self*-correction going on. All the spots at the barre are in front of mirrors, so I get a great view of my hunched shoulders and my dropped elbow, of the lifted leg that isn't lifted nearly as high as it should be. To say nothing of the critical eye I cast on the shape of my eyebrows and the arch of my feet—and everything in between. How does one unlearn that gaze? How does one work on improvement without the harsh criticism?

MAY 7. I go to the adult class. Miranda is teaching. It's just me, the thin woman who told me about her osteoporosis, and a shy, quiet Japanese high schooler. When I first thought about taking these classes, I figured all of us adults would bond over this humbling experience. But really we are all so intent on our own movements, our own posture, on working our joints and muscles in ways we don't normally work them that we hardly exchange a word. I miss Kim. I soldier on.

MAY 16. I wake up with a nervous stomach and that zap-and-zing electric current that travels down your arms to your fingertips—or my arms, my fingertips—when I'm anticipatory. Which is my euphemism for nervous. Half-awake, I think: *This is what I'm going to feel like, but even more so, when I go onstage.* I actually hadn't considered performance nerves until now, maybe because I'm accustomed to getting up in front of people, even crowds of people (to *talk*, that is). Maybe because I've been so focused on getting to the point where it would be possible for me to go onstage. But now that I feel that zing, I realize I'll face this challenge too.

The zap-and-zing I feel this morning, however, is not about ballet. It's about the 150-mile, 5,000-foot-elevation-gain bicycle ride I am embarking on with Zane, my middle son, tomorrow. He is on an epic cross-country trek from Pacific to Atlantic—a huge undertaking that is equal parts physical challenge and *What am I going to do with my life?* quest. I have to be a small part of this. I have to make room in my ballet-obsessed schedule to help launch him on this journey. I know that many dancers choose to not have children. Children don't fit easily into a ballerina's life. But I do have children, and this one needs me now. And the bike ride makes sense for me anyway. It's part of my ongoing effort to push myself, whenever I can, out of my comfort zone. I tell people nonchalantly about the trip. I am anything but nonchalant. I have never ridden more than thirty miles on my bike. And then there's that elevation gain.

MAY 21. Did it.

Sheeting rain the first day. Sleet over the 5,335-foot pass. We keep up our energy with almond butter and banana sandwiches and our spirits by yelling Twenty Questions at each other as we pedal single file along the narrow shoulders of two-lane highways. I stump him with Maria Tallchief. Which I realize is not fair. But when you're being drenched every few minutes by torrents of road water flung from the undercarriages of eighteen-wheelers, and you're soaked down to your underwear (despite expensive high-tech waterproof gear), you tend to play a little dirty.

Does it sound crazy to say this was fun? Probably. But it was.

MAY 24–JUNE 21. I travel to northern Europe for business (solo) and pleasure (with my husband) and manage to gain seven pounds in three weeks. To understand how extraordinary this accomplishment is, you should know that I walk more than ten miles every day. This is not some wild estimate. This is according to the pedometer clipped to my (expanding) waistband. However, my eating habits easily trump my physical exertions. It's not that I overindulge in the bear sausage, blood sausage, elk sausage, duck heart, reindeer heart, boiled pork in aspic jelly, wild boar, and deep-fried blood balls (I am not making this up) we encounter in Scandinavia and the Baltics. It's that, given this cuisine, I find I must console myself with bread and cheese and, especially in Stockholm, with kanelbulle, an addictively delicious cinnamon-and-cardamom roll. My mouth is watering as I write this. Alas, my eyes are watering too as I imagine how elephantine I will feel when I show up at my first private lesson with Tori, the EBC ballerina I hired to help me over the summer.

JULY 1. Have this dream: I am driving my car, alone, down a country road. I know with absolute surety that I am going to crash, to have an accident. In the dream, I think, *Okay, if I know, then I can prevent it from happening*. But I can't. Before I even have a chance to feel concerned about this, it also comes over me, with absolute surety, that I will be okay. So I crash, full force, into a tree. The front of the car looks like an accordion. I force open the door, get out, and assess the damage. The car is totaled. As I walk around to check all sides, I realize that there is not a scratch on me. Analyze *that*.

JULY 16. I meet Tori at 7:30 a.m. in a large studio in the athletic club we both belong to. Tori's boyfriend is the assistant athletic director, so we're cleared to use the space. It's the same space Marilyn uses for the Barre Fit class I took back in May. Barres run along two sides of the room. Behind them are floor-to-ceiling mirrors. Just last week I read a study in the *Journal of Rational-Emotive & Cognitive-Behavior Therapy* (not my usual bedside material, needless to say) about "mirror therapy." According to this study, mirror exposure therapy can significantly boost body esteem. This is news to me. Looking in the mirror is often, in my life, the best and fastest way to start the *How flawed am I? Let me count the ways* internal monologue. There's a way to turn this on its head?

Yes, according to the author of the study, Sabine Wilhelm, PhD, director of the Body Dysmorphic Disorder Clinic and Research Unit at Massachusetts General Hospital in Boston. Here's how it works: First, take a good, long look at your body, resisting the urge to zero in on body parts you dislike. Try to ignore your perceptions of fat, skinny, beautiful, and ugly. *(Okay, so unlearn a lifetime of cultural norms.)* Erase all the body-related chatter from your mind. *(I am not sure I have any other internal chatter.)* Just look at your body and try to see it simply and honestly. *(Um. Suppose, "simply" and "honestly," you have lumpy thighs?)* When you feel ready, state out loud at least five nonjudgmental things about yourself. If you have trouble getting started, simply saying "My hair is brown" works. Then, without skipping or dwelling on any particular body part, describe—objectively and out loud—how you look. Use color, texture, proportion, shape, and symmetry but not subjective words such as "gross" or "too big." (One suggestion offered in the study: "I have a heart-shaped face that is slightly red across the nose and cheeks.") When you feel ready, state five things about your appearance that you like and what you like about them.

Wow. You know how Woody Allen has been in therapy for, like, half a century? That is a conservative estimate of how long I'd have to work at this. While Tori is fiddling with her smart phone so we can have musical accompaniment, I stand at the barre and look at my reflection. I am wearing Nike running capris and a close-fitting workout tank. My eyes go directly to the bulge of my European-enhanced upper thigh. And what's with the pudgy knees? When did that happen? Damn. This is hard. I force my gaze upward. I look my reflection in the eyes. "My eyes are blue," I make myself say (to myself). Then: "My hair is brown." I'm on a roll. Maybe not. I cannot think of anything else nonjudgmental. Finally, something occurs to me: "I have ten fingers."

Tori starts us out with ten minutes of stretches during which I discover that the flexibility and elasticity I worked so hard to achieve through expensive Gyrotonics sessions have mysteriously disappeared. Well, not so mysteriously. I guess if you don't stretch or do yoga or anything other than walk and eat cinnamon buns for a month, it's pretty hard to sit V-legged on the floor, hinge from the waist, extend your arms in front of you, and inch your torso toward the floor. Why is it so arduous and time-consuming for the body to make headway and so effortless for it to regress? Here I am, a mere two months away from the start of ballet season when the company classes begin, and I feel creaky, stiff, and bloated. Take that, mirror exposure therapy.

Tori is kind and appears unjudgmental as we move to the barre. That's okay because I am judgmental enough for the two of us. As we begin with pliés, I am able to focus on something positive: I have an awesome turnout! My feet, in first position, almost make a straight line. I allow myself a little smile. Then back to business. The plié. I try not to sink down but rather slowly lower myself, back straight, knees rotated out, butt tucked. I watch myself in the mirror. Not too terribly awful, if somewhat mechanical. "Let's work on the port de bras at the same time," Tori says, referring to the controlled arm movements that accompany the pliés and the cycle through the positions.

Oh, the arms, the arms. There is so very much to the arms. It begins with the fingers, ever so slightly curved but also reaching long; the wrist, ever so slightly cocked but not "floppy," as Tori tells me, eyeing my first graceless port de bras. I need to elongate my hand position. My wrists move too much. In second position—the very best arm position in which to study one's bat wings—Tori instructs me to lift my elbows. When I do, my shoulders hunch. When I force my shoulders down, my elbows sink. When I manage to lift my elbows without the shoulder hunch, my wrists turn down. Tori gently rotates my lower arm so the palms of my hands face out. And then there's the rounding, the soft but precise rounding to the shape of the arms as they reach down in first position, out in second, and above the head in fifth. Nothing feels natural. Nothing comes easy. As soon as I direct my focus to my fingers, my elbows drop. As soon as I fix that, I lose the curve in my arm.

I try to remember when I first learned to play tennis—which I ended up playing quite well—how the grip of the racket felt alien to me, how I had to learn to swing not from the wrist, not from the shoulder, but with my entire torso. How my stance mattered, the bend in my knees, the position of my feet. It must have been painstaking to learn all this, right? I must have felt awkward. But at some point, this crazy-making focus on every little detail all at once suddenly clicked, and the movements were fluid, and I no longer attended to, or even thought about, what I was doing. I moved. I found a rhythm. I hit the ball. Will that happen in ballet? Or does this special magic happen only when you're eight years old?

We move on to tendus, an extension of the leg with pointed toe, which requires a perfect pointing of the toe, which requires the creation of a natural bow at the top of the foot. This is the articulation Miranda was working on with me, the exercises I was doing at home with the wide stretchy band. *Was* doing. Now, after my four-week hiatus, I feel the familiar cramp as soon as I bring my toe to the floor and attempt to create a convex position in my foot. This is hard. This is so hard that I forget my arms. "Soften those fingers," Tori says softly. "Relax the shoulders."

JULY 30. I take Tori to Barre3 with me this morning. It's Summer's class, the toughest there is, and this morning it seems exceptionally tough. Then, forty minutes in, something happens that's never happened before: I get called out for being particularly adept at something. It's a side plank with raised leg that is supposed to open your hip flexors, which are a good thing to open, here in Barre3 and most especially in ballet.

"Gorgeous, Lauren," Summer says as I assume the position. "Gorgeous" is her favorite word. "Lauren's hips are stacked one on top of another . . . really open," she adds. I am ridiculously thrilled by the shout-out. In months and months of Barre3, I've never been singled out. It's like getting a gold star. I try to savor the moment as I splatter my mat with big gobs of sweat. I wonder: Does this give me any cred with Tori?

AUGUST 6. In deep despair after my third private ballet lesson with Tori this morning. It's the same story: I attend to feet and lose hip turnout. I attend to elbow position and hands turn to claws. I soften hands and elbows drop. I raise elbows and shoulders hunch. Tori is a nymph, a sylph. I am this tree stump. There isn't a single moment during which I feel any sense of grace in my body.

My obsession today is my head. The tilt, but not too much. The raised chin, but only a suggestion. The expression, dreamy yet composed, ethereal—everything that belies the effort and focus. The head is so important. There's a beauty and elegance to movements when the head moves on a long, slender neck and the eyes follow the hand . . . *and the hand is not a claw.* My neck is not long, and not one of the head positions is coming "naturally." Tori says "natural" is not a part of ballet. "There's nothing natural about it," she says, and laughs. Then she demonstrates a simple, lilting pas de chat that looks effortless, almost instinctive. Which is to say: natural. The only glimmer of hope this morning is that the bow across the top of my foot is looking better. And, as a surprise bonus: no cramp.

I tell Tori that I have vowed not to say critical things about myself as we go through the barre work. But a few minutes in, I admit that I can't seem to halt the internal monologue. Tori says this is just how it is.

"With ballet, you can be 99 percent perfect and obsess 100 percent of the time about that last 1 percent," she says.

11

Perfection

I AM SITTING in Barbara Herman's cozy, welcoming, feng-shui-ish office talking about perfection. Barbara has been a therapist for thirty-two years. Most of her clients are women, and many of them are midlifers facing the various challenges and perils of, umm, midlife. I could be here as a client—perfection is certainly an "issue" in my life—but I'm here in the safer guise of a writer researching a story. Which suits me . . . *perfectly*.

I ask Barbara how many of the women she sees are in some way struggling with the notion of perfection. She laughs. "Pretty much everyone," she says. "I think it may underlie a lot of the issues that bring people to see me." She gives herself time to think more about that as she digs into her salad. She's managed to find a time slot for me, but it's during lunch. That's how busy the midlife therapy biz is these days. She tells me that women come to see her because they are depressed or anxious, overwhelmed or discouraged. But underneath these symptoms often lurks the push for perfection. Or rather the beating up of oneself that comes from never achieving perfection.

None of Barbara's clients are midlife women attempting to make themselves into perfect ballerinas so that they can dance *The Nutcracker* (Did I have to ask?), so the yearning for perfection, failure to achieve said perfection, and beating up of oneself for such failure manifest in more common ways. Like parenting. (If you don't raise the "perfect" kid, then obviously, you weren't the perfect mother.) Like midlife divorce. Like the (doomed to fail) striving for and preservation of the perfect body, which Barbara says "surfaces like a sea monster" when women hit middle age. Or, I might add, join a ballet company.

It's comforting—and, I must say, just a little amusing—to discover that even Barbara, wise, grounded, happy-with-herself therapist Barbara, has her own perfection issues. When I tell her about what compelled me to take on the ballet challenge, the whole shaking-it-up midlife itch that is at the core of this adventure, she tells me about her recent foray into pottery. She wanted to rediscover and cultivate an artsy-craftsy side that she'd let go fallow for decades. She wanted to have fun, she tells me. She wanted to shake it up, do something very different from her cerebral everyday life. Sounds good. The problem? "I couldn't tolerate not being excellent," she says. She laughs. Her laugh qualifies as "rueful." What began as a fun hobby rather quickly morphed into a push for perfection. It was not enough to relearn her pottery-wheel skills, to take pleasure in the activity. She was compelled to produce high-quality work, to produce beautiful work, to produce marketworthy work. To, in fact, market her work. "Actually, I am kind of disappointed in myself," she says. But I can also see, paradoxically, that she's kind of proud of herself—which is the trap, the allure of perfection.

AS I (ALONG with, apparently, most midlife women) struggle with the idea that I must be perfect, as I place myself in a rarefied world that is all about perfection, it might be time to face the music. And I don't mean Tchaikovsky. It's time to consider what "perfection" is all about, how it seems like a good thing (right?) but really isn't. How it is relentlessly presented to us as desirable and achievable— from creating the perfect meal to planning the perfect vacation to sustaining the perfect marriage—but is, wait a second, a false goal? And not just false but harmful? I'm slogging through a stack of female-focused magazines right now, from those targeting the hip high schooler to those with a bead on the young professional, with readerships ranging from fashionistas to homebodies to hardbodies. Finding the perfect hairstyle, running the perfect race, landing the perfect job, choosing the perfect accessories. And then there are the literally side-by-side "perfect" messages that conflict and confound and end up battering us coming and going. I open one magazine to find the recipe for and accompanying food-porn photo of an exquisitely caramelized pecan pie ("a perfect complement to your Thanksgiving table") across from a photograph of a reed-thin, wasp-waisted, coltish young woman sporting "the perfect look for fall." Can you sport that perfect look and eat that perfect pie? I think not. Can you drive yourself crazy—or into a therapist's office—because you feel compelled to make sumptuous dishes but not eat them, or feel guilty about eating them, or guilty about not cooking them? Or not looking coltish? I think so.

When you think about it (as I have, long and hard), the word itself, "perfect," contains within it the essence of the conflict that can drive us crazy. As a noun, "perfect" means flawless, ideal, the ultimate. As a verb, it means to improve, to make better. So, really, even when we *are* perfect (which, I guess, is never?), we are ensnared in the never-ending pursuit of perfecting ourselves. And it seems that the closer we are to what we think of as perfect, the more fixated we are on what we believe is not up to snuff. I keep thinking about what Tori had to say about this—Tori the graceful swan of a dancer—her words spoken with twenty-something innocence, the statement not yet burdened by (or even aware of) its own weight: *With ballet, you can be 99 percent perfect and obsess 100 percent of the time about that last 1 percent.*

Ballet and perfection. There may be more there there than I thought. Here's my latest insight: In ballet, it seems to me it may be both harder—and *easier*—to achieve perfection. It is harder for the obvious reasons: the extraordinary discipline, rigor, precision, and just plain difficulty of the art; the delicate balance between the aesthetic and the athletic; the decades of intense specialized training it takes to progress; the gutting-it-out perseverance; the ongoing battle between passion and pain that one must win every day, every hour. And then, of course, there is the body, the body one can work *with* and work *on*—but one must first be born with perfectible goods.

But it might also be that achieving perfection in ballet is, oddly, "easy" for some of the same reasons it is so challenging. Its very precision lays bare what perfection means and, in defining it, capturing it with exactitude, makes it at least theoretically attainable. Each step, each movement, every gesture is learnable and presumably perfectible (assuming talent and grace and perseverance and passion) because each is reducible to tiny details; each is the sum of all those details attended to with obsessive fastidiousness. And there are well-established, successful paths to the attainment of perfection: the famous curricula of schools of ballet, the hallowed teachings of enshrined instructors, the recorded performances of the greats that one can learn from. The rigor that perfection demands is enforced with daily drills and endless corrections, with classes and rehearsals, with a hermetic community of equally fanatical compatriots.

Ballet as an art form is, and dancers in particular are, definitely obsessed—and I use that word advisedly—with perfection. The ballet books I've started to read have something to say, often much to say, about perfection. There is, first of all, the distressingly recurrent theme of the perfection of body that focuses on harrowing tales of severely disordered eating: self-imposed starvation, anorexia, bulimia, outrageous Krispy Kreme binges paid for by days of ultrapunishing workouts, et cetera, et cetera. Gelsey Kirkland, whose memoir I read decades ago and just started rereading, writes about eating an apple a day. Not an-apple-a-day-to-keep-the-doctor-away. I mean, that is *all* she eats. One apple. Cut into quarters and portioned out across a grueling, high-calorie-burning day of classes and rehearsals. (Cocaine helps, apparently.) She also writes about choosing to undergo a number of plastic surgeries (many in her teens) to create what she believes to be the perfect body. She has a nose job. She has her earlobes clipped. She has two or three breast surgeries. She has silicone injected into her lips, her ankles. It's tempting to dismiss Kirkland as just a head case—and it seems that her compulsion for body perfection qualifies as a psychological disorder (or two or three)—but the idea, the goal, the operational everyday push for perfection seems to be a part of many ballet dancers' lives.

Away from the ballet studio, away from the floor-to-ceiling mirrors and the can't-hide-a-thing tights and leo, away from that roomful of poised, supple, lovely, and lean young women I will soon be joining, I may be able to think more clearly, more sanely, about this notion of perfection. Because in the thick of it—"thick" taking on added meaning when used by the likes of me with my midlife, mother-of-three waist—I am so obviously, startlingly, breathtakingly imperfect that it's hard not to entertain Gelseylike "solutions" to my various "problems." But that's not what this is all about, I remind myself. I am thrusting myself into this land of ultimate perfection to attempt to *challenge* my obsessions, not feed them. Can I do this while recognizing, while admitting, that I am (and am likely to always be) a borderline perfectionist?

Sequestered in my writer-in-jeans-and-T-shirt comfort zone, I apply reason—and research—to the idea of perfection. It is a *very* complicated and confounding subject. Perfection appears to be mostly indefinable, idiosyncratic, subjective, and entirely relative, as in being the Perfect Mother or finding the Perfect Career or baking the Perfect Chocolate Chip Cookie. (I do have a recipe for this.) But then there's ballet, where perfection is, sort of, definable. Of course, there's classic Russian perfection and Balanchine perfection and Royal Academy of Dance perfection and Imperial Classical Ballet perfection. But within each approach, there is a standard of excellence, a pinnacle of success.

But even if perfection is definable, is it achievable? Or maybe the question is: How do we define achieving? Is perfection a goal one must reach, a destination that one must arrive at in order to have truly achieved, in order to be satisfied with oneself? Or is it an always-beyond-one's-grasp ideal that stands as a beacon? I'm imagining a shining orb that casts a light, a light that illuminates a path, and that being on the path, progressing down the path, is what achievement is all about. But whether it is definable or not, whether it is an achievable goal or a never-ending quest, it seems that perfection can be a source of paralysis or a source of lifelong inspiration. Or maybe both.

Certainly, it can paralyze. It can trap and ensnare. That's what Barbara Herman sees in her practice: women who are stuck, women who believe they need to be perfect, who strive for some (unreachable) (ill-conceived) (meaningless) perfection. And fail. Or believe they fail. *I am imperfect, and I will never be perfect, which means I am a failure and unworthy and unlovable, and I will always and forever be so.* This perfection-as-paralysis can be a one-way ticket to the land of chronic stress, chronic disappointment, unhappiness, self-criticism, maybe even self-hatred. I see that path quite clearly, and occasionally, I have taken a step or two in that direction. But I want to believe it is possible to strive for perfection—to continue to raise the bar higher than I can reasonably, sensibly expect to reach—and not get tangled up in self-hatred. Self-criticism? Well, okay. I can handle that. It comes with the territory. And really, all this talk about positive affirmations aside, sometimes a good, swift (internal monologue) kick in the ass is just what we need. Or just what *I* need.

Right now I want and need to make a case for—and teach myself to firmly embrace—the idea of perfection as *motivator*. *Push*, not paralysis. I do this to override, or outshout, that too-loud voice that is telling me my neck is too short, my waist is too thick, my hip flexors are too tight, and my feet are too stiff. Also, says the voice, I lack natural musicality; I am slow to learn; I am far less graceful than I thought I was. And, oh, yes, I suffer mightily from the inability to give myself a break. That's right: I criticize myself for criticizing myself. How positively meta. I am reminded of the time I took an online "self-compassion" test, failed it, and then proceeded to scold myself, thus illustrating my lack of self-compassion for lacking self-compassion.

What I'm saying is: Perfection-as-motivation doesn't exactly come naturally. I have to work at it. And that's okay. That's part of this learning curve I'm on, which is so much more than training my body to move in certain ways. What I learn about reinterpreting and using criticism, especially self-criticism, as incentive and impetus will, I am betting, stay with me longer and be far more meaningful than what I learn about turnout and épaulement.

———ᘓ

AND SO I deliver this lecture to myself: Failure to reach perfection just means there is something more to do, something more to achieve. Which is a good thing. Life is about change and challenge, not about stasis and immobility—and this is necessary and healthy. Striving, but failing, to reach perfection can be interpreted as inching closer to a goal, with every inch a victory and a cause for celebration. Okay, maybe I'm overplaying it with the "celebration" idea. But I am working overtime to counter what I've been reading about us perfection-strivers, or, as Brooklyn psychotherapist Benzion Sorotzkin (my Internet find of the week) puts it, "those who strive compulsively and unremittingly toward goals beyond reach and reason."

Ouch.

We perfectionists are, he writes, the victims of dichotomous thinking who see the world (and ourselves) in a polarized fashion. Always or never. All or nothing. A lovely, graceful ballerina or a stumbling midlife oaf. For example. We are overgeneralizers who illogically reach conclusions based on a single incident. *(My performance at the barre this morning was awkward. I am and will forever be awkward.)* We have an "overly active system of self-commands" sometimes referred to as "the tyranny of the shoulds." As in: *I should be able to relearn ballet in a few months. I should be able to do a split. I should look as good as a twenty-year-old in my tights and leo.* And we are—*I* am—guilty of what Sorotzkin terms "overly moralistic self-evaluation." By "self-evaluation," he means blistering self-criticism, the kind of brutal self-talk that leads to crumbling (eventually nonexistent) self-esteem.

Not me! Not me! I refuse. I refuse to give up striving toward a lofty goal, even an unreachable and unreasonable one. And I refuse to let the striving (and the not-reaching) make me unhappy.

Although I didn't choose this particular challenge because I thought it could teach me something about my perfectionist tendencies, it seems to me now that ballet is the, well, *perfect*, educational milieu for me. First, it is, as I've said, all about perfection. So it kind of slaps you upside the head (if it were a ballet term: "une claque à la tête") with the concept. But it also gives you a non-Gelsey way of making your way through the perfection minefield. Because second, and perhaps even more important, ballet is about practice and perseverance. Dancers are always practicing. They are forever striving to be more graceful, more supple, more lyrical, to lift a leg half an inch higher, to hold an arabesque a second longer, to perform just one more (perfect) fouetté en tournant. Prima ballerinas, internationally renowned dancers at the apex of their careers, go to classes—every day— where they learn and practice and listen to corrections from their teachers. Their professional lives are about continual progress. Thus, despite the neurotic, obsessive, body-and-soul-damaging perfectionism expressed by certain individual dancers, it seems that ballet, as an art form, speaks to the idea of perfection as impetus, not paralysis.

Good. I must keep this in mind. I must keep *re*minding myself as I become increasingly more involved in the world of ballet. I want to learn life-enhancing lessons from this experience not feed my preexisting neuroses.

—☙

I NEED PRACTICE—and I don't mean at the barre. I need practice facing my perfection issues in my everyday world. I decide to mount an experiment: I will attempt to live One (subjectively) Perfect Day.

What do I mean by a Perfect Day? A goal must be clearly identified in order to be actionable. This Perfect Day should be (immediately the tyranny of the *shoulds*) intellectually, creatively, emotionally, and physically fulfilling according to my own high standards. It should be a day no other day could exceed in its wonderfulness. I'm not sure I even know how to think about that. At any rate, imagining perfection is a mighty tall order. And one that is impossible to fill without specifics. So here are the specifics of my personal Perfect Day:

> I will awake from a Perfect Night's Sleep, perfection a result of the perfect number of hours of sleep (7.5), the perfect room temperature (65), the perfect bed linen (freshly laundered, 450 or higher thread count).
>
> I will greet the day with a sense of adventure and wonder. In other words, my first thought will not be what's on the day's to-do list. And I will resist the temptation, as I brush my teeth, to craft a snarky e-mail I will never send to some ultra-annoying colleague.
>
> I will eat three Perfect Meals (nutritionally balanced, delicious, homemade, guilt-free).
>
> I will challenge my body with the perfect blend of physical activity.
>
> I will work happily and productively—thinking, researching, and writing—for the perfect number of hours (4.5)—during which I will stand, not sit.
>
> I will engage in any number of Perfect Interactions with family and friends, during which I will exude warmth, empathy, and interest.

I will end the day by reading passages from the Perfect
Book. (For me, that's Norman Maclean's *A River Runs
Through It*.)

Except for the "Perfect Interactions with Family and Friends"
thing, everything else on the Perfect List looks eminently doable.
But guess what?
It isn't.
First of all, the heat clicks on in the middle of the night and
warms the room to an imperfect 70 degrees. Then, as I lie in bed,
predawn, trying to overcome this perfection-robbing glitch, I can't
stop myself from contemplating the clever lie I will tell to get out
of a meeting I don't want to go to later that afternoon. And then I
think, *Maybe I should I tweet the progress of my perfect day.* Followed by: *Why don't I have more Twitter followers?* And then: *Do I
need to bolster my social media presence? Does my website need updat-
ing?* So much for waking with a sense of wonder. However, I can
report three lung-filling sun salutations (with only an errant
thought about why I should have broken up with my first boyfriend two years before I did) followed by a (near) Perfect Breakfast followed by the requisite number of hours spent in sweaty,
stretchy physical activity. Lunch is somewhat less than perfect,
but, in my defense (not sure who's attacking me), I do not eat
Kashi GoLean in handfuls straight from the box for an afternoon
snack. Work is performed standing up at my elevated desk (yes!),
but amazing research finds, brilliant insights, and masterful turns
of phrase for the most part elude me. Then I yell at my daughter
for throwing wet towels on top of a pile of clean laundry. Then I
yell at my husband for secretly turning up the thermostat settings.
Then we eat Thai takeout. With deep-fried spring-roll appetizers.
On the plus side, I get some good stretching in as I watch *The*

Walking Dead. And I do manage about twenty pages of Norman Maclean before lights out.

The not-surprising verdict: I did *not* live my (presumably achievable) Perfect Day.

But what did I learn in the not-living? I learned that planning and discipline can take you only so far. Life marches to its own beat. People, in clear violation of your plans, do what they are going to do. I learned that striving for perfection can be tiring, for me and for those annoyingly imperfect people around me. I learned that in keeping my "eyes on the prize"—the prize being the achievement of a Perfect Day—I didn't really or fully experience the day I did live. I was busy keeping score. I was focused on achieving/failing to achieve my series of self-defined benchmarks, always looking ahead. Not just looking ahead but looking ahead with blinders.

On the other hand, devising the Perfect Day plan gave me the opportunity to think through what I believe nourishes me. It helped me examine what I think is important and gave me important clues about achieving balance. Also, and not inconsequentially, it kept me from spending my all-too-usual hour scrolling through screens of shoes on Zappos.

But when I write "I learned," I am not fooling myself. I haven't *learned*, past tense. I am far from done with this tutorial on perfection. I know better. Big lessons like this are called *life* lessons because you spend your life studying, practicing, learning, and relearning them.

12

In the Company

THE EUGENE BALLET Company's seven-month season officially begins today, September 9, with the first company class scheduled for 8:00 a.m. Last night, for inspiration and in preparation, I started reading Maria Tallchief's autobiography. That's Maria, Balanchine's original Sugar Plum Fairy. But I'm afraid it had the opposite effect. She was taking lessons when she was three. At twelve she was studying with Bronislava Nijinska (yes, Nijinsky's sister), a graduate, like her incomparable brother, of the storied Imperial Theatre School in St. Petersburg. But, unlike her incomparable brother, not crazy. At seventeen, Tallchief was a company dancer with the Ballet Russe in New York. The photographs in the book take my breath away. Her elegance, her long line. She is regal in a way the iconic Russian ballerinas of old were regal: strong and commanding. Women of passion and substance, not like some of the will-o'-the-wisp dancers who came later, the ones who looked like a gentle breeze could blow them away, the ones who looked more like prepubescent girls than adult women. Tallchief's single-mindedness and passion put my long-ago overly romantic, soft-focus dreams in sharp contrast and illustrate what it *really* takes. I sleep fitfully, worried about how I should dress for class, how I will look to the others, what I will be able to do, if I will embarrass myself, if this ballet thing was one of the worst ideas I've had in recent years. The clock says 2:23, then 3:14, 4:19, 5:37. Am I really waking up every hour?

At 6:03 I give up, get out of bed, weigh myself (bad idea), and then try on my two new leotards—and spend a solid ten minutes stressing over the fit. They looked marginally okay in the Dancers' Closet fitting room, but now I'm not so sure. The least of my worries, I know, but looking the part builds confidence and, according to that "enclothed cognition" study I read a while back, actually could enhance performance. That's a lot to ask from a leo, but who am I to argue with science?

I scrape my hair back into what I consider a decent bun and apply mascara. I don't wear mascara even on those infrequent fancy occasions that might merit such cosmetic adornment. But what I have going for me, ballerinawise, is my long, dark, bunable hair, my acceptably oval face, and my big eyes. So I invest a minute or two enhancing what I've got. Besides, I know from talking with both Tori and Suzi that they and all the other ballerinas wear makeup to class. There's nothing *meaningful* I can do that would *actually* make me fit this morning. I can't turn back the clock thirty years or elongate my legs or narrow my rib cage or suddenly drop twenty—um, make that twenty-five—pounds. But I *can* dress the part and make my eyes look bigger.

I arrive at the EBC studios a half hour early, as Tory and Suzi tell me they do, to stretch. Maybe a dozen dancers are already there. One of the principals, a tiny young Japanese woman with thighs the circumference of my upper arms, is spread-eagled on the floor in that extraordinary position I now know is perfectly ordinary for a ballerina: legs pointing due east and due west to create a perfectly straight, as in 180-degree, line. She is hinged at the waist, her back ruler-straight, her entire torso flat on the floor, her arms stretched out long in front of her. She is holding her phone. She is texting. I try (unsuccessfully) not to stare. I spot Suzi sitting on the floor near the front of the studio, dressed in raggedly elegant, charmingly mismatched "junk," the hallmark of a veteran dancer, and thick socks. She is busy flexing and pointing her toes. I join her on the floor, stretching out as best I can. I place the thick elastic band my EBC teacher Miranda told me to buy under the arch of one foot and flex and point, flex and point, working on my "cashew" foot. I lie on my back, draw my knees to my chest, place the soles of my feet together, and press my knees to the floor. Well, near the floor. Meanwhile, I quiz Suzi about class etiquette.

I don't know where I belong. I mean literally. I don't know where to claim a place at the barre. She tells me that the returning dancers stake out specific spots, but she invites me to insert myself between her and the next dancer over, a big, handsome, tousle-haired blond guy named Mark Tucker. Sandwiched between them, I will have someone who knows the routines either direction I face. Suzi is looking out for me. I'm so pleased. And so *immediately* thankful. On the dot of 8:00, with a small smile and a curt nod of the head, Toni Pimble starts class. As I discover, she leads the class only one morning a week. Her responsibilities as artistic director are just too time- and energy-consuming for her to do otherwise. As I also discover, the dancers bring just a little extra to the class when she's in the front of the room. What Toni sees matters. Toni casts all the ballets. She decides who partners whom. She plucks dancers from the corps to take on key solos. She chooses principals from the corps—or decides to recruit from elsewhere. The fates and the careers of the new dancers—they are called "aspirants"—depend on her. So everyone wants to look very, very good.

I do too, of course, to justify her faith in me and to set myself up for securing a part, a real part, not a stand-in-the-background part, in *The Nutcracker*. But . . . *yikes*. It's immediately (and pain-fully) clear to me that company class is entirely different than the community classes I've been taking, classes that assume the rela-tive cluelessness of the participants with instructors who decon-struct every position and demonstrate every move. Toni, on the other hand, rattles off directions for each complicated sequence of moves *fastfastfast*—and of course in French. She demonstrates in quick, abbreviated steps and punctuates with staccato hand mo-tions. I catch some words I know—"tendu," "piqué," "attitude," "en l'air." But in between, it all just washes over me. It truly *is* a foreign language—and I don't just mean the French. I watch the other dancers as they watch and listen to Toni. Suzi and Mark just nod knowingly. Most of the others mark the steps with their hands, hands that are lovely, fluttery, and graceful even when not engaged in dance. Even the newbies, the aspirants, the handful of young women and men Toni has chosen to intern with the com-pany this year, even they seem completely at ease with these rapid-fire commands.

At the barre I am a full beat behind. I'm staring at Suzi's feet trying to approximate her movements, which of course means my head position is all wrong, and my chin is down, and I look most undancerlike. Suzi, on the other hand, gives every little movement her absolute attention, like she's not warming up in a class with barre exercises but performing onstage. She is quick and precise. The point of her toe in her beat-up canvas slippers. The soaring arch of her foot. Her extended leg, board-straight, shoulder height. Yes, I said shoulder. The soft, strong curve of her arm. The tilt of her head, *just so*. I could stand here and watch her all day. But, oh, right: I am supposed to be doing these barre exercises too.

Plié, fondu, battement, rond de jambe. At least I am in semi-familiar territory. But I am working so hard to follow the footwork that my arms begin to flail. I direct my attention to my arms, to the ports de bras that change with every position of the leg. And then I lose the leg. I stare at Suzi's back. Suzi's back is beautiful. Her scapula are like wings. She bends forward, brushes the floor with an arm that looks liquid, rights herself with grace and ease just as if—as Antonio explained in community class—she was being pulled by an invisible string on the top of her head. We turn at the barre, and now I am facing Mark. He has stripped off his junk pants and is wearing what I'm sure has a ballet name but to me looks like Calvin Klein black undies. Can I just say, for the record, that I could stare at this guy's butt all day? I can see the articulated muscles of his thighs, his calves. He looks like one of those Roman statues I saw outside the Uffizi. He is already sweating.

In fact, the room is beginning to smell, and I am reminded of that wonderful Chekhov quote about dancers smelling like racehorses. After an hour of increasingly difficult (for me, that is) and fast-paced barre routines, we are ready to move to the center, to floor work. Perhaps I should not use the inclusive pronoun here. I am not part of "we." I cannot follow—or begin to attempt—these floor routines at all. There are chassés and pas de chat and pas de cheval. There are grand jetés and pirouettes and double pirouettes and fouettés. Most of the women have exchanged their soft leather or canvas slippers for toe shoes. Toni fires off the instructions . . . six, seven, eight steps. The men go first, then the first group of women, then the second. I stand in the back, staying out of the way but trying to mark the steps when I can.

"I haven't done a pirouette in forty years," I tell Suzi as she returns, panting, from her time in the center. I try a turn, barely making it once around, forgetting the whole spotting-with-your-head thing and ending unsteadily and slightly dizzy. No one sees. Actually, no one is paying any attention to me at all. I am thrilled.

They are completely intent on their tasks. Totally self-involved. The only thing they see is their own reflection in the mirror.

—ᘓ

IT IS FASCINATING being this close to the work that goes behind the art. In the audience, you see the satin and tulle, the elegance and glamour, the graceful move, the jump that seems to come from nowhere and hovers, impossibly, in the air. Up close, it is muscles and tendons and sweat and stink. Out of costume with no scenery, each dancer is unique. Mark is big and muscular. His dance is all about power. Antonio is small and wiry. His dance is all about quickness. Yoshie, the little Japanese principal ballerina, is all detail and precision. Tori, a good half-foot taller, uses her long, long limbs to create fluidity. Danielle, another company dancer with classic ballet looks and extraordinary flexibility, manages to be both bold and elegant. Everyone is panting. Everyone is mopping at faces.

I try to find an analogy for what I'm seeing. I think it's as if an ordinary reader who had been transported by a piece of writing, the grace and ease of it, the seamless world it created, was all of a sudden stuck in a room with a real writer. A writer banging on a keyboard and cursing at the screen, fiddling with note cards, pacing, farting, I don't know . . . just working it, just being a hard-working creator in the act of creation. It is messy work. I love that. I love the magic that transforms the sweating, grunting work into what we see onstage—and on the page.

I am, let it be known, not as sweaty as everyone else because I haven't done the leaping, prancing floor work. But, hey, first day. I made it here. I did every barre exercise.

—ᘓ

I TELL MYSELF that the next morning as I stand at the barre between self-possessed and sculpted Suzi and magnificently muscled
Mark. But the image filling my mind right now is one of those
first grade workbooks, the ones with simple pictures—three
oranges and a baseball, three hats and a jacket—and instructions
to "circle the one that does not belong." I'm the one who does not
belong. That is, I don't belong if I think of myself as a dancer. But
as soon as I begin talking to Suzi and then Mark, I am in my
element—a reporter immersed in a story, a cultural-anthropologist-
without-portfolio delving into a subculture. I ask Suzi if what I
noticed yesterday is true. When Toni leads the class, as she does
every Tuesday, does Suzi feel she is performing, trying out for a
part, showing Toni just how good she is, how much work she's
done during the summer? She smiles, like I've discovered a secret
of hers. "It's inbred in us to want to please the teacher," she says, I
think a little ruefully.

On my other side is Mark with his thick blond hair and strong
profile. He looks like he could walk the streets of Kiev and blend
in. But as I engage him in what I hope feels more like a conversation than an interview, I discover that he is second-generation
Hawaiian. (Scotch-Irish, he quickly adds.) He's twenty-six, and
it's his fourth season with EBC. I ask him when he came to ballet.
So often with the boys it's later. The girls start at three or four.
Never the boys. Mark says he was nine when he started taking
musical theater dance classes and ten when he took his first ballet
class, the only boy in a roomful of seven-year-old girls. He hated
it. At thirteen, he finally took an all-male class, and he was
hooked. At sixteen, he left high school and Hawaii to enroll in
the famed North Carolina School of the Arts. Four years later, he
joined EBC. Reed, another of the male dancers, tells me later that
he didn't start ballet lessons until he was thirteen. He had been
taking tap, he says, and ballet was suggested as a way to achieve

greater strength and balance. "This Russian girl was teaching the class," he says, looking skyward for a moment, "and, well, that was that."

We get to work. Florabelle, one of Eugene Ballet Academy's teachers, is leading the class today. We start with a series of ballet stretches at the barre. Although I've been stretching for a half-hour before class, this feels wonderful, if "wonderful" can be used to describe that taut-wire pain that comes from asking the muscles along the backs of your legs to elongate. Florabelle rattles off the barre sequences even faster than Toni does. I imitate the others by marking the steps with little hand flourishes as she talks, although what I'm doing is mostly for show. I pretty much don't know what's going on. I will try to keep up by following Suzi and Mark.

There are a lot of arabesques and attitudes this morning. I raise my leg as high as it will go without assistance. Why can't I raise it higher than my waist? Why can't I hold it there for more than a nanosecond? I throw myself off balance. I modify so that I can pay attention to each position, especially to my arms and hands. When the class goes to the floor, I again stand at the back of the room out of everyone's way. Sometimes I mark the steps. Mostly I watch. But once, following along for part of a sequence, I practice my pas de chat—steps of the cat—a delicate move I half-remember from my Eglevsky days. It is beautiful on toe. Not that I will ever again be able to go on toe.

I am in the hallway just outside the studio working on grand battements when Mark comes out, smiling, panting, sweating after a set of floor exercises. I tell him I may never be able to do anything other than the barre work. "Hey," he says, "you have great turnout. I mean, you have better turnout than I do. I'm impressed." I try to keep myself from beaming. "You're not like some of the adults I see in the other classes," he says. "I can tell you took ballet when you were younger." Ninety percent of me is thrilled to pieces. *I've still got it! Booyah!* The other 10 percent lurking within is whispering, *Uh-oh, he's looking at me. Maybe they're all looking at me.*

But my realization today is that my being here for class every morning is not so much about relearning ballet and preparing myself for *The Nutcracker*—although that's obviously important. It is about immersing myself in the dancers' world to better understand it. It is about gaining the trust and respect of the company, letting the dancers know, by my actions, by my presence, that I care about and share their passion.

A FEW DAYS later, Mark doesn't show for class, and one of the other male dancers is absent. There is talk of muscle spasms and trips to chiropractors and physical therapists and appointments made at Slocum, the Center for Orthopedic and Sports Medicine, where Olympic athletes from all over the world come for treatment. Apparently, EBC dancers as well. Injury is a fact of life. Yet caution is not part of the dance vocabulary. Extreme precision and focus are what it's about. That and simultaneously giving yourself over to the music. Whatever this discipline calls for, I know I need to take special care of my much, much older body.

I awake in the dark at 5:30, make it to Barre3 in time for the 6:15 class—the idea being that I will warm up and stretch out my muscles—then to EBC in time for an additional half-hour of stretching before the 8:00 class begins. Because I spent more than an hour perusing a discount-dancewear site last night (and buying three leotards I probably don't need), I am very much aware that at least some of the dancers are wearing fashionable garb in the studio this morning. Suzi is in her signature "junk," but Tori and Danielle and some of the other women are wearing jewel-toned leotards with asymmetrical cutouts in the back. Antonio is sporting animal-print tights. I am in my simple spaghetti-strap, scoop-necked basic black. But soon, in the mail, I'll be getting cooler stuff.

Jenn Martin, an EBC principal dancer for eleven years who is now ballet mistress, is leading the class today. She would have kept dancing, but, as she tells me later with a kind of strained dispassion—an odd, clinical dissociation she obviously had to work hard to achieve—"the body degraded." Just a few years into her EBC dancing career, she sustained a third-degree ankle sprain. Because she was young and thought herself invulnerable and because dancing was everything, she was back on toe and on tour two and a half weeks later. But the sprain, she learned much later, had resulted in bone chips that damaged cartilage. And every year, it got worse. She'd dance in pain, stick her foot into an ice bucket as soon as she got offstage, go in for cortisone shots, and then do it all again. And that was just what was happening on the left side. On the right, the cartilage in her big toe was disappearing, the result of years and years en pointe. Toward the end, during her final two years of dancing, she was taking an anti-inflammatory cocktail and getting injections of the kind of lubricant administered to people with knee problems, and dancing hurt all the time. It was time, and she knew it.

But leaving ballet was not an option. It was the only life she knew, her sole passion. She had been dancing since she was three. Her parents had driven her an hour and a half each way to attend ballet classes. She'd had a private coach. She'd loitered by the stage door at the San Francisco Ballet to get her point shoes auto-graphed by the dancers. She'd gone to Russian training summer intensives, started with the Royal Winnipeg Ballet at seventeen. "I really don't know how to do anything else," she tells me later, over coffee, when we begin to get to know each other. And so, when the longtime EBC ballet master decided to leave, Jenn transitioned into that teaching role. She confides that she doesn't love it the way she loved dancing, but "I will *learn* to love it," she tells me, emphatically. There is an iron will behind that statement. It's the same iron will that kept her dancing through years of pain and kept her head above water last year when her then twenty-eight-year-old husband, Juan Carlos Amy-Cordero, an extraordinarily accomplished and charismatic dancer, committed suicide in their Eugene home. J.C., as he was called, was a principal with the company, having joined in 2002 after dancing with the Boston Ballet. He and Jenn married in 2010. The suicide was big news last summer. It shook the company to its core, not just because that's what the death of a young person does but because it was so unforeseen. Juan Carlos was "a jester on and offstage," Toni told a reporter covering the suicide. He was a joyous dancer, an accomplished photographer, and, as far as anyone knew, happy.

This messy, painful, stuff-of-life is a reminder that this ballet company—any company—is not merely a collection of hard-working, talented, genetically blessed young people. But it might be an overstatement to call the company "a family." To me, the company feels more like an ongoing play—with a little too much plot. There's J.C.'s suicide and Jenn's recovery and the miracle of her finding a new love right under her nose (EBC's business manager, Josh). There's Heather, a nine-year veteran of EBC, who surprised everyone by announcing her pregnancy right before the season began—and then promptly left the company. There's Mark and Danielle, who danced together for years before they became an item—so much of an item that they are getting married in a few months. And there's Suzi and Antonio, who as dance partners performed the unabashedly sensual Arabian dance in last year's *Nutcracker* and are now partner partners, seemingly inseparable.

And Cory and Beth, both company dancers, who've known each other since their student days and have recently been reunited via EBC. And a now maybe new couple among the newcomers, Jesse and Sonja, who are attracting the not-so-subtle interest of company veterans.

Some people think all (or most) men who dance ballet are gay. Is it because male dancers are graceful and sinuous and live in their bodies in a way we expect only from women? Is it because they wear makeup onstage? Tights? It's worth remembering that the world of ballet includes its share of both Nureyevs *and* Baryshnikovs (and that Nureyev bedded almost as many ballerinas as he did men). This relatively small company includes six straight couples. Given that most of the dancers' waking hours are devoted to dance, there seems to be an awful lot of action going on around the *edges*.

With significant relationship drama going on—and, presumably, sex—it may seem strange to say that I sometimes think of the company as a convent. (But with men.) And with the caveat that this convent-insight is based solely on my deep and impressive knowledge of convent life gleaned from multiple viewings of Audrey Hepburn in *The Nun's Story*. (Now, *there* was a woman with a ballerina neck.) But here's the point: The company, like the convent, is about discipline of the body and discipline of the mind. It is about essential daily routines (class/performance/rehearsal; lauds/matins/vespers), about giving yourself over to a higher power (art/God). It is about hierarchy (ballet mistress/mother superior). And years of proving yourself, moving up through the ranks. In the company, it's aspirant to corps to soloist to principal. In the convent, the path also begins as an aspirant, moving to postulant, novitiate, first vows, then final vows. Am I reaching here? I'm just working hard to understand this alien world. Or it could be that the company is like the military: hierarchical, suffused with strict discipline, a daily grind of readiness drills, an enterprise whose success hinges on both personal heroics and collaborative action, on both taking individual initiative and watching out for one other. On the battlefield as on the stage: Leave no one behind.

—♋

JENN'S BODY IS dancer-ageless, but her face is imprinted with tough times. When she begins to lead the class, however, she transforms. She is animated and lighthearted, youthful, excited. Toni is dead serious when she instructs. Hard to read, like any good Englishwoman. Florabelle is intent in the moment but slightly more fanciful. Jenn is a lovely combination of *Let's get down to business* and *Let's remember that this is the life we chose and the life we love.* She is demanding, but she has a sense of humor. Still, like Toni and Florabelle, she issues instructions so quickly that I give up trying to follow or mark or commit to memory, which everyone around me is doing with nonchalance. Here is Jenn cuing a barre routine. Instead of reading the sentence below to yourself, say it aloud with no pauses (I'm not going to tempt you with commas). Actually, don't so much say it as sing it with a lilt or recite it like poetry. And, oh, don't take a breath. Because Jenn didn't:

Fondu devant three piqués battement cloche derrière devant derrière devant derrière devant dégagé en croix dégagé to the first two times one dégagé à la second closing fifth back two quick retirés passé and reverse then switch sides.

(Full disclosure: I had her go through this for me, slowly, with repetition, when I had a notebook in front of me.) And then there are the frappés and the coupés, the développés and chassés, the bourrées, the pas de *this* and pas de *that*, the relevés in sous-sus. My head is exploding. I am grateful to have Suzi in front of me.

In between the relentless litany of steps and positions, Jenn makes little jokes as she demonstrates. She plays a Paula Abdul song. She walks the room, engaging with the dancers, making comments and small corrections. She does not bother to correct me, of course. That would take up the entire class. And the one after that. Ad pretty much infinitum. I keep up as best I can, feeling lost-er and lost-er as the routines get more and more complex, the combinations longer and longer. As I struggle, I think about a passage I just read in Toni Bentley's book *Winter Season*, her diary of a season with Balanchine's New York City Ballet. Here's what she has to say about going to class every morning: "As always, class proves to be a challenge beyond everything. Today I triumph; yesterday I did not. But back I go every day, however much fear I generate to deter me."

Yep.

13

The Ballet Book Club

KIM, WHO HAS taken to referring to herself as "that tall, mouthy redhead," has finally rehabbed her shoulder, the persistent injury that has kept her from what was supposed to be our regular Wednesday-night community ballet class. She's healed and ready, but it's too late to resume our schedule. I have started taking company classes every day now, with Barre3 as my 6:15 warm-up most mornings and afternoon Pilates twice a week to keep working on the "long line." Soon there will be late-morning and early-afternoon rehearsals for *The Nutcracker*. As important as it is to take the slow-moving adult all-comers class and get detailed instruction and correction, as much fun as it has been to attend the class with Kim, to bond and bitch and stretch the bounds of our friendship as we stretch just about everything else, I have no time now.

So, enterprising women that we are, friends without ballet benefits that we have found ourselves to be, we think of an alternative way to partner: We agree to start the Ballet Book Club—BBC for short. It absolutely suits my purpose right now: I need to continue to immerse myself—my head, that is, my time as a reader—in the world and culture and literature of ballet as I meanwhile, daily, immerse my body in its rigors. And it suits our friendship. We enjoy each other's company, and we love to talk. And by "talk" I mean mull over ideas—not just gossip (which we also love to do). The formation of the BBC may help assuage Kim's guilt for flaking out on me, if dislocating one's shoulder could be termed "flaking out." The astute reader will also note that the BBC gives Kim a reason to continue as a supporting character in the narrative.

As I sit on the living room floor gathering a pile of books for potential BBC consideration at tomorrow afternoon's first meeting, my daughter saunters by. I tell her about this new venture. Her own reading currently skews to the zombie genre. But she is kind enough to express a modicum of interest.

"So who's in this book club?" she asks.

"Kim and me," I say.

"I mean, like, who else? You know, the *club*?"

"Um, Kim and me." In truth, we haven't even discussed inviting other participants. This is our literary pas de deux.

Over the course of e-mails and Skypes, we decide to start with biographies of the greats: Pavlova, Nureyev, Fonteyn, Baryshnikov. Tallchief would make that list, but I tell Kim I've already read the book.

When the Fonteyn and Nureyev biographies arrive in the mail, each almost seven hundred pages long, we make a coexecutive decision to split the work, Kim reading Nureyev, I focused on Fonteyn, and share what we learned. Otherwise we can't hope to cover the terrain I was hoping to cover by *Nutcracker* time. I set our guidelines: We are not going to discuss the writing styles, the structure, the scene setting, and the character development, all those literary niceties one would expect to discuss in a book club. We are going to scour the books for insights about life and art, comb them for whatever lessons the lives of these famous dancers might teach us about our own lives. What can we learn about focus, discipline, and sacrifice, about pushing oneself, about raising the barre? That's the plan.

But the aforementioned agenda doesn't stand in the way of us beginning BBC meeting number one with a studious but nonetheless salacious discussion about whether bad-boy Rudi and Dame Margot's intimate artistic partnership was also a sexual partnering. I know, I know. This is beneath us. But there we are, I with my *Margot Fonteyn*, Margot peering out from the cover, huge doe eyes, gorgeous arched brows, looking simultaneously wistful and elegant, wearing a tiara. And there, right next to her, on the table at the coffee hang-out that will become BBC HQ, is Rudi on the cover of *Nureyev*. He's peering out from Kim's book with this trademarked *I am IT, and I know it* gaze, and those Tartar cheekbones and those lush lips, and he is (of course) stripped to the waist.

We can't help it. We just keep looking from book cover to cover. The cool, classy ballerina. The fiery enfant terrible. Their extraordinary union, she close to twenty years his senior playing Juliet to his Romeo. What follows is a (probably too loud) conversation about the likelihood that there was a partnering dans le boudoir—or, more likely, multiple boudoirs in multiple cities on various continents. We quote passages from our respective books. Kim remains dubious. I insist. "I think everybody slept with everybody," is the elegant way I put it. She considers the veracity of that statement, especially as it applies to her Russian, and grants that Margot may have succumbed. Or perhaps it was Rudi who succumbed. Enough already. We grudgingly move on to ideas more worthy of our attention.

During the almost three-month duration of the BBC, this is hardly our last off-topic discussion. At subsequent meetings, we salivate over photographs of and have anatomical debates about Baryshnikov's body. (How could fellow members of the Kirov Ballet have called the teenaged Misha "a short, stocky hockey puck" while partner/paramour Gelsey Kirkland used the word "god" an embarrassing number of times to describe him?) We count the number of times the magnificent Misty Copeland—who was, indeed, a prodigy—calls herself one in her memoir. And then there is Jenifer Ringer and God. And Kirkland—poor, frail, anorexic, depressed, cocaine-addicted, artistically tortured, plastic surgery–enhanced Gelsey Kirkland—who is sensible, sound, and well adjusted compared to the mad "God Nijinsky," as he calls himself. And then there are the season-in-the-life ballet-company books that dwell on the potent combination of pain and tedium that underlies a dancer's life. But mostly, over iced teas al fresco that become Americanos by the fireplace as early fall turns to late fall, we try to extract life lessons. We come up with a dozen. Here they are:

1. Turn Down the Volume on the Inner Body Critic. The most obvious lesson, the lesson that screams from the pages of all the ballet biographies and memoirs, is this: Obsession with one's body—and by that I mean the weight and shape of one's body, not its health or serviceability—is mentally, physically, and spiritually damaging. Not to mention dangerous. Dancers, of course, depend on their bodies. Their bodies are their instruments. Their bodies are the vehicles for their art. It is understandable (and necessary) for dancers to live body-centric lives. It is not necessary for dancers, or for any of us, to allow the mirror and the scale to rule our days—the "emotional terror of the mirror," Gelsey Kirkland calls it—to allow our bodies to define who we are; to endlessly, joylessly compare ourselves to an unattainable ideal; to forever focus on flaws; to starve ourselves.

It's one thing for me to scowl at my image in the mirror or read (in these very pages) about my foolish—tedious?—obsession with the extra skin that hangs beneath my triceps. In fact, my self-critiques are so firmly embedded in my life that they are like a software program always running in the background. I am, most times, consciously unaware of the gnawing away at self-esteem and self-worth going on at this deeper, hidden level. It takes reading Misty's dissing of her "too curvy" body—have you seen the *magnificence* of that body?—or Gelsey's pathological self-hatred of hers or even Dame Margot's fixation with her less-than-perfect feet to tune into my own trash talk. To discover that it *is* the background noise to my own life. I am wondering (I am hoping) whether all this reading about dancers' emotionally crippling obsessions with the shape, proportion, and weight of their bodies is a scary-enough cautionary tale to jolt me out of my chronic self-criticism. Okay, maybe not "jolt." That is too much to expect after years and years of reading "learn to love your body" advice columns and having them make not a bit of difference. Maybe just a little nudge?

2. The Life of the Mind Is as Important as the Life of the Body. There's a lesson to be learned in these books about the life-of-the-body/life-of-the-mind duality. Kim and I, both of the life-of-the-mind persuasion, are struck by how utterly brainless the life of dance (of the body) can be. I don't mean stupid, or that these dancers are stupid. Not at all. It's that they give themselves over to, lose themselves in, dance. They "think" through dance, feel through dance, communicate through dance. It is the body, not the mind—the body with its muscles and tendons, its movement and stillness, its strength, its pain—that asks the questions and provides the answers. This is magical to me, to both Kim and me. What we do is ponder, question, discuss, debate, research, analyze, codify. We talk. A lot. Our world is one of ideas, thoughts, and words, of conversations and books. (And, I have to add, because we are not quite the high-falutin' intellectuals this makes us sound like: Our world is also about binge-watching *Downton Abbey*.)

At various times in my life I have felt as if my body existed merely for the purpose of carting my brain around. At various times in my life I have felt the kind of severe, almost otherworldly disconnection between body and mind that someone who sits all day, reading and writing, can feel—without ever actually knowing that she is feeling it. That's how complete the disconnection is. The live-in-your-body life chronicled in these books comes through clearly (albeit via words), and it is a message worth listening to. It's one I am working hard to listen to as I catapult myself into not only this significant physical challenge but also this world inhabited by the body-centric.

But there's an alternate, and just as powerful, mind-body lesson from these books: A completely body-centric way of being does not allow us to be fully human. The life of the mind *is* important. In fact, it is vital. As Meredith Daneman, one of Margot Fonteyn's biographers, writes, "Entirely identified with the physical as Margot was, she had no idea how to find stimulation in the life of the mind." Or as Fonteyn herself is quoted as saying, "Mostly I just danced and danced." She knew so little about the world, about culture and politics and the ideas, big and small, that captivate the rest of us, that she truly didn't know what to do with herself when she wasn't dancing. Which may have been one of the major reasons she danced until she was sixty. Well, that and Rudi.

Former New York City Ballet dancer Toni Bentley writes bluntly (and harshly) about the paucity of the life of the mind. "Thinking is not a becoming stage image," she writes in her memoir of a season with the company. She calls the concentration that comes with thinking and reasoning "most un-ballerina-like," adding, "Perhaps our ethereal presence is achieved not because of our high level of consciousness but because of having none at all."

3. Appreciate Focus While Widening Horizons. Which brings us to the lesson(s) we can learn about focus from these books. I don't mean the garden-variety quieting-the-mind-and-zeroing-in kind of concentration we often strive for (and sometimes achieve) in our lives. I mean extreme, intense, laserlike focus. I mean the single-minded attention that is necessary to create great art, the obsessional focus that molds the lives of artists, that sculpts them, often painfully, as if all the parts deemed extraneous to the endeavor had to be chiseled away. It rendered Fonteyn, writes her biographer, "unequipped for the ways of ordinary society." It is a high price to pay. Yet they pay it, and we admire them for it.

I'm confused by this message. I thought being "well-rounded" was the ideal, which is the opposite of the lives led by these dancers. It makes me think—and not for the first time—about the line between "well-rounded"—which seems like a good idea—and "jack of all trades, master of none"—which sounds like mediocrity, or at least dilettantism. Is there such a thing as balancing diverse interests? Does balance preclude true excellence?

Where does focus end and blinders begin? Can you practice extreme focus without blinding yourself to the rest of life? "I only think of what I must do tomorrow—that I must dance *Swan Lake*, that I must dance *Sleeping Beauty*. I go from day to day," Fonteyn told a *New York Times* reporter in a 1972 interview. "I've always tended to reject everything in life which doesn't enrich or directly concern my single dominating passion," Nureyev is quoted as saying in the massive biography neither Kim nor I managed to finish reading. Can one actually live life that way? Does one want to?

But there is a lesson that seems clear enough for those of us at midlife, for those of us who have channeled all or most of our energy into one realm—the rigors of an all-consuming profession, the rigors of all-consuming parenting: Now might be just the time to widen the horizons. Being excellent at one thing is an enormous accomplishment. Is it time to move on?

4. Hard Work Is the Answer (to Just About Every Question). The books tell the stories of very different dancers, women and men, from different countries, born in different centuries. They come to dance for different reasons. They contribute in unique ways. But the metanarrative, and lesson number four, is: hard work, discipline, tenacity. It's all about blood, sweat, and tears—which I wish was not a cliché because it *is* literally about blood, sweat, and tears. And that is one powerful trifecta, cliché notwithstanding.

Yes, there is talent. Yes, there are the genetically blessed. But achieving greatness (or, for us mortals, doing something well or honorably) is, all the ballet books tell us, a matter of discipline and hard work. For Misha, who pursued a relentless work schedule, "the desire [to be a dancer] is the discipline of a career, and work is the language of that discipline." *Work is the language . . .* wow. The discipline of ballet—the "iron discipline of ballet," Fonteyn calls it—is undoubtedly more extreme than is required by many professions or midlife passions we might throw ourselves into. And ballet training is more exacting, more all-consuming, than many other undertakings. Pavlova likened her ballet academy to "a convent whence frivolity is banned, and where merciless discipline reigns." Nijinsky spoke of "the discipline of military drill" (which must have been particularly difficult to endure for a guy who believed he was God—not *a* god, but The God). But the lessons about looking inside for discipline, about showing up day after day, about bringing everything to every moment in order to push oneself, challenge oneself . . . these are lessons for us all.

The lives of these dancers are all studies in tenacity. It's not just their day-to-day determination, the doggedness of their routines, their nose-to-grindstone schedules of classes and practices and rehearsals and performances. It is manifested in other parts of their lives: Fonteyn's superhuman drive to keep dancing until she was sixty, holding on to a level of excellence and commitment and physicality without equal; Misty overcoming a tumultuous childhood, struggling back from a crippling injury, persisting against racial stereotypes; Gelsey fighting her addictions; Ringer and her triumph over body issues. It is having a vision of yourself and making that come true through force of will and harder work than you ever imagined. It is a deep, embedded, unshakable sense of self, which is a huge life lesson, and one I believe can and should be learned, relearned, and reiterated at midlife.

5. "Constructive Criticism" Is Not Just a Catch Phrase. This extraordinary, often punishing, discipline is not just about hard work and perseverance—as if these were not enough—but is also about opening oneself up to—*inviting*—correction and criticism. Now, *there's* a lesson. How many of us *invite* correction and criticism and consider them an important part, an essential part, a never-ending part, of the path to mastery or achievement or just plain old competence? Maybe we are eager for this input at the beginning of the learning curve, but soon (too soon) ego plays the trump card, and we no longer seek correction and criticism, or we ignore it. Or we grumble about it, take offense, are hurt by it.

The world of dance, however, has a different lesson to teach. Even the greatest dancers in the world, the reigning royalty of their day, attend daily classes where teachers dissect, correct, and critique their work. It is an integral part of their professional and artistic lives. This is very different from how most of us conduct our professional lives. Some jobs include periodic evaluations of performance. Some professions offer ongoing education. Outside critics comment on the work of writers, actors, musicians. But daily ongoing correction and criticism that are invited, not dreaded, that are part of the process, not after-the-fact evaluation, that are an expected and honored part of the lives of people even at the pinnacle of their careers? This would be, for most of us, a novel and very challenging way to approach what we do. It wouldn't just challenge our egos. It would challenge our ideas about being at "the top" of our fields, the apex of the learning curve. We may give lip service to the notion that "there is always more to learn," but how many of us, in midlife, embrace that on a daily basis?

6. Fear of Failing Stunts Growth. Worse yet for our delicate egos is the concept (let alone the reality) of falling, as the cliché goes, "flat on our faces"—which happens, more than I ever knew, in ballet. And, although falling is certainly a source of temporary embarrassment, it is, in the world of professional ballet, accepted as a more-than-occasional consequence of the endeavor. The books are sprinkled with anecdotes of the dancers falling on their faces, literally and in public. An overpolished stage, a missed cue, an unexpected added flourish, a turned ankle. In the midst of a performance, they fall. What happens? They get up and continue dancing. Balanchine, writes Suzanne Farrell, loved it when dancers fell. It showed exuberance. It showed a willingness to take risks.

We may not fear a literal fall, but we fear—especially I think at midlife, when we're supposed to have it mostly figured out—the figurative fall: failure. Especially in public. And this fear reins in our desire to take risks. So we stick with what we know, what is comfortable and safe, because it protects us from falling, from failing. Of course, it also "protects" us from growing and changing in ways we cannot imagine. The dancers have something important to teach us here, not just about getting up and carrying on after a fall but about the willingness to risk falling/failing in the first place.

Baryshnikov was already the most famous ballet dancer in the world when he took on the challenge of dancing an Alvin Ailey ballet. "All I could think of was that I looked like a cow on ice. . . . 'Don't look at me, don't look at me,' I said at the first rehearsals." With his exalted reputation and perhaps even more exalted ego at stake, he put himself at risk of falling (literally) and failing. Unsure and nervous right up to opening night, he—did we have any doubt?—nailed it. "It was a thrill," he writes. The thrill of risking failure, of pushing oneself into the *un*comfort zone, and of mastering a fear. You can't feel the thrill unless you take the risk. Now, there's a bumpersticker for you.

7. Find the Ease in Effort. I wonder about the "Never let them see you sweat" message Kim and I are getting from the ballet books. It's clear that in dance, as in many other creative endeavors, grindingly hard work underlies the beauty, the grace, and the artistry. Ballet, with its delicacy and refinement, is in fact grueling and relentless physical work. Yet dancers present onstage as effortless, floating, twirling, leaping otherworldly beings. We expect that of them. We are not interested in seeing the effort. Is this a life lesson? Should we attempt to show the world that life is smooth and we've got it absolutely all together, meanwhile toiling and grunting and angsting in private? Does doing this make us "inauthentic," a major sin in the self-help world? I struggle mightily with this.

That said, there's a way of turning this message on its head and extracting a very different lesson. Maybe Summer Spinner's

Barre3 mantra—"Find the ease within the effort"—is the better message. Maybe it's not about not letting them see you sweat. Maybe it's about that place where you acknowledge the intensity and then allow yourself to almost relax into it. You find a deep calm even as you are also in the midst of the turmoil of creation. It is finding the being in the act of doing.

8. There's Sacrifice, and Then There's *Sacrifice*. Reading about the sacrifices the dancers made, what they gave up in order to become who they became, it's hard not to consider the question: What are you really willing to give up to achieve what you say you want to achieve? The Russians (including my bête noire, Eglevsky) forsook family and homeland. All of the dancers gave up any semblance of a "normal" life. They didn't have hobbies or interests outside dance. They didn't have friendships outside dance. The rigors of the profession and its all-consuming, necessarily narcissistic bent appears to have meant that they gave up the hope of finding, building, and nurturing long-term, intimate relationships. The women, most of them, gave up (if they ever wanted it—and clearly, some did) motherhood. And the reading seems to point to something else, much bigger, that most of them sacrificed: happiness. None of these dancers seemed to be, in the simplest, most uncomplicated way, happy. Momentarily elated, yes. Occasionally (after a terrific performance) jubilant. But grounded in garden-variety happiness? I don't see much of it in the books, in their lives.

Even if Eglevsky had not booted me out of ballet, I wonder now, knowing what I know, whether I could have sacrificed what would have been necessary to become Laurissa Kesslova. Could I have sacrificed the future health of my joints, given up the years I ended up spending in grad school, which I loved, forsaken my enduring marriage, my occasionally seminormal eating habits? Coincidentally, I am writing this on the birthday of my oldest son. Life without him, life without his brother and sister, without the deep and enduring lessons I have learned from being a mother? I cannot and do not want to imagine that sacrifice.

9. Humility in the Face of Talent. What a Concept. With this recurring narrative of sacrifice and discipline and obsession, and the attendant rise to fame and celebrity, these dancers are, let's face it, not at all like you and me. But that doesn't mean that we don't know people (or sometimes *are* the people) who act a little like these dancers. That's right: prima donnas. Difficult, temperamental people who are convinced of their own importance. This makes me wonder, reading about the dancers' lives, whether it is possible to be a prima donna (in the best and literal sense of the word: a leading lady) without, you know, being a prima donna (in the worst, narcissistic, sense of the word). Is it possible to be talented and accomplished and celebrated and not be full of yourself? Does being an artist necessitate having "artistic temperament"—a euphemism for being arrogant, feeling entitled, and acting like a spoiled brat? I am wondering what we (I) can learn from the enormous ego of Nureyev ("Soon the whole word is going to know about me!" proclaimed a nineteen-year-old Rudi), the moodiness of Baryshnikov, Fonteyn's virtual oblivion to everything but the moment, Pavlova's choice to die rather than to stop dancing. How much do you have to suffer—or, more to the point, *be* insufferable, or make others suffer—for your art?

People react to ballet dancers (actors, rock stars, athletes) with fanatical adoration. How can you keep a head on your shoulders when everyone says you're great, and everyone says they love you? This is not really a problem most of us have ever encountered. But it does open the door to thinking about humility in the midst of achievement. Or humility in general. Being humble, I think, is one of the most underrated character traits around.

10. Take the Timely Exit. "Leave the stage before the stage leaves you," Tamara Karsavina, legendary star of the Mariinsky Ballet, famously said. This is such an elegant way of saying "Quit while you're ahead." It's understanding and coming to terms with one's own limits—*before* others see those limits. It's not defeat. Defeat would be staying too long. It is a triumph of self-examination, a successful struggle with the ego, a purposeful closing of one door while it is still wide open so that other doors may present themselves. What a truly excellent idea.

This is a ballet lesson immediately applicable to the nondancer. Don't wait until you are sick of the work you do, or you go stale, or you can no longer summon the effort. Move on before that happens. Move forward before you are pushed out. Move forward when moving forward is a creative, enriching choice, not the only option left to you, the sad consequence of staying too long.

11. Reinvention Keeps Us Young. Moving forward does not necessarily mean leaving the stage, however, as Dame Fonteyn's life illustrates so well. There is the "old dog new tricks" path she famously and successfully trod when, in her forties—retirement age for ballerinas, if they're lucky and their body holds out that long— she was rejuvenated, energized, and invigorated when she started dancing with Nureyev. She reinvented herself. She taught herself new tricks. She became a different ballerina with Rudi than she had been in her previous career. So the "Leave the stage before the stage leaves you" message needs to be tempered by the "It's not over till it's over" message.

The Nureyev-fueled, eighteen-year extension to Margot's acclaimed career also illustrates that it is possible to, essentially, turn back the hands of time. There is a phenomenon called "environmental aging." No, this does not refer to toxicity in the environment making you older and unhealthier (although, yes, it does). Instead, "environmental aging" is the documented *biological aging* of those who surround themselves with older people. That's right: You can accelerate the physical aging process by hanging around old people—that is, "old" people defined not by their birth dates but by their lack of vigor and vitality, their lack of excitement about the challenges of the future. It appears that the opposite could also be true, that hanging out (or dancing) with younger people might rejuvenate both attitude *and* body. How else to explain a hard-worked, sixty-year-old woman still dancing in top form? I do love this ballet-inspired lesson, which I am going to remember (for future reference) as the "Don't ever move to a gated retirement community" edict.

12. Love Is All You Need. Here's a final lesson from Suzanne Farrell's book, one that I am happy to be reminded of, one that I more than occasionally *need* to be reminded of: The love of the activity—in her case, obviously, the love of ballet—should trump everything. If you are truly passionate about and committed to what you do, you cannot care more about money, success, the opinions of others, or your own ego than you do about your art. When Balanchine ousted Farrell from his company, she had no place to go. The phone did not ring in her apartment. She got no offers to join another company. She could not find work. But she *had* to work. Her life was ballet. And so, a month after she was fired from NYCB, the country's prima ballerina danced on a small stage in front of an audience of children at a Long Island high school. For no money. Because she had to dance. Because dancing was what was important. Then she went to Europe and danced for a Belgian ballet company that created performances ballet historian Jennifer Homans describes as "sex, sweat and pretense masquerading as art." In other words, a far cry from her work with Balanchine on the New York stage. But she did it because it was an opportunity to dance, and dancing was what she did.

It was, and it remained, all about the work.

14

The Uncomfort Zone

THE WORK.

It continues.

The Ballet Book Club has been a place of ease where I get to stretch (and show off) the intellectual "muscle" I've spent much of my adult life building. And then there's class. My daily trek into the uncomfort zone, my morning reminder of what it means, what it *feels like*, to be a newbie in a room full of whiz kids . . . when you are old enough to be the whiz kids' mother.

SEPTEMBER 15. A week into the new schedule of company class every morning, and I am just remembering that, oh, yeah, I am not just your run-of-the-mill struggling midlife ballerina wannabe, I am an immersion reporter on assignment. Because the ballet itself, the positions, the steps, the postures, following along, is all so very challenging, I had almost forgotten my place here as Margaret Mead in tights and a leo, a student not just of dance but of the dancers themselves. Now, as I adjust, as I am ever-so-slightly less anxious in the studio—not more proficient, mind you, but less deer-in-the-headlights—I open myself to the energy and intensity in the room.

Suzi, standing in front of me at the barre, consistently performs every movement with such precision, grace, and artistic flair that watching her is a tutorial in dedication. Her body speaks this dedication more clearly, more forcefully, than any words I might extract from her in conversation. Meanwhile, just to my left, stationed at the long, portable barre the boys bring into the studio every morning to add necessary space for the company, Antonio has sweated through his t-shirt. As in soaked. This is noteworthy because at the barre we are not pirouetting or leaping. There are no big movements, no jumps, no lifts, nothing that would seem to start the heart racing and the perspiration flowing. The subtlety of Antonio's effort masks its intensity. And his body, like Suzi's, speaks.

This morning, in the five-minute break between barre and center work, I strike up a conversation with Danielle. Suzi told me last week to pay close attention to Danielle because she knows all the routines at the barre. Yes, she does. But then, so does Suzi. The fact that Suzi directed my attention to Danielle is interesting, I think. In the ballet books I've been reading, the dancers emerge as extraordinarily, almost blindingly, self-involved and very, very competitive. Suzi, by drawing my attention to another dancer and highlighting another's expertise, seems neither. Is it easier to be generous when the stakes are a little lower? EBC, after all, is not NYCB. Or are more openhearted dancers attracted to less pressure-cooker companies?

Danielle occupies a place at the barre set at a right angle to mine, so I can see her unobstructed. More than Suzi, who is henna-haired and compact, more than Tori, who is blond and maybe a touch too slender (if there is such a thing in ballet), Danielle is the ballerina poster girl: long-limbed, narrow-ribbed, Balanchineproportioned, with rich, dark hair, a composed oval face, and huge—I mean huge—dark, liquid eyes fringed by eyelashes that I swear must be false but aren't (yes, I ask). She's been dancing for almost a quarter of a century, which is pretty impressive given that she's twenty-seven years old. By the time she was six, she tells me, she was competing every weekend from January through April in tap, jazz, and lyric dance contests throughout the Northeast. She never won a title—her teacher blamed it on her bangs (which she no longer has)—but she did learn to love the stage. At eleven, perilously late, encouraged by another teacher who saw her potential, she started ballet. And it immediately consumed her.

After class, we continue our conversation at the espresso joint across the street. There I learn that in high school, Danielle—who, in case I wasn't clear about this, is drop-dead gorgeous—forsook a social life for a grueling schedule of dance classes and performances. She spent her summers away from her Connecticut home at ballet intensives. During her senior year, she went to scores of auditions—"cattle calls," she tells me. "I just didn't know any better"—until she reluctantly decided to go to college, where she majored in (of course) dance but also (for safety's sake) business management. She joined EBC after graduation as an apprentice— the oldest in her cohort. Three years later, she was hired into the corps. This is now her seventh season. I ask her if she is looking for another "promotion," a nice way of bringing up the sensitive subject of when, if ever, she might become a principal dancer with the company.

"Well," she says, her voice lowered to a whisper, "this isn't exactly public, but I'm dancing the Sugar Plum this season." The plum role. The role reserved for the principal female dancers. I offer congratulations.

"So this could be a big step," I say.

She smiles. "I really want to stay here." She tells me that Toni is not like any director she's ever worked with or heard about. "You can talk to her. You can offer ideas. She leads, but she doesn't intimidate. I don't want to leave." There is, however, another reason she might not want to leave: She and fellow dancer Mark are engaged. (Was Danielle's mother thrilled that she was planning to marry another struggling, half-year-employed dancer, I wonder? Probably no more than mine was when I announced that I was marrying a freelance writer.) They make a stunning couple, her dark to his light, both of them extraordinary physical specimens.

SEPTEMBER 18. After forty-five minutes to an hour of barre comes the floor work, which, as usual, I don't attempt. I marvel at the turns and leaps and long combinations of unfamiliar steps performed at great speed diagonally across the studio. The women are all on toe. Occasionally, I try a few of the combinations from my safe place in the hallway, where I dodge the benches and the clusters of gym bags and water bottles and spare ballet slippers on the floor. I stop the moment any dancer comes along. This morning, a young, sandy-haired guy with the short, compact, muscular build of a gymnast comes out of the studio, panting, and stands next to me. It's Cory. I recognize him from the online bios of the dancers, where I learned that he performed at Jacob's Pillow and danced last year with the Alaska Dance Theatre.

"The floor work is so far beyond me," I say, embarrassed because I think he may have seen me attempting a fouetté a moment before.

He laughs. "I feel that way too."

What a kind thing to say. What a sweetheart. I introduce myself. We haven't officially met—I haven't wanted to go around glad-handing all the dancers—but he knows who I am. Toni introduced me to the company at the first class.

"It's so nice having you here," he says. "It's nice having different energy in the room." Wow. The thought that I could be perceived as bringing energy to the room thrills me.

SEPTEMBER 23. Confession: I disappeared for almost a week to think and write and engage in possibly the single worst activity for my ballet muscles: I ran five miles every day. I couldn't help it. I was at the beach, and who can resist running on sand next to the mighty Pacific, breathing in the cleanest air on the continent? Now, as I stretch out on the floor before class, my winched-tight hamstrings are screaming at me. I confess this to Mark, and we joke about "hamstring augmentation surgery." Just a few inches, he says, that's all I need. As if.

After class I drive over to Barre3. Please remember that I am participating in only an hour at the barre in company class, not the additional hour of strenuous floor work, so it's not utterly ridiculous of me to follow up company class with more activity. Barre3, led this morning by the lovely, soft-voiced Evie Poole (just as tough as Summer but iron-fist-in-velvet-glove kind of tough), is surprisingly ballet-oriented, and I love it. We do pliés in fourth at the barre with a sort of tendu and a mini-arabesque. It's interesting. This morning Suzi said to me, "The first thing you learn is the plié, and it's the last thing you master." I am getting lots of practice today. In the locker room, a woman about my age comes up to me.

"Have you been doing this for very long?" she asks.

"A while," I say. She nods.

"You are just so strong," she says, not realizing that she has just made my day. Okay, my week.

SEPTEMBER 24. Fifteen minutes into the barre exercises, and Toni, who is the ballet mistress today, comes over to me to say hello. "Oh, I'm so sorry," she says. "I didn't even notice you before." She means it as an apology. I take it as an extraordinary compliment. She didn't notice me! I wasn't noticeable! I didn't stick out like that "Which one doesn't belong here?" item. It must be the cool new leotard I got from discountdance.com with the trendy low back. Either that or I'm not totally embarrassing myself with the fondus and dégagés. Nope. It's definitely the leo.

SEPTEMBER 25. At the barre this morning, I am struggling through a complicated (for me) routine led by Florabelle, the fast-talking former dancer who is our ballet mistress once a week. The routine involves half-turns so that the tendu, fondu, dégagé, chassé, pas de bourreé sequence can be seamlessly repeated on left and right. I can't figure out whether I'm supposed to turn into or away from the barre, what I'm supposed to do for ports de bras, how to move my head, where to look. In other words, I'm clueless, even for a half-turn. So I don't do it. After the sequence is over, and we're waiting for Florabelle to pick new music, Mark says, "You know, you really ought to do the turns." On the one hand, I'm not thrilled that he has noticed what I'm doing. Or not doing. I'm self-conscious enough. But on the other, I am delighted that he's taking an interest in me. So I ask him for help. Then I ask Suzi for a few pointers. I'm so lucky to be sandwiched between them.

Later, when barre is over and the rest of the corps is doing floor work, I stand in my usual position in the hallway. Florabelle puts on some lovely classical music, slow, and the dancers go through their paces. I move away from the window, close my eyes for a moment, and really hear the music. I move my arms—I don't know if it looks graceful, but it feels graceful. I try a few ronds de jambe en l'air. My leg is not high. It is, with effort, parallel to the floor. I try a few pirouettes. I used to be able to do this a billion years ago. But I still can't remember how to spot.

At 2:30 I return to the studio to check out the first afternoon of *Nutcracker* rehearsals. Thus far the afternoon rehearsals have focused on EBC's first show of the season, *Cinderella*. But today several of *The Nutcracker*'s Act II dances are being blocked, and I'm curious to see what a production looks like before it actually is a production. I left the studio five hours ago—wrote, ate lunch, ran errands—but these dancers have not left the building. They've been sealed in this bubble. They are sweaty and smelly and sprawled in the hallway massaging their legs with foam rollers, checking rehearsal schedules on their phones, eating meal replacement bars.

In one of the small studios, Jenn Martin is leading three dancers in the first rehearsal of the Russian dance, the hands-down favorite in Act II. In every production I watched all across the country, the Russians were the most beloved. There's a high viewing window into the small studio, and all of us in the hallway go over to watch them mark the dance. Toni, with Jenn's assistance, has choreographed something different this year, which includes Isaac, a new dancer, whipping around executing hugely impressive, seemingly endless (actually, there are twelve of them) turns à la seconde with little hops in the middle "to spice things up," Jenn tells me later. Isaac studied at the Academy of Russian Classical Ballet, so he's a natural for the centerpiece of this dance. And he apparently requested to do these turns that manage to look absolutely wild and completely controlled at the same time. Meanwhile, to his right and left, the two other dancers—Cory, the guy who looks like a gymnast, and Jesse, very young, very slender— are doing what are called "coffee grinders." It's a lightning-fast double-leg rotation performed while in a squat. Break dancing à la

Russe. Three other male dancers are standing next to me, watching. They are mightily impressed. They are also good-naturedly disgruntled.

"It doesn't matter what they do," says Reed, "they get all the applause anyway."

"Yeah," says Mark, "if I went out onstage and did a striptease after those Russians, no one would notice."

I beg to differ.

At 4:00 I head over to a Pilates class because I know I should. It's a dancer thing. But it's just such a weird discipline for me, so controlled, so small, with moves that look like moves I know from yoga but aren't. It's confusing. And you don't get the endorphin rush. Today Marilyn is teaching, and although I don't much like the class, I like her and her expert cuing. It forces me to focus on individual muscles in the core. How could such tiny movements be so exhausting? I soldier through the ninety minutes—although I am not sure soldiers could actually make it through this ninety-minute Pilates class—because I want to be around for the class that follows this one, Ashtanga yoga, taught by Gyro Jean. It's the class Danielle has raved about to me. "It's improved my dancing so much," she told me this morning.

And here she is, looking like a gazelle in spandex, her eye makeup as perfect as it was at 7:30 this morning. Those enormous eyes. It's hard not to get lost in those eyes. Yeah, I know this sounds like a girl crush. In class, Jean takes us through increasingly challenging asanas. Danielle executes each pose as if she were dancing, which is to say with strength and grace and seeming lack of effort. She lifts her leg higher than her chin. She "binds"—that curious, almost off-putting pretzely thing that yoginis do—as if her hinge joints were socket joints, as if her tendons were twice as long as everyone else's. They probably are. I last for fifty minutes. (It's an hour-and-a-half class.) Even the *modifications* of the modifications are too much for me.

SEPTEMBER 26. Uh-oh. I just found out that there is a particular way to construct a ballet bun that Toni insists on and that I know nothing about. As I know virtually nothing about how to do anything with my voluminous hair, the ignorance itself is not surprising. Apparently, I need to go to the Dancers' Closet and purchase Bunhead-brand pins. And a net. Hairspray is also a thing.

Much more terrifying is the makeup. I also discovered that all the dancers do all their own makeup, and it's stage makeup, and everyone, I mean everyone including the lowliest seventeen-year-old aspirant, knows how to do this. I quiz Suzi about cosmetics as we stretch out on the floor. She reels off a litany of products, none of which I've ever used, and starts naming brands, none of which I've ever heard of. I hadn't bargained for *this* learning curve.

On the positive side, at the *other* barre, Barre3, this morning, Evie, whom I am beginning to love as much as Summer, says, "True strength is finding the connection between mind and body and working the edge." *Thank you.*

SEPTEMBER 27. I went into the studio today, Saturday, to watch the children's auditions for *The Nutcracker*. Toni and Jenn will choose first and second casts for the Party Scene and Bon Bons. They select two complete casts for the kids in order to give as many talented youngsters as possible a chance to dance. And there are two casts for the company itself, Toni tells me. EBC puts on so many *Nutcracker* shows that it would be impossible—not to mention dangerous, injurious—for only one dancer to dance Sugar Plum or Cavalier or some of the other superdemanding parts every night.

Thirty girls from the Eugene Ballet Academy, ranging in age from seven to fifteen, ranging in size from hipless sixty-pounds-when-soaking-wet prepubescents to sturdily built, borderline womanly high schoolers, go through the paces while Toni and Jenn sit at the front of the room, watching, taking notes, and occasionally conferring. They are all bunned up, all pink-tightsed and pink-slippered. The youngest girls wear rose-colored leos. The middle schoolers are in sky blue. The older girls wear black. It's the ballet school uniform. Before they entered the studio, the little ones were loud and giggly, doing little tricks, hugging each other. Now they are all focused and intent, facing forward in four long lines. You can tell, even at this dance school level, even at single-digit age, who is meant for ballet and who is not, to whom dance is already a known language and to whom ballet will always be a struggle. It's not just about shape and size, but it's a lot about size and shape. Gravity just does not tug at the slim-as-a-willow girls the way it does at the rest of us, the way it does at the girls who have already become women with breasts and hips, with thighs. This is how Eglevsky must have seen me. It was not, however, in my borderline-pubescent innocence, how I saw myself. I was gloriously oblivious. Until the moment I was not.

After the auditions I stop by the Dancers' Closet, where Tori is working this afternoon. She steers me to a display of supersturdy Bunhead-brand hairpins that everyone uses to keep buns in place. I also buy a new leo. Not that I need one. Oh, and a flirty, sheer, very short black wraparound skirt. Which I truly don't need. But it's sort of amazing how much better I look when you can't see the tops of my thighs.

SEPTEMBER 28. "I am going shopping for makeup at the mall" is a sentence I have never, until today, uttered. Or, really, imagined myself uttering. But here I am, at 5:30 p.m. on a sunny autumn Sunday, scanning the aisles at Sephora for Tori, who has generously agreed to meet me—after a full day of classes and *Cinderella* rehearsals—to assist in the purchase of stage makeup. I sent an e-mail to Tori and Suzi yesterday with the subject line "Make-up freak-out." They both responded, in excruciating detail. Here's what Suzi recommended for me:

SEPHORA

- Color FX Total Cover Cream Foundation (ask them to match your skin color there)
- Color FX pressed powder that matches the foundation color
- Foundation brush
- Kabuki brush (for the powder)

RITE AID/TARGET/ETC.

(I also use ULTA.com for some cheaper makeup.)

- Powder blush in a fairly obnoxious pink color
- Bronzer powder (usually sold near the blush) to contour the cheeks and neck
- Blush brush, angled blush brush, foam eye-shadow brush, angled eye-shadow brush if they don't come in the package with the products (Sonia Kashuk brand at Target has pretty good brushes)
- Bright pearly white eye shadow (I got some at Dancers' Closet, Ben Nye brand . . . very good for stage)
- Brown eye shadow (at least one very dark brown—or a palette that has several brown options)
- Mascara (black)
- Liquid eyeliner (I use Maybelline's waterproof liquid liner—then it doesn't sweat off)

- Lipstick—a red that's a little darker than fire engine colored
- Makeup remover wipes
- Dark brown eyebrow pencil (or you can just use the brown eye shadow)

SALLY BEAUTY SUPPLY
- Tube of eyelash glue (make sure you get clear colored— and not the "individual lash glue")
- Eyelashes (I like #118 the best—but any style that is black, long, and not so dense that it looks like a plate over your eye)

Tori's list was similarly heart-stopping.

There must be other women like me, right? Women who never cared about, were curious about, or experimented with cosmetics? In eighth grade, while other girls were pleading with their mothers to allow them to wear eyeliner to school, I was running away from my lipstick-wielding mother, who used to chase me around the house brandishing a tube of Revlon and yelling, "Color! You need color!" So, of course, I never wore lipstick. Or powder, blush, eyeliner, eye shadow, etc. Those days are about to end.

I spot Tori scanning the shelves of one of the more-than-dozen aisles that crowd this small store. Her blond hair is scraped back in a not-overly-neat ponytail, and she is wearing well-worn jeans and a Nebraska Cornhuskers T-shirt. And she looks elegant. That's what great posture, a long neck, and two decades of ballet will do for you. We spend the next hour and a half—yes, I said *hour and a half*—looking at a dizzying array of products in a dizzying array of brands while several heavily made-up saleswomen take turns dabbing and sponging and brushing me with products and suggesting even more products than are already on our extensive list. One salesperson who has done herself up like Catwoman (although, I fear, not on purpose) sponges three different cream foundations on my jaw. They look like varying shades of calamine lotion to me. Catwoman and Tori lift my chin this way and that, squint, confer with each other, and come to a consensus. The $29 little compact goes in the handy shopping tote provided by the ever-attentive Catwoman.

Now it's on to powder to cover the foundation. "Translucent, of course," Tori says. Of course. Catwoman leads us to something called HD powder, which is specially formulated, she says, to look good under lights or if one is being photographed. And I need blush. As we stroll over to examine various shades of blush—from "blushing bride" to "orgasm"—Tori educates me about contouring. Apparently, with the blush (my shade is "seduction") I will need a brownish powder to apply under the cheekbone, which I will then blend with the blush to accentuate, for the faraway audience, my bone structure. Tori tells me I will have to do this along my jawline as well. "Up close it kinda looks like you have a beard," she says. Which is a cruel thing to say to a woman old enough to be tweezing chin hairs.

We go hunting for eye shadow. I may need three or four different colors. There's white on the lid, brown in the crease, a lighter brown or copper above that, and then white again in the space under the brow. The brow, of course, has been emboldened and darkened with its own special powder applied with its own special little brush. That makes four brushes I need to buy, really five if I want to do it up right. Six counting eyeliner (our next stop). Seven if I want one for lipstick, our final purchase. Or I think it is our final purchase. We hear the "closing in ten minutes" announcement on the P.A. system just as Tori selects the "raspberry" shade for me. We are now being assisted by another young woman. I like her a lot better because her face doesn't look like a Halloween mask.

"Wait," she says as Tori and I head over to the checkout counter. "You'll want primer, won't you?" *Primer? Like what you put on a wall before you paint it?* I don't realize I say this out loud until I hear our new saleswoman laugh. "Yeah, kinda," she says, handing me a small pump bottle. Then she explains that you put a thin layer of the stuff on your face before foundation. It creates a slick surface, lays down a thin barrier that protects your pores, and makes the foundation just glide on. Tori nods enthusiastically. Four minutes and $216 later, we're done. All that remains—ha!— is for me to learn how to use the bagful of products I'm taking home with me.

15

Going Native

THIS MORNING, A Barre3 epiphany: I am—I have become—one of "them." Months ago, I started out here as the chunky-muscled aging tomboy who was used to hanging out with other aging tomboys as we grunted and hefted weights in gyms that smelled like iron and sweat. In Barre3 I was surrounded by these strange creatures, both fit and fashionable. They didn't grunt. They wore makeup. They were mani-ed and pedi-ed. They wore really cute workout clothes. They wore bangle bracelets and toe rings. And . . . they got the job done. They held the two-minute planks. They balanced on little squishy balls and did killer crunches. I had to give them their due.

I worked hard in class. (Still do.) I gave it everything. (Still do.) But part of me was outside the experience, an observer—not always a kind one—to this girly fitness subculture. But it now appears that I have "adopted the lifestyle or outlook of local inhabitants," as they say in cultural anthropology circles. I have gone native. It comes to me as a revelation in this morning's class that I . . . *fit in*. I'm not just talking about the *important* ways I fit in, that my body is lengthening and loosening, that my spine is straighter, my shoulders less hunched, my core stronger, that I know how to activate my hamstrings so my quads don't always take over. I'm talking about the embarrassingly superficial way I now fit in. I understand, thanks to ballet, the whole looking-good-while-you-do-it thing. I mean, I have four leos and a little skirt. I wear a cute cropped shirt for the first few minutes of barre warm-ups. I get it. This morning, readying myself for my usual 6:15 Barre3 class, I take a minute to apply mascara. Yep. Predawn cosmetic enhancement. On the way out, I grab a rose-and-gold-colored infinity scarf and wrap it around my neck. Not because it is cold outside. But because it looks good. I am making a fashion statement. I am making a fashion statement on my way to a tough workout.

And I am especially glad this morning when I arrive at the EBC studios after Barre3 that I'm sporting (reapplied) mascara and wearing the infinity scarf (not to mention the periwinkle leo and flirty little black skirt). I am Dressed for Success. And success is what awaits me. Toni has posted the cast lists for *The Nutcracker* on the bulletin board, and there it is:

Clara's Maiden Aunt Rose . . . Lauren Kessler

I get a named part! I'm not just one of the guests at the party, which was what I expected Toni would assign me. I don't know what it will mean, onstage, to *be* Aunt Rose, to dance Aunt Rose. But I won't think about that today. I'll think about that tomorrow.

Meanwhile: I'm Clara's aunt! I remember that Misty Cope-land mentions in her memoir that Debbie Allen played Clara's aunt in a production of *The Chocolate Nutcracker*. Debbie Allen! The two-time Tony Award winner! The star of *Fame*! I am playing a part Debbie Allen once played! (Okay, no more exclamation points.) I note that Mark is playing Clara's father, which means

I'm his sister—or sister-in-law. But it's more amusing to think I am his sister. I go into the big studio to warm up and to tell Mark the news. It takes him a moment, but he gets the joke. Then, as we stretch (and he goads me into attempting a full split), we discuss how we might be siblings. He is fair-skinned and golden-haired, tall, broad-shouldered, and, um, twenty-six years old.

"Let's see, how *can* this work?" I ask, folding myself over into pigeon position after futile attempts at a full split. We've already rejected the obvious: adoption, different mothers, blended families.

"I know," says Mark, "our mother got pregnant with you when she was fifteen."

"Yeah," I say, warming to the idea. "She had to drop out of school, but," I quickly add, "she was a great reader, and she educated herself."

"So, she married our father . . . " Mark says, moving the story forward.

"And they had, like, four or five daughters," I say. He looks skeptical. "But then, in her forties, she really, really wanted a son." He nods, encouraging the thought. "So they did in vitro fertilization . . . and you were born. Voilà! My blood brother!"

To celebrate my ascendance to Named Character, I wear another of my new leos to class the next day.

On the subject of tights and leos, I'd like to mention the delicate but all-important issue of going to the bathroom. Please feel free to skip this section. So, there you are—*here I am*—with a little warm-up shirt over my pretty leo which is pulled over my tights. And I have to pee. One could remove the shirt, shimmy out of the sweaty, clinging-to-the-body leo, squirm out of the skin-tight tights, and proceed. Or one could be in a hurry, having left the studio midbarre and not wanting to miss the progression of routines. In the latter case, it is possible (but not easy) to reach up under the leo leg opening, inch the hand up to the waist, grab the waistband of the tights, gently pull one side down under the leo, and carefully position the fabric about three inches down the thigh. The trick is to do this while not poking a fingernail through the tights and starting a run. While holding the tights in place, one then grabs the crotch of the leo and pulls it over to the opposite side. Yes! The only task that remains is to not pee on any piece of clothing. As I do this—with great success, I might add—I have but one thought: *I bet Dame Margot Fonteyn did this too.*

A few days later, I broach the bathroom subject with Suzi while we wait for Florabelle to find the right music for the next barre routine. Suzi nods knowingly, laughs, and then tells me this story: Several seasons ago, she was dancing in *Cinderella*, sharing a fairy part—and a costume—with another girl. The costume was a complicated affair with a swirly, diaphanous, knee-length skirt constructed from layers of tulle and dotted with flowers and assorted doodads. When the matinee was over, the other dancer handed over the costume with hesitation. "I'm really, really sorry," she told Suzi. And Suzi knew what was coming. Happily, the bottom of the skirt had fallen into a *clean* toilet. Or so the other dancer told her.

ON BREAK BETWEEN barre and center, I am standing in the hallway watching as Reed, a fourth-season company dancer, puts on a brand new pair of bright red ballet slippers. I don't know him very well, but he always smiles, and we often exchange minor pleasantries. He's a friendly kid, actually a local boy from a small town forty miles north of here who studied at the Jacqueline Kennedy Onassis School of the American Ballet Theatre. That's a mouthful. And major cred.

"Nice shoes," I say, smiling. He tells me that they are for his part in *Cinderella*. "Be careful," I say, "once you put them on, you won't be able to take them off, and you won't be able to stop dancing." He thinks that's funny. Really funny. And I think, *How many other twenty-something guys from an Oregon cow town would get a* Red Shoes *reference?* I could get used to hanging out with these guys.

———◯———

FALL DEEPENS. THE rains come. Sunrise is at 7:45 this morning. At least I think the sun rose. Mostly the thick, charcoal-gray, flannelly blanket of sky lightened ever so slightly to ash as I made my way from Barre3 to company class. In Oregon you get to know fifty shades of gray, and you either embrace the palette or move to California. I'm still here. The company has been away off and on for a few weeks, performing a dozen *Cinderella* shows on the road. This past weekend, while I was engaged in the kind of public performance well within my comfort zone (I was reading onstage at a book festival in California), EBC performed its only in-town *Cinderella* shows.

Meanwhile, in between EBC's travels and my own, I manage to wedge in another private session with Tori. I am (again) floored by her patience. I marvel at the lack of judgment in her tone when she tells me, for the umpteenth time, to unclench my fingers and unhunch my shoulders and lift my chin—all those pesky "details" that get lost as I focus on pliés and tendus. I have asked her to teach me some of the simpler sequences Toni and Florabelle and Jenn call out during company class. And, as she guides me through them, slowly, repeatedly, and with explanation, I begin to actually understand what we do at the barre. These are well-thought-out sequences meant to progressively warm muscles and stretch tendons and get the blood flowing. I know that sounds obvious—and, in retrospect, *is* obvious—but it was lost on me. I was so intent on following each individual step that I didn't see how they made sense, orchestrated sense, together. I am not sure, after our session, that I have made any improvements in technique, but I do feel a little less lost about the whole barre experience.

Now it is back to company class. Yesterday was a rare day off, so this morning spirits are high. Often, during the first few minutes in the studio, with everyone sleepy-eyed and going through their stretches, the atmosphere is subdued. Not today. People are downright chatty. I ask Mark what he did on his day off.

"It was awesome," he tells me. "I rolled out twice!" He is referring to massaging his muscles by moving back and forth over a foam roller. Not the height of awesomeness as far as I'm concerned, but such is the life of the dancer. "Then I read *Harry Potter* out loud to Danielle. . . . " He pauses and looks over at his fiancée. She is standing at the barre, holding her foot in her hand. Her foot is maybe two inches from her ear. Basically, she is standing up doing a split. "So I read out loud to Danielle," he says, nodding to her, "*while she cleaned the kitchen.*" Danielle laughs. (Without releasing her foot.) It's hard to imagine these gorgeous young dancers, these rare, exotic birds, Formula 409ing countertops or degreasing ovens. But apparently, their kitchens get dirty too.

JENN IS LEADING class today. She is, as I've noticed before, the most relaxed and casual of the morning instructors, probably because it has been only a few years since she too stood at the barre taking class. She may be the ballet mistress now, but in her heart, she is still a dancer. This morning she is sitting on the floor at the front of the room swiping her thumb across her phone screen as she chuckles. "Okay, guys," she says. "I'm going to have to read this out loud. It's just hysterical." Most everyone—I am the exception here—is already in on the joke. It has to do with "dance belts," the main topic of unusually lively conversation this morning. I don't know what a dance belt is, but I am about to find out.

Jenn starts to read: "The male genitals must be kept out of harm's way. Fifth position, beats, and sautés changement can crush an errant testicle left hanging below the crotch line." She pauses for effect. "The penis must be tightly controlled." Laughter fills the studio, but it's not titillated laughter or embarrassed laughter. It's good-natured, let's-laugh-at-the-odd-particulars-of-our-rarefied-world laughter. They are enjoying a shared intimacy, a G-rated in-joke masked in language that might make others blush. Bodies mean something so different to dancers than to the rest of us. It's not just—although this is hardly a *just*—that their bodies are their instruments. It's not *just* the extraordinary attention they must pay to their bodies to keep them strong and healthy and able to withstand the punishment of their art, to keep them perfect and beautiful. It's that they see their bodies as working machines with definable parts that need scrupulous attention. And not only their personal selves but also the bodies of their fellow dancers. As Meredith Daneman writes with such sharp-edged elegance in her biography of Fonteyn, "Dancers must breathe hard into each other's faces, bathe and slither in each other's sweat; she must split her legs for him without propriety, and his hand must go wherever it will to gain the grip he needs." The mentioning of an errant testicle or two is hardly a blip on the radar.

But I confess: I have long wondered about what Dr. Dance Belt (the author of the passage Jenn is quoting from) calls "the idealized male bulge." While the female dancers seem to want to be as flat in the front body as possible, the men present, shall we say, more boldly. It turns out they're not showing off (well, maybe a *little*?); they are protecting their delicate parts from work-related injuries. And it's the dance belt—a specialized, supersupportive, butt-flossing uberjockstrap—that does it. A secondary benefit, Dr. D. explains, deadpan (at least it reads deadpan on his website), is the contraption's "ability to hide any visible evidence of a spontaneous erection."

Jenn is reading aloud again: "Your penis is supposed to end up facing upwards towards your belly button. Next comes the process dancers call the 'swoop and scoop.'"

"What was that?" someone yells from the back of the room.

"'Swoop and scoop,'" Jenn calls out.

"Oh, like *one* guy in the world calls it 'scoop and swoop,'" Mark says, scoffing.

"I'm sorry," Jenn says, laughing. "I just can't read this next part out loud." But that's not going to stop *me* from quoting it from Dr. D.'s website because there are just some things one ought to know, and I believe "swoop and scoop" is one of them. Or two.

"Reach inside the dance belt and pull your scrotum up inside the pouch. Your testicles need to be up and front, above the crotch line and well clear of their usual dangling position. Adjust your penis position to face straight up ('North')." More directions follow, including some painful instructions related to giving oneself a monumental wedgie.

Wow. This really puts into perspective my ongoing attempts to pee while not removing my dance togs.

16

Humble Pie

I ARRIVE AT the EBC studios this morning warm and limber from an hour of Barre3, high (or as high as one can be in the rain-soaked predawn) from the boost I get knowing that I am beginning to master the routines. Well, "master" is an overstatement. But I see improvement, a transition from what has been a plodding *do this, now attend to this, now move this way* linear focus to the beginning of a flow. It's what happens when the details no longer overwhelm you, when you can begin to see and feel and give yourself over to the whole. It's that moment when you realize the mind and the body have actually connected and are talking to each other on some level you no longer have to consciously attend to, that particularly tantalizing moment on the learning curve when what had been a hard, sweaty, sometimes dispiriting slog begins to feel like it *could* become instinct and intuition. It has been a long time since I've placed myself at the beginning of a learning curve like this, which makes this Barre3 moment especially lovely.

And so I arrive at EBC this morning feeling particularly empowered, a feeling intensified by discovering that the outside door is locked, and I must enter the six-digit code to get in. Why is this empowering? Because I *know* the six-digit code, the code given only to the dancers and company employees. My elation lasts through warm-up and barre work. I am no longer completely and utterly clueless about the intricate barre routines (thanks to that half-hour tutorial with Tori last week). It's not so much that my technique has improved, but I now better understand the progression of barre exercises and can discern the repeating patterns. My ballet vocabulary has broadened a bit too. Company class doesn't terrify me quite as much as it used to.

But terror is about to return. Terror is clearly marked on today's rehearsal sheet posted in the little hallway leading to the dancers' "lounge," and by lounge I mean long, narrow, airless, odoriferous room stuffed with costumes and old toe shoes. This is what terror looks like:

10:15–11: Kessler, Haag, Tucker, studio B

Haag is Suzi. Tucker is Mark. Toni has assigned them to teach me one of the dances Aunt Rose will be performing in the Party Scene. This is my first clue about what I will be doing onstage. It's called the Grandfather Dance—although, as I discover, no grandfather is involved. I don't care what the dance is called. I care only about not making a fool of myself in front of these two lovely, graceful people I have come to know. I care about not clopping about like a Clydesdale. I care about not creating wind currents with the flapping bat wings under my arms. I care about my ability to perform, and remember, a complicated series of steps. "Complicated" is relative. Apparently, the company dancers hardly even need to practice these Party Scene dances. The steps are rudimentary compared to the choreographic and physiological complexities of Snow or Flowers, Spanish or Arabian. But to me, there is nothing rudimentary about this.

I am—having yet to expend any effort, merely standing as I watch Suzi and Mark perform the dance for me—sweating profusely. I am not exaggerating for dramatic tension or comic relief. I am sweating. A lot. But my hands are ice. I ask them to repeat the dance. And again. And a fourth time. Each time I watch, it seems the steps get more complicated. Each time I watch, my confidence—that Barre3-bolstered self-assurance I arrived with—shrinks a little more. I'd better make an attempt before I am completely frozen in place. Suzi smiles and nods encouragingly. I take a deep breath and offer one icy hand to Mark as he calls to me with a theatrical flourish that begins the dance. I take way too many steps to reach him and swing out far too wide to circle around him. This is not even a ballet move. It is just gracefully covering some ground to position myself to *begin* the actual dance. Minus the gracefully. Mark, my "brother," will actually be my partner in the Grandfather Dance. He is kind and patient, as is Suzi. We do the call-to-dance move several times until I stop feeling like a complete klutz.

Next are a series of ports de bras that I manage to overdo, depriving them of both charm and grace. I then execute a little turn, which, miraculously, my body seems to know how to accomplish. This is followed by a step-up-step-back-fondu routine that I again overdo, dipping too deeply, which has the effect of bringing unnecessary attention to my hindquarters. We take it from the top. But now I extend the wrong icy hand to Mark. So we do it again. And now, following the extension of the correct icy hand, I fail to present from the heart with a controlled sweep of the arm. So we do it again. Again. And again.

After the call-to-dance and the presenting and the little turn that I can do and the front-back routine comes a much harder two-times-around twirl of a turn that ends in an open-to-the-audience, arabesquelike posture, only without the raised leg. Then it's chassé, chassé, tombé, pas de bourrée left (I mess up on the feet); chassé, chassé, tombé, pas de bourrée right to set up a two-and-a-half-times-around turn (I am dizzy. I need to start spotting), which leads to a sort of do-si-do with some elegant ports de bras (well, elegant when Suzi demos them). Then there's another turn. By the time we go through the whole thing, I have forgotten what I learned ten minutes before. I present the wrong hand. I end on the wrong leg. I take an extra step that positions me incorrectly and gets us off beat.

Mark and Suzi are so kind—"Good job," "You've got this"—that I am beginning to be suspicious. Their cheery encouragement in the face of my dismal performance reminds me of that first KidSports baseball game my son played when he was in second grade. His team lost 28–0, while all us parents were making ourselves hoarse yelling "Good job," "Great effort," "Way to go." Am I really making progress here? Am I beginning to get this at all? I can't tell. I ask Mark to be blunt. He tells me I'm doing fine, but I should "go with the music and the movement" and stop thinking so much about the individual steps.

I absolutely get what he means. I get it *intellectually* because thinking is what I'm good at. But getting it *intellectually* is actually the problem. I know that he wants me to be at the magic moment in the learning curve that I experienced a mere three hours ago, back when I arrived at EBC suffused with Barre3 bravado. But I am not there. I am at the very bottom of this Grandfather Dance learning curve, where obsessive overthinking leads to stiffness and self-consciousness. I am at the point where the internal monologue (*Move right foot—no, right foot, you dummy—brush the floor, point the toe, watch that arm, unclaw the fingers*) drowns out the quieter conversation that needs to happen between mind and body. I try to explain this to Mark. He wants to understand. But he is most fluent in, most attuned to, the language of dance, and I am speaking some other language, some cerebral, analytical, my-body-is-just-functioning-to-cart-my-brain-around language.

Part of me wants to stay in this very uncomfortable space, to carefully ponder and puzzle through and learn from this humbling experience. I get that there are important life lessons here. I know this is about facing fear and taming the ego. I know this is good for me. But it feels like shit. And I want it to be over. I want to learn this dance right now and be good at it. I hand Suzi my phone and ask her to video Mark and me doing one last run-through. That way I can study it at home.

That afternoon, at home, I watch the video.

And wish I hadn't.

I look at my one-inch self decked out in my best leo and the sheer little confidence-boosting, upper-thigh-obscuring wrap skirt, and I see that I am trying *so* hard. I am exaggerating all the steps—and not in a cool, theatrical-flourish kind of way. More in a clodhopping, uncomfortable-in-my-skin kind of way. I am painfully, painfully far from any reasonable person's definition of graceful. I call Kim and attempt not to wail. She tells me to give myself a break. She says all kinds of encouraging things that I don't hear. Then I do myself a favor: I delete the video from my phone.

I'm in my writing room, alone, trying hard not to berate myself. I have to get out of my head. As in right now. I move away from my desk and stand quiet and still. I unhunch my shoulders. I try to feel the gentle, upward pull of the imaginary string at the top of my head. Then I close my eyes, hum the Grandfather Dance tune, and visualize the steps. I see myself dancing, really dancing, with fluid arms and lilting steps, with tight, swift turns, with a smile. I open my eyes, imagine Mark beckoning to me. "Sister!" he calls out. And I hesitate just a second. I am, after all, the maiden aunt. I am a little bashful. I run on demi-pointe across my writing room floor, circling the imaginary Mark. I try to work through the next series of moves, but I'm concerned that I have not remembered everything I need to remember, and I don't want to imprint the wrong footwork. I need more practice.

Dear Toni: Could you please please please see if you can schedule another rehearsal for me with Mark? Also, can you tell me (1) in addition to the Grandfather's Dance, what other dances will Aunt Rose be performing? (2) any hint about dates for costume decision/fitting? Avec reverence, Lauren

Hi Lauren: I started working on a schedule and will try to get further ahead with that tomorrow and will look for a possible rehearsal with Mark. Aunt Rose will also be dancing in the gallop, which is the dance before Herr Drosselmeyer's entrance in the party scene. We will be starting to pull costumes the week after next at which point we may be able to do a costume fitting for you.

Hi Toni. Hope the tour this week goes well. I didn't see any rehearsal time for me and Mark for the following week. —Lauren

Hi Lauren: Hmmm . . . has Aunt Rose been at the gin again. . . . I think she is confused. Don't panic you have time.

Toni: Aunt Rose is partial to a brandy cup now and again. I'll try to keep her in check.—Lauren

Lauren: Can you rehearse next week Tuesday & Wednesday 10:15–11:00 a.m.? TP

Toni: Yesyes! Aunt Rose sends her sincere thanks and promises not to be a pain in the neck.

Lauren: Pain in the derrière perhaps . . . but never a pain in the neck. :)

Whew. More rehearsal time. But meanwhile, this week, no rehearsals and, even worse, no company classes, as the troupe is traveling with *Cinderella.* I am on my own, and I'm feeling a bit like an alcoholic whose regular AA meeting has been canceled. *I need to find a meeting!* I mean a class. Online I find Eugene Ballet Academy's "Adv Adult" class taught by Florabelle on Wednesday night. I attempt, unsuccessfully—despite my finely honed guilt-tripping techniques—to strong-arm Kim into coming with me. She has, she insists, a "prior commitment," something having to do with her husband's work. Really? She is choosing her husband over me? I'm miffed. I have to go it alone.

In the studio I find mostly older high school–aged girls and twenty-somethings with perhaps two women in their thirties. The class is also full, with almost every place taken at the barre that runs along three sides of the big studio. The good news is that I am already slightly familiar with Florabelle's routines. The good news is that she talks slower and spends just a little more time demonstrating the routines in this class than she does in company class. The good news is that, unlike in company class, which is designed to help professional dancers limber up before a full day of rehearsal, this is an actual class with instruction and correction. The good news—yes, I tell myself, this is good news—is that most of these "adv adult" dancers don't need that much instruction and correction, so Florabelle is free to focus on me. And boy, does she ever. It's one thing to have a sense in your body that you are not executing a move with anything close to perfection. It's another to have someone on your ass (literally) correcting derrière position, hip placement, knee rotation, turnout, spine alignment, elbow lift, arm curvature, chin tilt. It's amazing how long an hour can be.

She is right about everything, of course. And I am grateful for the corrections, really I am. But the whole beginning-of-the-learning-curve thing is getting a little old. When I call Kim the next day to tell her about the class, she says the fact that Florabelle paid attention to me means I am worth paying attention to. (You see why she is my wingwoman.) Other friends bolster me with comments about how brave I am to court this uncomfortable place. But secretly (well, not so secretly anymore), I am more fretful than fearless, more apprehensive than adventurous. To tell the truth, I am kind of a sniveling whiner. *In my head*, that is. To the outside world I am amusingly self-deprecating.

WHILE AWAITING THE company's return, I repeatedly watch the very bad, murky video recording of last year's *Nutcracker* that Toni made available for me. The camera is static, the footage looks as if it were shot underwater, and the audio . . . well, poor Tchaikovsky. But watch it I do. Three or four times a night for the remainder of the five days the company is away. I watch the entire show three or four times a night, but I watch "my" dances—the Grandfather Dance I am trying to learn and the Gallop, which I have yet to attempt—close to a dozen times. *A night.* This gives new meaning to "binge-watching." Or obsessive-compulsive behavior. In between viewings of the Grandfather Dance (my twenty-four seconds of glory . . . or infamy) I practice the steps in my office, offering my hand to and circling around Invisible Mark. If I can just get the steps down so I can start actually hearing the music, start feeling the dance itself, start imagining myself as a Victorian lady on Christmas Eve at the Stahlbaums' party, start inhabiting my little part. I don't think this is too much to ask. I am not aspiring to be Pavlova here. This, by the way, is Agnes de Mille's description of Pavlova's technique: "All her gestures were liquid and possessed of an inner rhythm that flowed to inevitable completion with the finality of architecture." Gee, and all I want to do is not look like a jerk.

Sunday night the company returns from yet another road trip. Just a few more shows before everyone can truly focus on *The Nutcracker.* I, of course, am already focused. As in obsessed. Today, Tuesday, the dancers' first day back in the studio in more than a week, I make it to my usual predawn Barre3 class to warm my body, set my intentions, and sop up some self-esteem. ("Lovely, Lauren," Summer says as she walks by my open-hip side plank.) In company class, led this morning by Toni, who looks more overworked than usual, I kind of keep up. But I don't even attempt the pirouette. Mark notices and gives me a hard time. "I turned," I tell him. "I just turned so fast you didn't see it."

After the barre routine, I leave the dancers to the far more complicated floor work while I walk across the street to self-caffeinate, text Kim with my latest insecurities, and contemplate the Barre3 mantras I am trying to embed in my brain: *Find the ease in the effort. Find the calm within the chaos.*

THERE'S SOMETHING TO this. There *really is* something to this. When I walk back over to the studio to begin my forty-five minutes of rehearsal with Mark and Danielle (Suzi is scheduled to rehearse Arabian, so Danielle is substituting), I am just a little calmer and looser than I was at the first rehearsal. Of course I've been practicing all week with ghost Mark in my writing room, and that helps a lot, but it's more about my attitude. We gather around Danielle's iPad to study a video clip of the dance, playing it again and again as Danielle comments on arm positions, head tilts, the way the big ballroom costumes change how you have to move. I point at the dress I am hoping Toni will assign to me, the burgundy one I've had my eye on for a while. "That's my favorite too," says Danielle. We watch the dance again.

"You know, sister," Mark says to me, with a gentle bump into my shoulder, "everyone will be taking their cues from us."

"Huh?"

"We're downstage center," he says. "As close to the audience as it gets. Look." He reruns the dance and points at the screen. It's true. Because Mark is Clara's father, and he is the host of this Christmas party, he and his partner—meaning me—lead the dance. I am, surprisingly, only mildly freaked about this news. I really trust Mark. And I have to trust that the costume will transform me, that the stage makeup will mask me, that the music will transport me. At least this is how, this morning, this calm-within-the-chaos morning, I am choosing to look at this.

"Shall we take it from the top? Do the whole thing?" Mark asks. I nod and take my place. Danielle restarts the clip so we have music. Mark calls to me. I mime surprise—you want to dance with *me*, your spinster sister?—and we begin. I make it through the first two turns and the first chassé to the left, miraculously putting the correct foot forward. Then I miss the beat. "There's a tombé there," Danielle says helpfully. "And *then* the pas de bourrée." I walk through the steps and see how that little tombé I was forgetting makes all the difference. We start from the top. I get through the left and right chassés–tombé–pas de bourrée this time but take too long with the next series. Danielle demonstrates. We start from the top again. This time we get through it all, but I end the curtsy on the wrong foot. Still, I am very, very pleased with myself.

"I can tell you've been practicing," Mark says. What a sweetheart. He suggests that I sing while we dance. "That way you're engaging more of your brain." We try it with me alternately humming and then singing the steps as I dance. When it comes to the most challenging part toward the end, the two-and-a-half turns that I have trouble with because (1) I am not (yet) light enough on my feet, and (2) I haven't worked enough on my spotting, and thus (3) the turns make me dizzy, I stop singing. I don't notice this, but Mark does. "Sing through it," he says. "You'll see." So we take it from the top, again. And I hum and sing. And he's right: I am forging some connection that is working. I am also still making myself dizzy. But it's been good. Much better than last time.

—

SUZI AND ANTONIO are sitting side-by-side on a bench outside studio B. They're recovering from their twenty-minute Arabian rehearsal. I love Arabian. It's my favorite dance in the second act, so fluid, so sensual.

"How did it go?" asks Suzi.

"My twenty-four seconds of fame," I say to them, joking. I still can't believe the entire Grandfather Dance is less than half a minute long. It seems so inconsequential given the entire performance.

"Hey," says Antonio, "that twenty-four seconds is important. Don't think it isn't."

—

THE NEXT DAY, after company class, Mark, Danielle, and I are in studio B at it again. And, just let me say this: I *nail* that Grandfather Dance, which is to say I go through the dance three times without making any errors. In fact, I do so well that, after four run-throughs, we begin rehearsing the Gallop. The Gallop is a lot of very quick chassés and a lot of turns. But the whole thing is a partner dance, and Mark knows what he's doing. And, unlike most of the other male dancers in the company, he is big. Which makes me feel little. In a good way. In a ballerina-sylph way. So I relax into his strength, and I let him whip me around. The trick here is to stay light on my feet, to take nimble, sprightly steps. Which is easier if you weigh 100 pounds and not 140. But I can do this. I am doing this. The Gallop is exhilarating. I'm all smiling and adrenalized and pretty damned pleased with myself. At the end of rehearsal, I chassé out of the studio and into the bathroom, where I manage to pee all over the waistband of my new tights.

17

Rehearsals

I STARTED THIS project in awe of the beauty and grace of ballet as seen at a distance, my view from the audience. I am now in awe of the sweat, the grit, the sheer will that gets them through nine-hour days and ten-hour bus trips and sixteen-city tours. To say "You have to love it to do it" is an understatement so colossal as to be meaningless. Yes, I know they are not out there curing cancer or feeding the homeless, but these dancers have committed them-selves heart and mind, body and soul to an enterprise, and they do it *every single day*. Days when they are hurting. Days when the sun is shining, and they'd rather not be stuck in a windowless studio. Days when it's wet and gray (like, for example, today), and bed looks like the best option. Days when life conspires against you. And still, they get up and do it. It is a lesson to us all—certainly to me—and not just a lesson about ballet and what I need to bring to class and rehearsals. It's about what it takes, really takes, to do something well. Forget "waiting for the Muse." It's about daily commitment.

This week the dancers are not only rehearsing for the solo and second-act dances in *The Nutcracker*, they are also learning and rehearsing a contemporary dance staged by a visiting choreographer. He is in town for a fast-and-furious visit, sitting in the front of the room watching their floor work, casting the show, teaching it, and then overseeing preliminary rehearsals—all within three days. That show won't be performed until after *The Nutcracker*, but Toni had to sandwich this session in now because it was the only time the choreographer was available.

Given all this activity, I am surprised (and delighted) when Toni sends an e-mail saying that she's arranged two more rehearsals for me later in the week. She is being incredibly accommodating and very generous. (Or, alternatively, she has heard disturbing reports about me from Mark, Suzi, and/or Danielle.) I know extra rehearsals put a strain on an already complicated schedule, and I know it takes away time from Mark and Danielle, who've now been permanently assigned to me. Thus, I feel grateful and guilty and stressed all at once. I want to justify Toni's investment in me. I want to make Mark and Danielle proud. And, when I dance onstage, I don't want to be the one person the audience notices because she looks like a cow on ice.

IT'S WEDNESDAY MIDMORNING, rehearsal time for me, but it turns out that all three studios are being used. Suzi and Antonio are rehearsing Arabian upstairs; Brian (Cavalier) and Yoshie (who shares the Sugar Plum Fairy part with Danielle) are pas de deux-ing in the big studio. In the other studio an adult tap class is in session. The only place for us is the long, narrow hallway that runs between the two downstairs studios. It's an awkward space made even more awkward (for me) by the presence of the half-a-dozen dancers who are sitting on the wooden benches that line the hallway. An audience that is beyond the footlights is one thing. Onlookers ten feet away is quite another. But when Mark calls to me, "Sister!" and I rush toward him, trying to be delicate and light-footed about it, and we make eye contact, I am pulled into the moment. I am pulled in because he is there, oblivious to the circumstances, to the coat hooks that graze our shoulders, to the low-hanging pipes in the ceiling, to the chatter of the other dancers. My feet remember most of the steps. "Yes!" Danielle calls out with enthusiasm when I remember to take the extra tombé that sets up the third turn. Mark notices and comments on my attempt to spot the final turn. Danielle gives me an important arm-position correction that will help with the turn.

But this tantalizing whiff of self-confidence dissipates rapidly as the adult tappers clear out of one of the studios and we make our way into the empty space to continue rehearsal. Only it is not empty. Toni is perched on a folding chair in the front of the room. When did she sneak in? She looks up expectantly, and I realize that she's there to observe me. And I freak out. Quietly, that is. With the sangfroid my character, a Victorian-era spinster aunt, might exhibit in this circumstance, I lift my chin and walk toward her slowly with balletic grace (or so I imagine). "I will be ready for you next week," I say. "But please, please, not this week." She smiles good-naturedly (I hope it's a good-natured smile) and leaves. I breathe.

We're going to rehearse the Gallop now, which I love because the steps are easy and the music is absolutely rousing. I am disappointed to learn that Mark won't actually be my partner for this dance in the stage performances. He will be dancing it with his *Nutcracker* wife (Tori, my Sephora partner and erstwhile private tutor). Who will be my partner? Mark and Danielle think it will be Jesse, one of the first-year aspirants. Mark goes out into the hallway to round him up. Jesse is a sweet kid, very young, a slip of a fellow. I am accustomed to being whipped around by the six-foot-two, muscled Mark. Dancing with Jesse (whom I am pretty sure I outweigh) reminds me that I am not a slip of a girl.

Later that afternoon I meet up with Kim. It's not our official Ballet Book Club meeting. That's not scheduled for another week to give us time to catch up on our respective reading assignments. I am currently mired in Nijinsky's unexpurgated diary, which has almost nothing to do with dancing and everything to do with world-class psychosis. It is like the proverbial accident on the side of the road that you hate yourself for slowing down to watch—but you do. Kim asks me how rehearsal is going, and I launch into an account of my progress in the Grandfather Dance and the fun and freedom of the Gallop.

"I can't believe the difference I see in you," Kim says, shaking her head. "You're beginning to believe in yourself."

—⟋⟍—

ALL OF A sudden it's November. Mon Dieu! I'd say "Merde!," but that's how dancers wish each other luck (their version of "Break a leg," which, of course, is not something you'd dare say to a dancer). What I mean, though, is: *Holy Shit*. It's November. My first performance is sixteen days away. Toni e-mails me that she's scheduling costume fittings this week. I text Suzi and beg her to come over to give me a lesson in how to apply stage makeup.

The next afternoon, after a full day of rehearsals, Suzi drives out to my house for an hour of staring-in-the-mirror instruction. Moisturizer, primer, foundation (everywhere), shimmery powder, liquid eyebrow paint to create dramatic dark arches, massive amounts of white eye shadow to open up the eye, brown in the crease, bronze feathered in, more white, eyeliner above that follows the lashes and then sweeps up toward the brow, eyeliner below that follows the lashes and then heads straight out toward the temple, brown shadow along the cheekbones to define the face, scarlet lipstick applied outside the lines to exaggerate. I don't think I've ever stared at my face for so long. I almost stop seeing who I am.

Suzi says I'm a fast learner, but I think she's just being nice. She also says I need to buy three more brushes (to add to those I've already purchased on that buying spree with Tori), rose-colored eye shadow, a volumizing mascara (mine apparently does not volumize enough), makeup remover wipes, Q-tips, and a mirror with a stand. The next afternoon, I hand the list to the sales clerk at Sally Beauty Supply, and her eyes—enhanced with a more-than-generous application of Sally products, I can't help but notice—light up. She leads me up and down the aisles. We stop to study a six-foot-high display of brushes in more sizes and shapes than there are sizes and shapes. We linger at the vast array of false eyelashes (with feathers, with sequins, double-layered). We debate the necessity of purchasing both eye-makeup remover and makeup-makeup remover. (I win. One remover is remover enough.) But she scores a late victory by upselling me on a Sally card for all the future purchases I hope I never make.

AT REHEARSAL THIS morning, both Mark and Danielle point out (unnecessarily) that I'm making this dance look too much like work. I am button-down serious, intent on getting everything right. I am rigid, not so much in my body as in my head. I am supposed to be a fancy Victorian lady having a lovely time at an

elegant Christmas party. Instead, I'm a self-conscious midlife in-
terloper trying desperately to not screw up in rehearsal. Danielle
stops the music. They double-team me.

"You have to have fun with it," Mark says, tilting his head,
smiling, waving his arms expansively.

"The *audience* is there to have fun," Danielle adds. "They want
to see *you* enjoying yourself."

I hear what they're saying—and I agree—but I don't know
how to do it. How do I "have fun"? Immediately, I defer to the
way I approach just about everything: I make a mental list. How
to Have Fun While Dancing: *Listen to the music. Relax your shoulders. Lift your chin. Smile.* Oh, wait. I am replacing one set of instructions with another. I just leaped from my rigid "Just Do It"
mantra to an equally lockstep "Just (Look Like You) Enjoy Doing
It" refrain. But that's not how one enjoys something, is it? How
does one find joy without *working* to find joy . . . which takes the
joy out of the joy? This rehearsal has morphed into a life lesson. A
life lesson delivered to me by two twenty-somethings. Which
makes it a double life lesson.

I walk a few paces away from them, turn my back, and close my
eyes. I call up an image of the Party Scene. I've seen *The Nutcracker*
so many times over so many years in so many different venues that
the image immediately materializes, clear and bright: the elaborate
set, the fanciful arrangement of props, the soft lighting, the stage
full of dancers in elegant costumes. It is the holiday season, and the
people out there beyond the footlights—the mothers and their
daughters, the ones who dream of being dancers, the ones who've
never seen a ballet before, maybe guys like Victor LaRossa, the
Brooklynite who'd never before seen a ballet—they are all ready to
be charmed and entertained. This ballet, this night, is part of their
holiday celebration. The audience wants—deserves—to see their
joy reflected in the faces of the dancers. "The stage is not the place

to remind the audience that one is human," Suzanne Farrell writes in her memoir. "Illusion is what they are paying for."

"Let's *do it*, sistah!" Mark calls from across the room. Danielle touches the iPad and restarts the music. We dance the Grandfather Dance once again. And, yes, it *is* different. I realize, as I step through the first series of pas de bourreé, that I'm dancing because of the music, not because I told myself it was now time to take the steps I am supposed to take. But, in that moment of realization, I become self-conscious again. Still, I force myself to look up and out, not down. This is harder than it sounds, and not just because I am so accustomed to staring at my own feet. It's also hard because looking "out" in the studio means looking straight into a mirror and seeing yourself. I have studiously avoided doing this both in class and in rehearsals. I'm afraid that will turn up the volume on the inner critique so high as to truly deafen me. I force myself to look forward into the mirror as I dance the Grandfather Dance this morning, but I train my eyes on a spot above my head and gaze at a reflection of the back of the studio.

"Good, good," says Danielle, nodding. "That's more like it."

We go on to the Gallop. Jesse is rehearsing in the other studio, so Mark is my partner again. We prance back and forth diagonally across the room. Because the steps are so simple—two chassés, half-turn, two chassés, half-turn—it's easy to let the music take me away. The challenge is to be both elegant and sprightly, to cover a lot of ground with energy and also grace. The grace is a lot harder than the energy. I struggle with the slightly complicated ending, and we have to run through it three times before I finally figure out how to complete the sequence facing the right direction. At the end of the dance, Mark and I are holding hands, our arms aloft, having promenaded across the studio to get to the correct stage position. I'm feeling pretty okay about the whole thing.

Mark turns his head toward me, smiles. "You'd make a great man," he says. He says it completely without affect. It's not a compliment. It's not a criticism. It's a statement. I look up at him, waiting for his explanation. Instead, he says, "My job is to lead you and keep you safe and make you look good. Your job is to trust me." Ah, I get it. I am trying to *lead*.

———◦っ———

AFTER REHEARSAL I have my fitting, which I have been looking forward to—who doesn't want to wear a gorgeous Victorian gown?—and dreading—what midlife woman would not quake with fear at the thought of having to fit into a costume made for a twenty-year-old ballerina? Shaunna, the company's seamstress and dresser, has my costume off the rack and waiting for me when I finish rehearsal. I had been hoping for a particularly elegant-looking burgundy-colored gown that Tori wore in last year's performance. But alas, the dress I've been assigned is not that one. It's a fanciful gown the color that maple leaves turn in the fall, a kind of burnt orange. The dress has a deep scoop neck trimmed with a six-inch-wide flounce of lace. The bodice is tight and lacy, blinged out with sparkly amber-colored buttons and another wide flounce of lace at the waist. The skirt is satiny and voluminous with an over-skirt (called a "peplum," Shaunna tells me) of heavily embroidered tulle dotted with appliquéd flowers the color of butternut squash.

Shaunna cradles the dress in her hands and approaches me. I have never had anyone dress me. I feel like Lady Mary in *Down-ton Abbey*. I raise my arms, and she eases the gown over my head, gently pulling it down, adjusting the neck and shoulders, attempting (unsuccessfully) to secure the bodice in back, and fanning out the skirt over the big, stiff hoop I am wearing underneath. Things are not as bad as they might be.

"The bodice almost fits!" Shaunna exclaims as she almost fastens it, and I almost manage to breathe. As she measures the gaps that must be closed, she entertains me with a story about a "larger" dancer and what she, Shaunna, had to do to make this woman's costume fit. There was not enough material to let out in the seams, so Shaunna crisscrossed black ribbon back and forth across the gap in the back and had the dancer wear a black leo to hide the juryrigging. "But we don't have to do that!" she says excitedly. "I can find what I need in the seams. I can make this work!" She'll have to find extra fabric in the upper arms too. But the good news is, the costume has three-quarter sleeves, which means total upper-arm coverage! Those flaps I was so worried about, those underarm bat wings that jiggle with every port de bras? They will be encased and contained in satin and lace.

─ႱჁ

A FEW DAYS later, I wake up to a gray, rainy, typical Oregon November morning, make myself a cup of tea, and look through my calendar for the week.

What?

One week from today is my first performance of The Nutcracker?

Sharp intake of breath. Thump of heart. Of course I knew this day was coming. Yes, I've been working and planning for months and months—in fact, very close to a year now—but the reality of it, the almost-here of it—turns my hands to ice. I immediately shift into overdrive. I have to make an appointment at the hair salon for a hot-oil treatment. Suzi told me last week (in the kindest of terms) that my hair was too flyaway and that the stage lights would catch all the frizz and wisps and make me look all furry. And I have to practice putting on stage makeup again. And again. Not to mention those false eyelashes. With that thin line of glue that must be not too much and not too little and must dry to a special, fleeting state of perfect tackiness that somehow I must learn to recognize. I'll have less than forty-five minutes before the shows to get makeup done. And get myself in costume. Which reminds me: I need to practice walking around in my two-and-a-half-inch-high character shoes. The ones I'm going to be dancing in. And I need to buy a pair of pink tights for under my ball gown. Which I hope fits after Shaunna's seam-expansion efforts. Is it possible to lose another pound or two? Is this what a freak-out feels like?

I think so.

I call Kim so she can talk me down, but she doesn't answer any of her three numbers.

Nut minus four.

I SPEND MOST of the morning parading around the house in my character shoes (I didn't realize how high two-and-a-half inches could be) and practicing applying stage makeup and those damn eyelashes. It takes me 22:46 to put on *half* a face. Yes, I am timing myself. My husband ignores me. My daughter doesn't understand why I'm so stressed about applying cosmetics. She is—inexplicably, given her lack of an in-house role model—an expert. Every morning, in her bathroom crammed with just about every product Sally Beauty Supply sells, she applies foundation and dusts her soft, dewy cheeks with powder and makes up her eyes with liner and shadows and mascara. She hums as she does this. She enjoys doing it. And she looks wonderful. I don't ask for her help. I need to learn how to do this myself.

Nut minus two.

This afternoon is my first full rehearsal. I've practiced the two partnered dances I will perform in Act I dozens of times, but I've never been through a rehearsal of the whole Party Scene with the cast. I actually have almost no idea what I am supposed to do in between the Gallop and the Grandfather Dance. I've watched the EBC video, so I know there's a lot of graceful partylike movement, the swishing of skirts, curtsying, smiling, miming conversation, toasting empty champagne glasses. But when and where this happens for Aunt Rose onstage, and with whom, is a mystery to me.

When I arrive for rehearsal, Jenn tells me she's designed a headdress and jewelry to go along with my costume. Wow. More stuff! The headdress is lovely, ribbons and bows and flowers and a glittery leaf that hugs my ear and follows the curve of my jaw. It's showy, not tacky. The jewelry consists of drop earrings and a double-strand necklace made with amber-toned beads that bling out my already blinged-out ball gown. I take my whole getup into the bathroom. This is a dress rehearsal, and I need to be dressed. The good news is I don't have to be in makeup.

But the *really* good news is that the upper arms of the costume fit the upper arms of my body. Thank you, Shaunna. I find Jenn and enlist her to hook up the back. The waist is a bit of a challenge, about as snug as it could possibly be while still allowing me to breathe. But the hooks hook. I am *in*. I put on the jewelry, slip my feet into the character shoes, smooth my hair, and take a long, hypercritical look at myself in the mirror. The glamour is perhaps best seen at a distance of twenty feet. That's what I tell myself.

Okay, so I said it was a dress rehearsal. But apparently, it is dress rehearsal for me only. I am *the only one* in costume. The rest of the dancers, all gathered in the big studio waiting for the run-through to begin, are wearing the "junk" they wear to company class. And here I am in full regalia. As if I needed to stand out even more. A scene comes to me from one of my all-time favorite silly movies, *Start the Revolution without Me*. It's when poor, bumbling King Louis (the google-eyed actor Hugh Griffith) shows up at a royal ball wearing a full-on rooster costume. He looks out over a sea of guests, all of whom are attired in appropriate eighteenth-century royal-party dress, turns to Marie Antoinette—who has set him up for this humiliation—and says, "But I thought it was a *costume* ball." At this moment, I know exactly how King Louis felt. On the other hand, it is so over-the-top ridiculous that I have to laugh. Out loud. It is also worth noting that, with the possible exception of Mark, Danielle, and Suzi, who have the most invested in me, no one seems to actually notice.

Nut minus one.

Half an hour before rehearsal, the final one, Jenn brushes and twists and braids and buns and curls and sprays and nets my hair. It looks gorgeous and balletlike. And I will never, ever be able to replicate it. I am all hooped and bejeweled and gowned. And I flub the Gallop, missing a turn and thus working from the wrong foot for the last quarter of the dance. No one can see because the ball gown hides my feet. But I know it, and Jesse, my partner, knows it. And I feel awkward and out of control. I'm slowly catching on to the acting and miming—but too slowly, I fear. With no one in costume and two casts, I'm not sure who is who among the Party Scene characters. And, without the children (we'll perform with different casts of local children at each venue), I'm not getting a feel for the action onstage. So I stand around with my gorgeous hair and my dazzling dress, and I am clueless. Flat-footed and clueless.

It is time for the Grandfather Dance. Mark calls to me. I perform in a workmanlike fashion with only one misstep on that pesky chassé-tombé combination. (Later Danielle tells me she never would have known except I let it show on my face. "Whatever happens, just smile," she says.) My big mistake of the afternoon comes right after the dance is over, and I am supposed to promenade with Mark stage left. I let go of his hand and stride off, by myself, stage right. I don't know why. I am in some kind of altered state: tense, on high alert, just waiting to make a mistake. So of course I do.

When the Party Scene is finally, mercifully over, I hike up my skirt and walk back to the smelly, crowded dancers' "lounge," where I've stashed my street clothes. I am close to tears. And just so mad at myself. What I'd like to do right now is drown my sorrows and/or numb my pain—pick the appropriate cliché—by eating my way through, say, a pound of salted cashews. But I can't, dammit, or the dress won't fit. Instead I get in my car and drive around for an hour listening to talk radio. I don't know who is talking or what is being talked about, but words fill the car, which prevents me from saying words to myself. Words like, for example: *You suck, you loser.*

When I get home, I e-mail Kim that I am having a meltdown. Seconds, literally seconds, after I press "send," my phone rings. It's Kim. She launches into the best pep talk imaginable. It is sincere and loving but also no-nonsense. She reminds me of who I am and how hard I've worked. She says I am brave, and because I trust her and she knows me and she's been with this project almost since the beginning, I have to believe her. She tells me I've earned the right to have fun with this. That I should go and have fun. Right: *fun*. I forgot about that. Then her husband, Tim, grabs the phone and delivers this rousing, gale-force call to arms that at first stuns me and then, despite myself, inspires me. Kim is back with final words: "Just go out there and do it. It's your 'fuck-you' to that Russian guy . . . what's his name?"

"André Eglevsky," I say. "His name is André Eglevsky."

18

On the Road

"WE HAVE ONLY one rule on the bus," Sara tells me. Sara, one of the company dancers, is my newest EBC friend, a lively, light-hearted girl with an infectious sense of humor. It's just past noon on this mid-November day, and we are queuing up to board the charter bus that will take us to Florence, a small coastal town where we'll be performing tonight. It is EBC's second *Nutcracker* road show—and my first. It is Aunt Rose's debut. Years ago, immersed in another book project, I traveled with a college basketball team and discovered that there was a deeply entrenched but unspoken on-the-bus code of etiquette. So I am careful to check that out before I step on board today.

When I quizzed Suzi and Tori just a few minutes ago, they told me about the Rules of Seating: Everyone gets his or her own double seat on the bus. No one sits next to each other, although couples sit either across the aisle from each other or directly in back or in front of one another. Toni and Jenn get the first seats in the bus, followed closely by the principal dancers. Then come the newer company dancers mixed in with the aspirants. The old hands—Tori, Suzi, Antonio, Danielle, and Mark—all have "reserved" seats in the back of the bus. In the middle there's a sort of no-man's-land. It is suggested that I hang back and wait for people to settle in before I find a place somewhere in this uncharted territory. As I wait to board the bus, Sara informs me of yet another rule of the road, the one she says—accompanied by her wonderful laugh—is the single, unbreakable EBC travel imperative: *There is no number two on the bus.* The dancers have decreed this after several unpleasant experiences with the less-than-vigorous ventilation system in the tiny rear bathroom. Duly noted.

The bus leaves on the dot of 12:15, exactly as stated in the much-anticipated Nut Book, the thirty-seven-page touring bible that lays out our lives for the next month. In it are the details of the company's thirty performances in fifteen venues in five western states. It will be a long, hard tour, just as it is every year for EBC. The company depends on this ballet for income, and the many small communities that host performances depend on EBC for their dose of holiday High Art. I will be dancing in about half of the performances. I wish I could be part of the entire tour, but I just can't figure out how to juggle some of the lengthiest out-of-town trips given my teaching schedule and family responsibilities. Aunt Rose will be missed, I'm sure, but Toni has figured out alternate choreography for the shows I won't be dancing in. With separate travel schedules for crew and cast, detailed production timetables, scene-by-scene rehearsal schedules, accommodation information, and the two bits of intel the dancers most care about—whether there will be "hospitality" (aka food) at the venue and where the nearest grocery store is—the Nut Book, like the ballet itself, is a masterful production months in the making. It owes its life to Josh, EBC's hardworking manager and ballet mistress Jenn's soon-to-be husband.

On the bus, the dancers are all chowing down. I mean seriously chowing down. I've read so many literary accounts of obsessive dancer dieting and ballerina bulimia ("Our lives revolve around what we don't eat," writes former NYCB dancer Toni Bentley) that it is heartening to see big appetites in the process of being happily satisfied. There are massive sandwiches being consumed. Danielle is busy spooning something healthy from a commodious Tupperware tub. Tori is attacking what looks like a one-and-a-half-pound apple. Cory and Beth, seated across from and behind me, make their way through a big bag of something crunchy and salty. The bodice of my Party Scene ball gown fits like a corset. I cannot afford even an eighth of an inch expansion in my waist. I slug water and nibble at the lowest-calorie, highest-protein bar I could find.

To silence the saliva-inducing crunchings around me, I put in my earbuds and crank up the Moscow Symphony Orchestra's rendition of *The Nutcracker* that I downloaded on my phone last night. As the bus makes its way out of town, past miles of unlovely strip malls, into open land and then across the timbered coastal mountains, I try to let the music weave its magic. Which it does. That is, until I hear the Gallop music, and I am reminded of the rear-of-the-stage turnaround I missed in rehearsal. And then I hear the intro to the Grandfather Dance, and all I can think of is how I am always late for that cue, and what I must look like racing halfway across the stage to join hands with Mark on beat. I force myself to think positive, fleet-footed ballerina thoughts. I listen again to No. 3, "Petit Galop: Presto-Andante-Allegro." What joyous music. Please let me be joyous dancing it. I jump ahead and listen to No. 5, "Scène et Danse du Grand-père: Andante." Please let me not look like a fool. Please let me stop thinking about all this! I switch from the Moscow Orchestra to the Indigo Girls. "The less I seek my source for some definitive / The closer I am to fine." I so want to be fine.

Am I? I don't know. I know that the preshow run-through goes well. I know that a combination of lighthearted chatter in the crowded dressing room and my own laser focus on applying layers of stage makeup keeps (most of) my first-performance jitters at bay. I know that onstage I become part of an artfully choreographed tableau, surrounded by lovely young dancers, enchanted by the music. But the performance, *my* performance, my *debut* performance, is mostly a blur. I was expecting an epiphany, a wow-here-you-are-and-this-is-it moment. But my time onstage whisks by. I am all body, no mind. This is a good thing. This is how it should be. I should be so caught up in the moment that I am unconscious of its particulars. Well, almost unconscious. In fact, for a terrifying ten seconds in the middle of the Grandfather Dance I am very conscious of my performance. That's because I mess up. It's the timing of those tombés/pas de bourrée, the step combination I continue to have trouble with. Onstage, my ball gown hides my clumsiness, and it is all over in a flash. Mark is holding my hand as we parade stage left, and I let him lead me, and I am mindless (in a good way) again, and I curtsy. And that's it. I've done it. It is less of an accomplishment than I had hoped but not the disaster I had feared.

The following day, we travel north for an hour to Corvallis for an evening performance, and I nail it—*absolutely nail it*—during rehearsal. I am dancing in my insulated REI booties (worn by close to half the company). The auditorium is cold; the stage is cold; and dancers are (rightly) fixated on the health and well-being of their feet. They have fully researched the warm-feet alternatives, and this dorky, slightly cushiony après-ski footwear is the bootie of choice. I want warm feet too. But more than that, I want to be part of the "in" crowd. Last week I rushed out to the local REI and grabbed a pair. At this afternoon's rehearsal I am decked out in my personal version of dancer "junk": knee-length sweats over footless tights; Writers' Dojo tee over long-sleeved tech shirt with hobo hands. And the aforementioned booties.

I feel more professional, more a part of the company, now that I am finally comfortable enough to dress down, to leave those lovely leos in my closet at home. It is true that Danielle never wears junk and always looks elegant, and may in fact be incapable of looking anything other than elegant, in the studio, in rehearsal, on the bus, and, for all I know, mopping the floor. And some dancers' "junk" is so mindfully chosen as to belie the term: Suzi's hand-knit scarf that she always wraps around her waist; the over-the-top fake-fur coat that Yoshie wears to every rehearsal. It's the kind of coat a Real Housewife of New Jersey would wear, the kind of coat that goes with big hair and a loud voice. Only Yoshie is maybe four foot eleven and maybe ninety pounds, and everything about her (except the coat) is delicate. She wears the coat, but really, the coat wears her.

In rehearsal this afternoon, I hit every musical cue. I dance lightly. I smile. Which all goes to prove the cliché: good rehearsal, bad show. (Actually, I think the cliché is the opposite, but it works both ways.) In the show, Jesse and I almost collide with another couple as we gallop diagonally across stage, which gets us a half-beat behind, which messes up our turn. Then, in my "star" turn center stage, I pick up late on Mark's cue, and he has to pretty much whip me around so I'm in position for the beginning of our dance. The whipping around throws me off balance. I feel myself wobble on my two-and-a-half-inch-high character shoes as I struggle to adjust, and I never truly feel graceful during the rest of the dance. I never lose myself in the performance.

What's most interesting about this second show, though, is not my bumbling mediocrity but the contrast between the performance tonight and the last time I was on this very stage. Yes, I have performed in this 1,200-seat auditorium on the Oregon State University campus before. In fact, twice. On two past book tours I stood on the stage I danced on tonight, poised behind a podium, speaking with ease, making eye contact, gesturing, ad-libbing, working the crowd. Comfortable. The opposite of tonight. That said, on the bus ride home, I am practically knocked over by a wave of joy. More like a tsunami of joy—that's how powerful it is. Where did *that* come from?

It occurs to me, suddenly and delightfully, that regardless of my own stumblings and self-doubt, I love being around these young, unjaded people, these twenty-something dancers who live in the moment and love what they do. My everyday midlife world is populated by disgruntled writers who rail against the Amazon monopoly and dis their editors and bristle at the rise of the "content provider," and disgruntled university professors who rail against the hijacking of faculty governance and dis their colleagues and bristle at being tapped to serve on yet another ineffectual committee. What a delight to be temporarily part of this other—it seems to me simpler—world. I am not romanticizing the world of ballet. These dancers do not live glamorous lives, and they do not make a very good living, and they get injured with distressing regularity, and touring is grueling. I know all this. What I am delighted about is being around people whose passion for what they do trumps . . . well, everything.

And then there are the unexpected pleasures of the girl thing, the girl thing I never experienced as a girl and am now suddenly in the thick of: the random chatter in dressing rooms so cramped that we sit, literally, shoulder to shoulder in front of long, far too brightly illuminated mirrors, staring at our faces, making faces at our faces, tweezing, assessing blemishes, trading contouring techniques, borrowing bobby pins, gossiping about what "the boys" do in their dressing room, debating the lash-lengthening power of various mascaras. *Has anyone seen my pink tights? Could you zip me up? Where's that necklace? If I hear that Katy Perry song another time,*

I'll explode. The rooms are tiny, airless, and, thanks to the rows and rows of makeup lights, very, very hot. There is no place to move. The space is always jammed with the bulky rolling racks that hold our costumes. The floor is covered with our underskirts and hoops, our travel bags and ballet shoes. In that hour or two between the end of the onstage company class (yes, there is class on the road before every performance) and curtain time, the dressing room is our home. The atmosphere veers between professional tour and pajama party, and I love both.

When the Party Scene is over, I return to this hothouse because there is really no other place to go. I try to take up as little room as possible as the dancers rush back to make quick costume changes. I breathe in the atmosphere—the air thick with sweat and hairspray, the room buzzing with performance energy. I scribble notes as the girls rush in and out, leapfrogging over obstacles, panting and flushed. They change for mice, for snow, for Spanish, Arabian, and Chinese, for flowers. They fix their hair, reapply lipstick. Sometimes they scold themselves aloud for missteps; other times they radiate quiet confidence. Always they slug vitamin water.

And then it's over. Just like that. And we are lugging our gear bags and our makeup kits and our plastic sacks of snack food out the stage door and into the rainy night. I step up onto the waiting bus, Mark and Danielle ahead of me, Sara behind me, and a long line of dancers behind her. Everyone is wired and tired. Running on empty.

—◌

ON THE BUS to our next venue, another small Oregon burg that would never get to see ballet if we didn't bring it to them, the dancers alternately eat, text, and doze. Cory and Beth, limbs intertwined, whisper and canoodle. Mark plays Peggle on his iPad. I stare out the rain-splattered window. I have ample time, maybe too much time, for self-reflection. And what I reflect upon is the whole notion of "learning curve," the idea of progressing toward accomplishment over time, the notion that you get inexorably better, more skillful, the more you practice, the more you try, the more you do something. But I am now convinced that the learning curve also means something else: It means you are on a path that offers all kinds of new opportunities to make different mistakes, and the longer you stay on the path, the more mistakes you get to make. Which doesn't feel like progress at all.

I think about my lackluster performance in Corvallis. Those mistakes were all about timing. When you are a half-beat ahead, you end up standing flat-footed. When you are a half-beat behind, you trip over yourself to catch up. In Coos Bay, tonight's performance, I correct the timing error by keeping careful track of the music in my head with the unhappy result that I rob my movements of spontaneity. Who knows what new errors I will commit tomorrow during our matinee in Roseburg?

What's so interesting about these "mistakes" is how easily the audience can be fooled. Danielle says that most people who watch ballet see dancers from the waist up. If you have lovely posture and smile, you can get away with all kinds of egregious footwork. Danielle told me this in rehearsal, but I didn't really understand it until I was onstage, until I realized that, in the Party Scene, if you are wearing a gorgeous, glittery gown, hardly anyone in the audience notices anything else. This is comforting. But it doesn't make me want to stop trying to be perfect. The audiences in Florence, Corvallis, Coos Bay, and Roseburg are enchanted by the spectacle and just happy to be there. Knowing that doesn't give me permission to slack off. It merely locates my quest for perfection, my goal to ascend the learning curve, where it belongs: in my head. In learning to perform for others, my insight is that I am really performing for myself.

―co―

FOR WHATEVER REASON—and I'm betting it is not the lousy night's sleep I get in a local motel—the next day, the Roseburg matinee goes well. For a few magical, un-self-conscious moments, I actually feel as if I am at a party. At intermission, instead of removing my makeup and changing into my traveling sweats, which is what I have been doing, I sashay out to the lobby. Sashay is absolutely the right verb. If you've ever covered ground in a four-foot-diameter hoop skirt under a heavy satin gown, you know sashay. Out in the lobby, at every performance, the EBC, like just about every ballet company out there, sets up a boutique to sell *Nutcracker* merch. There is a crowd around the table, which this afternoon is staffed by Sara; my Gallop partner, Jesse; and a delightful aspirant named Izzy, who is Jesse's Party Scene wife. Business is brisk, which is good. It means extra income for the company and a small stipend for the dancers who take care of the sales. I make my way around the perimeter of the crowd, nodding and smiling and trying to act all Aunt Rose–ish.

A little girl in a red velvet dress with matching headband tugs at her mother's arm, pulling her toward me. "She thinks yours is the most beautiful dress," the mother says. The little girl lowers her chin shyly. "Can I take a picture of you with her?" Of course, I tell her. I put my white-gloved hand on the little girl's shoulder and smile with my lipsticked lips. The scene repeats itself three times as I work my way through the crowd. The little girls are awestruck. Their mothers are treating me like a real ballerina. Wow. I could get used to this.

But alas, my puffed-up ego is forced to take a rest.

Two days after returning from our mini-Oregon tour, the company heads off to Anchorage without me. They will do seven shows in Alaska, then fly to eastern Washington, where they will travel many miles by bus to perform in towns in Wyoming and Idaho. This is the leg of the tour I just can't manage, as it coincides with the most work-intensive part of the writing seminar I'm teaching and, just as important, with Thanksgiving, which is a very big deal at our house. So Aunt Rose stays home, where she keeps up with the company via Facebook updates.

—⟨⟩—

I SETTLE BACK into my "real" life—my teacher-mother-wife life—so easily, so seamlessly that it is disconcerting. On the one hand, I love being back in my element, where I feel (relatively) smart again and (sort of) in control. It is so very tiring being a beginner. I love sleeping in my own bed and having dinner every night with the family. I rejoice at the prospect of no makeup for two weeks. No twenty-pound dress with a bodice that fits like a wetsuit. No sprayed-to-within-an-inch-of-its life bun.

On the other hand, I'm on edge. I feel anxious away from the discipline to which I've become accustomed. I do thirty minutes of predawn yoga at home. I go to Barre3 just about every morning. I slog through afternoon Pilates classes. I make it to several evening community ballet classes. And I still feel like a couch potato. Without the two-hour company class and the rehearsals (and the shows), I am not using my body in the extreme ways it has (sort of) gotten used to. I stand at the kitchen counter waiting for the tea water to boil and do my pliés, my ronds de jambe.

And I watch what I eat. Obsessively. Thanksgiving comes. I toast with carbonated water, not wine. I don't touch the buttery mashed potatoes my husband makes. I don't partake of even one of my daughter's toothsome garlic biscuits. I carefully measure a measly half-cup of my homemade stuffing and plop it down on my plate next to the triple portion of undressed green salad and the slice of gravyless turkey breast. Yeahyeahyeah, I'm thankful. *Just not for the dinner.*

But Thanksgiving isn't the worst of it. My husband and I give one party a year, a holiday singing event that, in addition to featuring friends on electric and bass guitars vamping Elvis's "Blue Christmas," is noteworthy for its spread of home-baked cakes, bars, brownies, and cookies. And by home-baked, I mean baked in my home by me. Everything. (Although these past few years I've gotten able assistance from my daughter, Lizzie.) Thus I must endure a two-day immersion in the forbidden land of white flour, white sugar, butter, chocolate, and did I mention butter? I am talking about epic Raw Dough vs. Aunt Rose battles. The name of the party, by the way, is "The Annual Song Fest and Glucose Tolerance Test." That's what the invitations say.

As if I were not obsessing about this *enough*, the day before the party, I get an e-mail from Toni, who is not traveling with the company on this part of the tour and so rsvp'd that she'll be coming to the party. Her P.S., which I pray she means as a joke, is: "Don't forget you have to squeeze back into Aunt Rose's costume on December 12th." Right. Like I was going to forget.

At the party, I sing and circulate. I drink hot tea and chain-chew Orbit Sweet Mint Gum. I make sure that Toni sees me not eating, which is not to say that I don't sample at least one (small) piece of, yes, everything. Because I do. And, although I am successful in not beating myself up about the extra and completely unnecessary calories, I do feel sort of awful lying in bed that night, jittery and borderline nauseated from the sugar spike. The following morning, mea culpa, I take back-to-back Barre3 classes, then head to the gym for an additional hour of cardio.

—☙—

PACKING FOR THE second leg of the tour later that day, I print out the relevant ten pages of the Nut Book so I can review what my life will be like for the next two weeks. And I have a deeply disturbing OMFG moment when I go through, marking with my yellow highlighter, and see what I'm in for. Friday: a six-hour car trip with Toni as we travel to meet up with the company in eastern Washington, arriving just in time for a full-show dress rehearsal. Saturday: matinee and evening performances. Sunday: on the bus for three hours, then a matinee performance, followed by another two-and-a-half-hour trip to the next venue. Monday: evening performance. Tuesday: eight hours on the bus back to Eugene. Wednesday: an hour and a half up and back to Salem for an evening performance. Thursday: same thing again. Friday: in Eugene for the final four-show run beginning with an evening performance. Saturday: matinee and evening. Sunday: matinee.

That's five cities, four motels, ten performances, almost twenty-four hours of travel, and another roughly twelve hours of applying makeup and fussing with hair. It feels as if the dancing itself, the being onstage and Galloping and Grandfathering, is a minor part of the experience. And the experience—just thinking about the experience of the next ten days—is overwhelming.

19

Road Warriors

IN A SEPARATE caravan of trucks and vans, the crew precedes us. They are a hardworking, nose-to-the-grindstone bunch, not chatty—at least not with the dancers—and idiosyncratic as hell. There is Elliot, the impossible-to-miss six-foot-five kilted electrician with his footlong braided red beard and his enormous steel-toed boots. Counter to this how-can-you-not-gawk-at-me appearance, he is an unassuming, soft-spoken professional who gets the job done on tour in circumstances that would throw others into either rage or panic or both. And there's Earendil, the rigger, carpenter, and prop master, who is no slouch either. Buff—and I mean *buff*—her supersculpted shoulders and arms covered in gorgeous tattoos, she does everything from hoist scenery to haul hefty prop crates to hand-paint, glue, and repair mouse heads. Backstage, she is everywhere, all focus, no wasted movement. Earendil (an important figure in Middle Earth during the second and third age, in case you didn't know) is her real name, not a hippie moniker she adopted. Her parents were over-the-top Tolkien enthusiasts.

Shaunna is on the tour also. She is the wardrobe mistress who worked magic to make my Party Scene gown fit. On tour she cares for more than a hundred costumes, ironing, sewing, and repairing as needed, doing everyone's laundry (thus making her the most popular member of the crew), dressing and herding the little girls (and an occasional little boy) who dance with us in each town. David is the unflappable stage director. At least I've never seen him flap. In fact, he moves like a dancer, graceful, light on his feet, seemingly—and, apparently, *really*—in control, his voice reassuringly, consistently calm as he orchestrates the magic of lighting and scenery and keeps us all on schedule.

Mike, technical director for the tour, seems plucked from a different era, maybe the 1930s. Gruff, lovably cranky, a union man, a heavy smoker, he rules backstage. He looks and moves like the Oscar-winning actor J. K. Simmons, the tyrannical teacher in the movie *Whiplash*, but he doesn't yell. That much. A story circulates that Mike yelled at one of the little girls from a local dance studio and made her cry before a performance. Mike vehemently denies making the little girl cry, but he seems to like telling and retelling this story. I watch him boss around the local stagehands and stare down dancers who commit the sin of standing too close to props. I hear him grumble sotto voce. And I think I have him figured out. Then he comes back from what I thought was yet another smoke break holding a Starbucks paper cup, which he sweetly and somewhat ceremoniously delivers to Yoshie, the principal, the little dancer dressed in the Real Housewives of New Jersey fake-fur coat. He does this at every venue. He goes out and gets her coffee and hand-delivers it.

On the road, at each stop, as we dancers set ourselves up in our dressing rooms, as we familiarize ourselves with the layout, the dimensions and feel of each new stage, as we hunt for food, we see the guts of the operation laid bare. We see the workings of the crew, these people who do the unglamorous jobs that create the glamour onstage. They follow different schedules than the troupe so that when we arrive at a venue, they are already unpacking prop crates, delivering racks of costumes to dressing rooms, laying and taping the Marley floor, rigging our backdrops, setting up the lights and the sound system, running massive electrical cords everywhere, rolling in the props stage right or stage left.

It takes the crew a good three times longer to set up than we are onstage dancing. Each stage is different, each setup with its unique challenges. Meanwhile, we dancers arrive on our separate bus and begin the long, often tedious preparation for the performance. For 3:00 p.m. matinees, we arrive at 9:30 or 10:00. For 7:00 evening performances, we're at the theater by 2:00. We get in makeup, familiarize ourselves with the place, run through the entire Party Scene with the new batch of kids we'll be working with, mark a number of other dances on the stage (a necessity because the stages differ so drastically in their size and dimensions), gather for a ninety-minute company class onstage (we travel with our own barres), refresh our makeup, get in costume, and then, only then, only after five or more long hours, do we hear the opening strains of Tchaikovsky and get to do what we came here to do. I thought the challenge of being on tour would be all the performances. That's not the challenge. The challenge is the tour itself: the tedious bus rides, the grocery-store meals, the long hours in cold theaters waiting for the curtain to go up.

But whenever I start thinking that our little *Nutcracker* tour is tough, I remind myself of what I read about the legendary Anna Pavlova and her U.S. tours. In 1910, for example, her troupe performed 224 shows in 36 cities in 26 weeks. That's right, on the road—and consider what that might mean in 1910—for half a year. In the 1920s, the tour schedule continued apace. Pavlova performed one-night stands, runs of three performances (two evenings with a matinee on the second day), or, in major cities such as Chicago, San Francisco, Los Angeles, and New York, runs of between one and six weeks. As one of the dancers who toured with her in those days wrote, "I began to wonder how many towns there were in the states, for there were new ones on every tour—Kalamazoo, Battle Creek, Sedalia, Walla Walla—on and on we went, performing in temples, mosques, Academies of Music, halls, auditoriums, and occasionally a real theatre or an opera house."

In Jackson, Mississippi, they performed in a garage that had been adapted for a movie theater with a rat-infested cellar for a changing room. But, as Pavlova said—and as I'm sure Toni would second: "How can people in these little places see [ballet] if I don't come here to dance?"

The rigors of our tour may pale by comparison to the great Pavlova's, but we are nonetheless in the midst of a singularly unglamorous experience, an experience made odder, and perhaps even less glamorous, because the enterprise we're engaged in—the performance of *The Nutcracker*—is itself so very glamorous. We are the people who sit on the bus in sweats, faces half-scrubbed, hair crunchy from too much spray, stuffing down Safeway deli sandwiches. And we are also the people who dance on beautifully lit stages in stunning costumes and elegant headdresses and exquisite makeup, moving with precision and grace to some of the most famous music in the world. The yin and the yang of it on a daily, sometimes hourly, basis is disorienting, almost crazy-making if you stop to think about it. I may be the only one who stops to think about it. For the dancers, this is what the life is about, and you just go ahead and live it.

THE GLAMOROUS TOURING life continues with a six-hour drive, the last two in the sheeting rain, ending at a Holiday Inn Express on the outskirts of Walla Walla. At the theater, there is no hospitality. And the "rehearsal" listed in the Nut Book turns out to be an actual, full-on with costumes and makeup performance—with the parents of the Bon Bons and mice in the audience. There's a real orchestra, not the recorded music we're used to dancing to, which should be wonderful. But isn't. The conductor has his own idea about tempo, which is not the idea the dancers have. There is much grumbling about sluggish music. And no food. I don't perform well. It seems impossible that I could actually have forgotten some of the steps during my two-week hiatus, but I have. Maybe it's because I'm starving. Or because the music is off. Or because I didn't think we were actually performing tonight.

After the lackluster rehearsal-that-was-actually-a-show, the bus drives us to a local Safeway, where we invade the store like the starving horde we are. With attention to Aunt Rose's waistline, I buy yogurt, an apple, a package of sliced deli turkey, and microwave popcorn. I consume this feast sitting cross-legged on my Holiday Inn Express bed while watching *International House Hunters*.

The next day we perform a matinee and then an evening show, which means we are at the theater (an auditorium on the Whitman College campus) from 10:00 in the morning until 10:00 at night. I slip away for an hour in between shows in search of a triple-shot Americano. I don't have time to take off my makeup, which includes my inch-long fake eyelashes and blood-red lips, so I stroll the streets of downtown Walla Walla in my elasticized-ankle polyester harem pants (standard-issue dancer "junk"), an oversized sweatshirt, and a puffy down vest, looking like . . . well, you get the picture.

The next morning it's back on the bus. We pull into Pullman an hour late. The fog is so dense, the visibility nonexistent, that our veteran bus driver is forced to slow to forty then thirty then twenty miles an hour for much of the 115-mile trek. It turns out that we'll be performing our matinee the next day in Washington State University's basketball arena. One-half of the stadium is curtained off, with our stage created by the crew in the other half. The small (half-court) stage faces a steep wall of stadium seating. Yes, bleachers. The place smells like where hot dogs go to die. Our dressing room is actually one of the men's locker rooms—probably the one assigned to the visiting team—and is not dancer-friendly. It's a square, empty room lined with burly benches for guys to sit on while they lace up their size 17 Nikes. Apparently, basketball players don't need mirrors. The room is—or feels as if it is—a half-mile from the entrance to the arena.

Rehearsal is rushed. Company class is rushed. Makeup is rushed. The only mirror is over the sink in the one-stall bathroom adjoining the locker room. Those who know what they're doing (as in everyone but me) sit on the floor with the little makeup mirrors they brought with them perched on the athletes' benches, and, in the allotted time, maybe fifteen minutes, they are face-ready. But it takes me close to fifteen minutes just to put on my eyelashes. And that's when I'm sitting down in front of a big, well-lit expanse of mirror. I freak out quietly and do the best I can. Which is, in truth, better than I thought I could manage.

Onstage, if you can call the half-court space covered with our rolled-out Marley a stage, things fall apart for me almost immediately. My hoop gets stuck under the couch I sit on when the Party Scene begins, and so, after I mime reading a book to the party children gathered at my feet and attempt to arise gracefully, I am yanked back and land with an audible thud on my Victorian ass. This is front-of-stage stuff. I finally manage to free myself and then spend the next several minutes colliding with said couch as I try to mix and mingle with the other party guests. The stage is a weird shape. I keep being surprised at where I find the couch. And I am distracted by the sounds coming from the bleachers dead ahead. Hundreds of people in our *Nutcracker* audience are eating the popcorn they bought at the concession stands in the stadium, rustling the grease-stained paper sacks, crunching.

Then, in the Gallop, I do something I've never done before: I trip on the hem of my dress. Twice. Jesse saves me by gripping my hand. My not-that-noticeable gaff is followed by Beth, a truly lovely dancer, slipping and falling to the floor as she dances the mechanical doll. I know dancers fall onstage during performances. I've read about this happening to the ballet elite: Balanchine dancers performing at Lincoln Center. I've just never seen it happen. Beth, the professional that she is, gets up and dances the rest of the number flawlessly. But I am unnerved. I continue my witless, graceless performance by stepping on the hem of my dress, again, as I move quickly across the stage to begin my dance with Mark. Then I manage to screw up the easier of my two turns, spinning once rather than twice. Mark makes it work so effortlessly that I almost doubt I have done anything wrong. I remember him telling me at the end of one of our rehearsals back at the EBC studio, "My job is to make you look good." This afternoon, he does one hell of a job.

—☙

WE DON'T GO back to the motel after the performance. We've got some miles to rack up to get to our next venue and tomorrow night's show. So, after dressing down and packing up our gear, and after the obligatory quick stop at a nearby Safeway, we're winding along a dark secondary road that skirts two national forests as it follows the Washington-Idaho border. It must be lovely out there. A few seats behind me, Mark and Danielle take turns reading aloud from a Harry Potter book. I stare out the window into blackness and tell myself: *Okay, fine. You got all* that *out of your system.*

After three very long hours, we arrive at our motel in Sandpoint, Idaho, a slightly musty, rustic-without-the-charm establishment that makes the Holiday Inn Express look like the Plaza. You know the kind of place where the walls are not quite at right angles, and the washcloths are thin and scratchy? That kind of place. Much worse news: *No microwave in the room.* This is so very unfortunate. At our second stop of the night at our second Safeway, I had decided that I'd eaten enough yogurt and deli meat and needed an actual hot meal. I bought a frozen, microwavable Chicken Lime Lean Cuisine and, for a treat, popcorn. Microwave popcorn. It's 10:00 p.m. on a Sunday night in Sandpoint, Idaho. I sit on my slightly lumpy bed, watch *Say Yes to the Dress*, and eat a pound of pea pods from a plastic bag. For dessert: Orbit Sweet Mint gum.

—◌

SANDPOINT TURNS OUT to be a charming little resort town on the shores of a forty-three-mile-long lake with a backdrop of three major mountain ranges. *USA Today* anointed it "the Most Beautiful Small Town in America" in 2012. The downtown is authentically quaint, as is our performance venue, the Panida, a lovingly restored and repurposed 1927 vaudeville and movie theater. It's a 540-seat gem, the lush interior all red and gold with fanciful period chandeliers. The stage is diminutive, however, so small that it requires a different set of props. The Panida is the only performing arts center in the area and enormously popular with locals and visitors. All the veteran dancers say that the Sandpoint audience is the best audience on the entire tour. Everybody loves Sandpoint.

And everybody *talks about* Sandpoint. I've been hearing Sandpoint stories for months. "Something always happens to us in Sandpoint," Toni told me months ago when we were discussing which performances I should make sure not to miss. One year one of the techs tripped over a tangle of wires, not surprising, as there is almost no room to maneuver in the cramped wings. The wires went to the speakers. The speakers went dead. This was midperformance. The dancers kept dancing, humming aloud and counting for each other. Two years ago, during the battle of the mice at the end of Act I, one of the combatants actually drew blood. (The swords are metal, so they can make a resounding clang, but they are not sharp.) Somehow a dancer got his finger sliced and, according to three separate reports (I asked for independent verification on this one), ended up bleeding all over the sleeve of his costume, the costume of another dancer, and the stage. The blood on the stage found its way onto various dancers' slippers. The way they describe this unfortunate accident makes it sound like the prom scene from the movie *Carrie*. I don't know how a finger can possibly bleed this much. Maybe it's that Sandpoint juju. "You must go to Sandpoint," Toni told me. So here I am.

And something happens.

What happens doesn't happen because the stage is so tiny that the mini-version of my couch (a prop constructed just for this space) creates a major obstacle by occupying a good third of the dancing area. And it doesn't happen as a result of all fifteen of us female dancers being shoehorned into an airless twelve-foot-square basement dressing room. It happens because we love coffee. And it happens because the trek from the dressing-room catacombs to backstage means navigating a narrow, curved set of stone stairs to a postage-stamp landing and then more narrow stairs to backstage. On the landing, someone has kindly set up a small table with a bowl of fruit and a thirty-cup coffee urn.

When the Party Scene ends, Danielle, dressed in her voluminous ball gown, dashes down the first set of stairs and rounds the tight corner on the landing. As she makes the turn, her big hooped skirt catches the edge of the thirty-cup coffee urn. Roughly twenty-six cups of hot coffee splash onto the tiny landing, puddle, and then cascade down the second set of narrow stone stairs. The coffee grounds—probably two cups' worth when first measured and now, water-soaked and brewed, at least double that—cover the little landing and the first few steps with a carpet of brown grit. Here's where I mention that several of the dancers have heaped their mouse costumes in the corner of this landing so as to facilitate a quick change. (Remember the postage-stamp dressing room.)

Sara, one of the dancers who must make a two-minute costume change, has her toe shoes and big mouse head waiting in the corner of the landing. She rushes up from the dressing room, unaware of the spill, and the first thing she sees is her pink toe shoes. They are blotched with brown stains and sprinkled with coffee grit. She surveys the mess. She says a few choice words. But the show must go on. (No, these are not the few choice words.) She makes the only decision she can, given the approximately thirty seconds she has to be onstage. She decides to dance barefoot. She grabs her mouse head and upturns it, positioning it quickly over her head. Coffee grounds rain down, sprinkling her hair, her shoulders, her costume. She says a few more choice words, shakes out the head, puts it back on, and goes out to dance.

And that is the Sandpoint story for *this* season. I think it is so much better than the wounded-bloody-mouse story, and certainly far, far better than the dancing-with-no-music story. Best yet, I am here to witness it.

In Sandpoint's favor, I must add that the hospitality is outstanding, with trays of hot food and platters of home-baked goods that Aunt Rose should not eat but does. Also, the Sandpoint audience is, as everyone told me it would be, wildly appreciative. There's nothing like a two-minute-long standing ovation to make you forget what ails you. I try to hold on to that feeling as we board the bus at 10:00, stop you-know-where for you-know-what, and drive a few hours to Spokane, where we spend the night in a motel hard by the freeway. Bright and early the next morning we're on the bus again for an eight-hour drive back to Eugene.

ALTHOUGH WE'RE FINISHED trekking to the hinterlands and enriching the coffers of local Safeways for this season, the company still has two shows in Salem before our four-performance finale on the home stage. And so, after one night in my own bed and a perfectly ordinary morning that, by comparison to the last week, feels downright self-indulgent, I am on the way to the studio to catch the bus to our final on-the-road venue. It's a mercifully quick hour-long drive up the freeway. I've got my makeup done (ah, the luxury of one's own bathroom), my false eyelashes glued on, my ballet bag packed with pink tights and my special nude (with transparent straps) leo and my long white gloves and my uncomfortable character shoes and my "junk" for company class. I make a quick stop for an Americano. The barista admires my "Cleopatra eyes" and kind of fawns over me when I tell her why I am in stage makeup. And while she's exclaiming, I'm thinking, *Yeah, yeah, another day, another show.* I mean I am really thinking that, and then I catch myself thinking that. And it startles me. Apparently, I'm in the zone, and I didn't even know it. I feel almost, well, comfortable.

Which is funny, and not funny-ha-ha, because just hours later, costumed and onstage at the Elsinore—a restored Tudor Gothic castle of a theater (yes, really)—I am suddenly, inexplicably, overcome with amnesia. I cannot remember the entire middle of the Grandfather Dance, and I am terrified. I feel goose bumps on my arms as a trickle of sweat runs down my back. My mind is utterly blank. Then I hear the music that signals the beginning of the dance, and I see Mark do the theatrical flourish that beckons me center stage, and I go out and dance the best Grandfather Dance I've ever danced.

The next night at the Elsinore, we suffer a Sandpoint-worthy mishap onstage when Fritz, Clara's misbehaving brother, spins around with the nutcracker, and the head, which is supposed to detach but remain dangling by a thread when Fritz knocks the nutcracker on the stage, instead, propelled by centrifugal force, flies off and hits a lady seated in the front row. The girl playing the Fritz part soldiers on, and everything continues as if the nutcracker still had its head. So Fritz knocks the headless prop on the stage and pretends the (nonexistent) head comes off, and Herr Drosselmeyer does his magic thing where he presumably reattaches the head, only there is no head to reattach. Now Clara starts dancing with the supposedly repaired nutcracker and, as the ballet calls for, showing it off with pride to all the party guests.

She is *not* happy.

The nutcracker is not too thrilled either.

Sara, Jesse, Izzy, and I, standing together midstage, are trying to look like we're admiring the decapitated nutcracker and trying very hard not to laugh. Meanwhile, an audience member kindly retrieves the head and places it on the front of the stage, and somehow—it's a mystery to me how this happens so smoothly—Danielle picks up the head, takes the headless nutcracker from Clara, and delivers both to Jesse, who retreats to a position behind us, reattaches the head, and hands it back to Danielle, who hands it to Clara.

Jesse is grinning an out-of-character grin. He catches himself, tightens his lips, and says, ventriloquist-style (which is how we talk to each other onstage), "Oh, yeah, oh, yeah, I saved the day!"

And the show goes on.

20

The Life of the Party

OUR FOUR-SHOW HOMETOWN run begins tonight, and I am more nervous than I ought to be. After all, Aunt Rose is a veteran now. She and I know the ropes. We've been through good performances and bad, danced on cramped stages and basketball courts, endured overheated, closet-sized dressing rooms, popcorn-munching audiences, and eight-hour bus trips. We've tripped, stumbled, bumped into props, missed cues—and occasionally gotten everything just right. What's there to be nervous about?

I'm contemplating this as I drive myself downtown to the Hult Center for the Performing Arts for this evening's show. It's mid-afternoon and already getting dark, although what that means in the winter in the Pacific Northwest is just that the dove-gray sky has now deepened to a steel-gray sky. Sure, I'm on edge because I'll know people in the audience—*lots* of people. But there's something else going on. I think it has to do with the venue itself. The Hult is the real deal, a 2,500-seat world-class concert hall with a soaring, three-story lobby and a serious stage and tiers of burnished-wood curvilinear balconies. It's not nineteenth-century ornate like the halls in Chicago, Boston, and San Francisco where

I sat in the audience, just a year ago, cocooning myself in all things *Nutcracker*. But this hall has, well, gravitas. It feels as if you should *be* somebody to perform here.

Am I somebody?

During the almost five-hour-long lead-up to the Friday-evening show, the weird hurry-up-and-wait rhythm that I am still not used to, I am alternately restless and excited, bored and anxious, at ease and deeply uneasy, sometimes, it seems, simultaneously. I set up in one of the three—that's right, three!—dressing rooms assigned to the female dancers. What opulence: a well-lit, well-ventilated, expansively mirrored room with only four other dancers. I may not be sure if I am somebody in a grander sense, but I know on this day I am somebody who earned a place in an honest-to-God professional dressing room. As I spread out my stuff—oh, the counter space!—and put on my makeup, no longer a cortisol-drenched experience, I strike up a conversation with Beth. She's the one company ballerina I haven't really gotten to know. It might be because she and Cory are such an insular pair. Or it may be that she's just not as chatty as some of the other women. In any case, as I paint my face and listen to Beth's backstory, it comes as a strange, you've-come-full-circle surprise to learn that she studied and danced with the Eglevsky Ballet on Long Island. Yes, that Eglevsky. Well, actually, not *that* Eglevsky. André was long dead by then, and Marina, his daughter who took over, had by Beth's time sold the company and its name to someone else. Still, to be dancing onstage in *The Nutcracker* with an "Eglevsky" ballerina feels like a personal victory. Or perhaps just sweet revenge. Either one works for me.

My makeup, I can't help but notice, is stellar. My costume zips. I go out onstage to do my thing.

This evening's production feels entirely different from all the other performances, the dozen on-the-road shows I've been a part of. And it's not just because I'm a veteran now. Or maybe it is, but in an unexpected way. Maybe it is precisely because I'm a veteran—even though I'm battling a case of hometown-audience nerves—that I have this unexpected holistic experience. It is not all about me. It is not about my position onstage or whether I bring enough energy to the Gallop or whether I anticipate the cue from Mark. It is not about whether I nail the damn tombé-pas de bourrée. It is the whole *Nutcrackery* gestalt.

The Hult stage is huge. We're using all of our beautiful, full-sized props and scenery drops. The lighting is magical. And the music—the music is amazing. A Julliard-trained music professor has put together and is conducting a stellar orchestra of professional musicians paired with top student talent from the university. The sound is rich and bold, both crisp and lyrical. The tempo is spot-on. From my perch on the prop couch at the front of the stage, I pretend-read to the party children spread out at my feet and steal glances at Brian McWhorter, the conductor. With his shaved head, engagingly goofy jug-ears, and Elvis Costello eyewear, he is an arresting sight. I watch him track the dancers as he simultaneously attends to his musicians. He is as much a part of what is happening onstage as if he were up here with us instead of in the pit. Tonight the music is not just what we dance to, which is how I've felt about it at the other performances. It is the ballet. It is us.

Without me realizing it, Brian is apparently also watching me during the first act. At intermission he finds me backstage and tells me I have "great stage presence." You could heat a large room with the glow that emanates from my face. I take my glow and go upstairs to the lobby to greet the friends who've come to see me, the very most important of whom are Kim and her husband, Tim. They say nice things—of course they do—and we take pictures to commemorate the moment. As I stand next to Kim in my ball gown the color of autumn leaves with my flashy costume jewelry and my over-the-elbow white gloves and my elegant ribbon-and-bow headdress, I remember the day we tried on plain black leotards at the Dancers' Closet. I give her the best hug someone wearing a hoop skirt and trying not to smear her makeup can give a person. I know—and she knows—I wouldn't be here without her.

⸻

THE FOLLOWING DAY, the matinee goes well. The sold-out audience is packed with kids, little girls in their holiday dresses with bows in their hair who pressure their moms to buy them *Nut* trinkets during intermission. I circulate for the meet 'n' greet, shamelessly soaking up the adoration of these girls, who shyly hold on to my skirt and look up at me with wide eyes and seem to think I am a real-deal ballerina. Their moms whip out phones to take our picture.

For the Saturday-evening performance, it seems that cast and crew and orchestra, *everybody*, steps it up, bringing their very best selves to the show. It is our prime-time performance in our prime venue at the end of a long run, and it feels absolutely right, from curtain rise to curtain fall. My family is out there in the expensive center-section-rear-orchestra seats I bought for them—my two sons, my daughter, even my ballet-averse husband—and I'm glad they get to see us at our best. I am glad too that they've never seen a rehearsal or seen me in costume before tonight. It's all a surprise for them. *An Evening at the Ballet*. All magic. All Oz. I love that. I am a small part of the show, but with my placement downstage right and my front-and-center dance with "brother" Mark, I am a visible part, more visible, more identifiable than my family thought I'd be. I like that this too comes as a surprise to them.

This evening, I am not thinking about my family or anyone in the audience or, really, oddly, even the show itself. I am not thinking about anything. I am in the scene, at the party, more fully engaged, more in the moment than I have ever been. It is a gift to get lost in the moment; I know that. And I also know it is a temporary gift, which is okay. It means you value the magic, when it happens, even more. Tonight I feel tall, regal, even, and it's not the two-and-half-inch character shoes. That string attached to the top of my head pulling me skyward, the image Antonio tried to plant in my brain a year ago? It's there! That elongated spine from my Barre3 practice? I feel it! That light step, that quickness I struggled with in practically every rehearsal? Yes. It really is all about patience and hard work. And more patience. And more hard work. It is possible to do what you didn't think you could do, what others may have told you you couldn't do, what you told yourself, in moments of discouragement, you were incapable of doing.

"That was your best ever," Mark says, putting his arm around my shoulders as we walk offstage together at the end of the Party Scene.

After the show, there's a knock on the dressing-room door. Jenn opens the door a crack. I have visitors, she says. It's one of my sons, Zane, and Liza, his girlfriend, who have somehow managed to talk their way backstage. With appropriate fanfare, they present me with a bouquet of roses in pastel pinks and corals. I respond with a deep *reverence*—the formal ballerina curtsy—and manage to trip on the hem of my hoop. Of course I do.

—ᠺ᠍᠍ᢒ᠍

THE LAST PERFORMANCE, the Sunday matinee, is over. As I shimmy out of my ball gown and scurry around the hallway looking for the big plastic bin to deposit the character shoes I'll never wear again, a clichéd bit of advice pops into my head: Play to your strengths. And I think about how wrong that is. You should, I tell myself, intend to remind myself from now on, play to your *weaknesses*. Because that's what stretches you.

—☙

I LEAVE THE theater in inky blackness at 4:30 p.m. Today is the shortest day of the year, the solstice. Tomorrow brings the light. It's raining, of course, a soft Oregon winter rain that dampens my crunchy, three-day, four-show, overhairsprayed hair, still pulled back tight in a bun. My skin, gloriously naked to the elements, no primer, no concealer, no foundation, no blush, no contour lines, no hi-def powder, drinks in the moisture. I've been hurrying from one place to another these past ten days, from dressing room to stage, from home to theater, from hotel to bus, from city to city. Now I'm done hurrying. I stand flat-footed on the steps of the theater. I look down at my feet. They are slightly splayed—a nicer way to put that would be "turned out"—like ballerina feet. I make myself stand perfectly still. I take a deep, rich, damp, misty breath. And another.

  Fuckin' A.

—☙

ON THE WAY home, I decide, uncharacteristically, to stop for a drink. I should just get back to the house, take a shower, put in a load of laundry, check the freezer to see if there's any more of that homemade chili I can defrost for dinner, slog through the e-mail clogging the inbox. My life, my old life, awaits. Watching junk TV in one or another second-rate motel room in the hinterlands, I sometimes yearned for the comfort of domestic routine. Or at least the comfort of high-thread-count bed linen and hot meals. Now I'm suddenly in no hurry. I want, I need, to mark this moment, to sit with it for a while. So I stop at a neighborhood watering hole.

I'm dressed in postshow dancer grunge: sweats, three-season-ago Ugg boots, the puffy winter vest I rescued from my daughter's closet, a red velvet scarf far too fashionable for the rest of the outfit. I scrubbed my skin after the show, but I didn't take the time to remove my eye makeup. Under superdark arched eyebrows, my lids are blanketed with snowy, sparkly white powder blended with shimmery copper and a hint of rose and lined with thick, blacker-than-black eyeliner, top and bottom. And, of course, there are the lashes, the uberdramatic, one-inch false fringes that took me most of the season to figure how to apply correctly. I look, well, ridiculous.

So what?

I think about calling Kim and asking her to meet me at the bar. I think about calling my husband. But I don't. Me and my baggy sweats and my over-the-top eye makeup walk into the bar and sit between an old guy eating a burger and a young hipster nursing an IPA. And they don't know who I am or where I've been or what I've done. And that is just as it should be. Because the only person who knows what this means to me, the only person who can truly celebrate this moment with me, is me.

We're fools whether we dance or not, so we might as well dance.

—JAPANESE PROVERB

Acknowledgments

I HAVE TO admit that I unfailingly read the Acknowledgments section of every single book I pick up. In fact, it's the very first section I turn to. I read through all those names that mean everything to the author and almost always nothing to me because I am and continue to be fascinated by how many people contribute to the life of a book.

What amazes me is how writing a book—one of the more intensely solitary experiences there is—can involve so many people. Without the generous, smart, and supportive engagement of the people I want to thank here, this book would not be what it is. And, really, neither would my life.

For starters, the book never would have/could have happened without the encouragement and support—not to mention patience and good humor—of Eugene Ballet Company Artistic Director Toni Pimble. She gave me the chance. She didn't have to. It made more work for her. But she allowed me to join the company, created a part for me, assigned me rehearsal partners, and, most of all, believed in me. Riley Grannan, managing director and EBC cofounder, extended a warm welcome. Jenn Martin, ballet mistress, taught me (about ballet, yes, but also about passion and resilience), cheered me on, and designed a gorgeous headpiece for Aunt Rose. Josh Neckels, production manager and author of the indispensable Nut Book, made my touring life possible. Shaunna Dowling Durham, EBC seamstress extraordinaire, managed to get me into a costume designed for a ballerina. Jerril Nilson helped spread the word.

I owe an enormous debt of gratitude to the talented, hardworking, and oh-so-generous EBC dancers who accepted me into their midst and helped me understand their world. I particularly want to thank Suzanne Haag, a constant source of inspiration, for being my everyday teacher-at-the-barre and for initiating me into the mysteries of stage makeup, and Victoria Harvey, a lovely dancer and an even lovelier person, for the tutorials and the eye-opening trip to Sephora. Without the generosity, good humor, and superhuman patience of Danielle Tolmie (who, let's face it, defines elegance) and Mark Tucker (my oh-so-wise and strong big little brother), Aunt Rose would never have made it to the stage. Without the ethereal instruction of Antonio Anacan, she would forever have been a prisoner of gravity. I thank my intrepid Gallop partner, Jesse Griffin, and my Party Scene BFs Sara Stockwell and Izzy Mick. And I thank Beth Maslinoff, Cory Betts, Reed Souther, Isaac Jones, and Marilyn Brady for their friendship and goodwill. These dancers, all of them, combine talent and humility, sophistication and sweat, and manage somehow to be both intense and playful. I'm in awe.

And then there were the people who whipped me into some semblance of ballet shape, foremost the amazing and inspirational Barre3 Eugene crew of Summer Spinner, Evie Poole, Jodi Auxier, Brenda Watson—and especially Jessica Neely, who made the whole thing work every single day. I thank intro to intro to intro ballet instructor Miranda Atkinson; take-no-prisoners Pilates instructors

Marilyn Hanson and Judith Schlacter; Gyro Queen Jean Nelson; boxing buddy Roma "Panther" Pawelek; and the crew at Movara, aka Fitness Ridge. Randy Davis and the Sweat Chicas: It's because of you that I had the strength and the stamina to even consider doing this.

Thanks to Barbara Herman, Linda Sapadin, and Zanne Miller for helping me better understand the psychology of midlife challenges. Thanks to Lizzie Reis for the children's book that helped reawaken my ballet self; Barb Bolsen for the warm hospitality and even warmer clothes; Gayle Appel Doll for traveling two thousand miles to see me perform; Amelia Unsicker for ongoing inspiration; and Perrie Patterson, Jen Morton, Liba Stafl, Pam Cytrynbaum, Katherine Sherif, Teresa Barker, and Tim Sheehan for believing in me, even when evidence was to the contrary.

Kim Sheehan, true friend, spirited coconspirator, stalwart wingwoman, first reader, and all-around phenom: You get your own paragraph. And a permanent place in my heart. Merci, merci, ma belle copine!

To the good folks at DaCapo/Perseus: The pleasure was all mine. Big thanks to John Radziewicz, Jonathan Sainbury, Kate Burke, Kevin Hanover, Amber Morris, and Connie Oehring. The cover is beautiful, Carrie May: Thank you.

Renee Sedliar, best editor in the known universe, you get your own paragraph too. Your notes were so good and so right-on. You saw the forest *and* the trees. This book is infinitely better for having been filtered through your intelligence, your book sense, your good sense, and that semidark and quirky sense of humor we share.

David Black, profound thanks for guiding my literary career and finding great homes for my books. For this one in particular, I especially thank Sarah Smith for seeing more ballet in this story than I originally did.

As for the fam: Thank you, Lizzie, for humoring me, indulging me, accompanying me—and continuing the mother-daughter *Nutcracker* tradition. Thank you, Zane, for the shot-in-the-arm, yes-I-can-do-this bike trek that stretched my definition of what I was capable of. Thank you, Jackson, for your unlikely love of dance—and for bringing a real ballerina into our lives. And thank you, Tom, for weathering the storms and for always knowing the correct answer to "Does this leo make my butt look big?"